BEING
DHARMA

BEING DHARMA

—

The Essence of the Buddha's Teachings

AjAHN CHAH

TRANSLATED BY PAUL BREITER

SHAMBHALA

Boston & London

2001

Shambhala Publications, Inc.
Horticultural Hall
300 Massachusetts Avenue
Boston, Massachusetts 02115
www.shambhala.com

14   13   12   11   10   9   8   7   6   5

Printed in the United States of America

⊗ This edition is printed on acid-free paper that meets
the American National Standards Institute z39.48 Standard.
Distributed in the United States by Random House, Inc.,
and in Canada by Random House of Canada Ltd

Book Design by Ruth Kolbert

Library of Congress Cataloging-in-Publication Data
Chah, Achaan.
Being dharma : the essence of the Buddha's teachings / Ajahn chah ;
translated by Paul Breiter ; foreword by Jack Kornfield.—1st ed.
p.   cm.
Includes index.
ISBN 978-1-57062-808-5 (pbk.)
1. Spiritual life—Buddhism   2. Buddhism—Doctrines.
I. Breiter, Paul
BQ5650 .C43   2001
294.3'42041—DC21
2001020065

*Dedicated to the long life
of all genuine spiritual masters
and the preservation
of their pure and authentic traditions.*

CONTENTS

———

Contents

FOREWORD

WHEN THE FIRST WESTERN DISCIPLES arrived at Wat Pah Pong in the 1960s, Ajahn Chah did not give them the special admiration and treatment that Western monks often received in Thailand. He did not excuse them from any of the demanding challenges and strict training of the monastery. Seated on a wooden bench at the foot of his cottage in the center of a huge forest, he peered at them like a watchmaker taking off the cover of an intriguing new piece, and demanded to know whether they understood suffering or how to find peace in this world. Then he would laugh in welcome and bid them to listen, and if they dared, to join him in practice for a while.

In those years, the monastic community was relatively small and Ajahn Chah was still unknown as a teacher. Twenty-five years later, he had become one of the most honored and revered forest masters of the century, and in 1993, nearly a million people joined the king and queen of Thailand at his funeral in order to pay their last respects at his temple. By then, his influence had

spread worldwide, with a hundred branch monasteries and re-
spected disciples teaching internationally.

Ajahn Chah's natural wisdom expressed itself in the wide
range of skillful means he used to bring students to freedom.
The demanding discipline and mindful dignity of the monastery
were his first line of practice. In the community, he also taught
by anecdote and example, by story and piercing, koanlike questioning. He used humor and poked fun at the delusions of the
world and those he mentored. He taught by close-knit relation-
ship, by compassionate understanding and insightful no-holds-
barred dialogue. Though his way of practice involved strict
training of virtue, precepts, renunciation, and concentration, he
taught them with a light heart, and all were done in the service
of wisdom and freedom.

From the start, his teaching of meditation focused on this
freedom. While he instructed students in many traditional practices of mindfulness and concentration, he deliberately chose
not to emphasize remarkable meditation experiences, samadhi,
jhana, or special insight stages. Meditation was a tool, a means to
sit and examine ourselves, to quiet the mind and open the heart.
He instructed students "to abide in the one who knows," to discover the natural peace within. From a base of inner stillness, he
pointed out, we can more directly see the truth, "the way things
are." We can recognize the impermanent, ungraspable nature of
life; we can study suffering, its cause, and its end. He taught that
meditation is a way for us to let go, to stop the war, to put down
the struggle, to be at peace no matter what the circumstances.

Each day, the monastery had periods of chanting and mindful
work, walking and sitting meditation, silence and community
practice, all interspersed with informal guidance from the master. On occasion, usually after evening chanting, Ajahn Chah
would close his eyes and give a more extensive Dharma talk, instructions to his monks, nuns, and other devoted disciples. These
discourses could last from one to five hours. The new monks
would call the longer ones "endurance sessions."

Now Paul Breiter, a longtime student and beloved disciple of
Ajahn Chah, has translated some of these discourses from Thai

Photographer unknown

Ajahn Chah (seated) with, from left, Doug Burns,
Ajahn Sumedho, and Jack Kornfield; circa 1970.

and Lao for Western readers. It is a blessing to have these teachings, the meat and potatoes of Ajahn Chah's Dharma, the
evening trainings where he would take the gloves off and challenge us to look squarely at human life. As you read these pages,

you can imagine yourself deep in the forest in the early evening after two hours of meditation and sonorous chanting. The light is flickering from the candles, there is a quiet rustling of forest creatures settling down, the evening cicadas are singing—the time has come to reflect on your commitment to a life of wakefulness and truth.

Now the master addresses you sincerely, describing the nature of this existence. He knows that you too can awaken. "All situations are uncertain. This is the central truth in this worldly realm." He goes on, "Live with things as they are. Don't get drunk, carried away, lost in your desires, intoxicated by your situation, by ideas, plans, the way you think things should be." He expresses the truth in simple ways. "You don't own anything. Even your thoughts and body are not your possessions; they are mostly out of your control. You must care for them with compassion, but all things are subject to the laws of change and not your wishes for them. When you truly understand this, you can be at peace in any surrounding."

In speaking to the nuns and monks at his temple, Ajahn Chah urged them to live up to the nobility of their station, to uphold the monastery's reputation as sincere followers of the Buddha's way. He urged a determination in their practice and a fearless self-honesty. He asked them to reflect: Have I truly taken the teachings to heart? Am I willing to remove all forms of greed, hatred, and delusion, to let go, to be free? Do I unwaveringly honor the practice of virtue and compassion, no matter how difficult? Am I one who is easy to speak to, easy to reach, not proud or rigid? "Don't take the teachings for granted," he went on. "They are not philosophy or ideals. Examine yourself, examine your mind and heart. Release your entanglement with pleasure and pain, and rest in the Middle Way, in the heart of freedom. Let the saffron robes you wear be a banner of the Buddha to demonstrate the living reality of peace and wisdom in the world."

When he offered Dharma instructions to the lay practitioners, government officials, and military officers who visited, it was also the straight scoop, no holds barred. He didn't go along with the superficial practices of devotion and merit-making that were common for lay visitors. He demanded that they embody the Dharma, live with virtue and compassion, purify their hearts, and let go of craving and delusion. These were what he insisted are the true blessings and genuine merit to be found in the Buddha's way.

In all his teachings Ajahn Chah reminds us that liberation is possible. With sincere intention and diligent effort, each of us can awaken, each of us can discover the freedom and peace of the Buddha.

As you read, take these teachings to heart. Digest them slowly. Let them be an inspiration for inquiry. Let them be medicine for your spirit. Let them be a source of guidance for your unshakable deliverance.

May the words of Ajahn Chah carry the clear light of truth into the world. May they bring blessings and awakening to all who read them.

JACK KORNFIELD
Spirit Rock Center
2000

TRANSLATOR'S PREFACE

———

AMONG CONTEMPORARY Thai Buddhist masters, perhaps none have been as influential with Western students of Dharma as Ajahn Chah (1919–1992). One reason for his popularity is certainly the clarity and accessibility of his words to people of widely diverse cultural backgrounds and to followers of different Buddhist lineages. Hopefully, some of this will come across in the translations set forth in this book. *Luang Por,* as he was known to his disciples, could teach using the traditional concepts of Dharma, but he also put the truth into analogies and fables using animals, trees, and the events of everyday living in a way that penetrated the hearts of his listeners; he did so with much warmth and humor and without sacrificing anything in the way of profundity. "Simple yet profound" has perhaps become an overused and hackneyed phrase, but it applies to much of Ajahn Chah's teaching.

Over the course of some twenty-five years of teaching and training, Ajahn Chah was able, as his senior Western disciple

Ajahn Sumedho put it, to teach the ideas of Buddhism in a way that even an uneducated rice farmer could understand. Yet he was also able to answer the questions of upper-class Thai people and attract and train skeptical Westerners, many of whom stayed under his guidance for ten years or more and still continue the monastic life today.

Beliefs about Practice

AJAHN CHAH CONSTANTLY PUSHED people past what they were likely to consider their limits. The practice in his monasteries did not always follow what might seem to be reasonable, and the routine was always changing. He sometimes recounted his own difficulties in practice and the resolve with which he faced them and spurred himself on:

> Before I started to practice, I thought to myself, "The Buddhist religion is here, available for all, yet why do only some people practice it while others don't? Or if they do practice, they do so for only a short while and then give it up. And those who don't give up still don't knuckle down and do the practice. Why is this?" So I resolved to myself, "Okay . . . I'll give up body and mind for this lifetime and try to follow the teaching of the Buddha down to the last detail. I'll reach understanding in this lifetime . . . because if I don't, I'll still be sunk in suffering. I'll let go of everything else and make a determined effort. No matter how much difficulty or suffering I have to endure, I'll persevere. If I don't do it, I'll just keep on doubting."
>
> Thinking like this, I got down to practice. No matter how much difficulty I had to endure, I did it. I looked on my whole life as if it were only one day and a night. I gave it up. "I'll follow the teaching of the Buddha. I'll follow the Dharma to understanding why this world is

Photograph by Irving and Barbara Breiter

Paul Breiter, translator and editor of Being Dharma,
in Thailand in 1974.

so wretched." I wanted to know. I wanted to see the
truth, so I turned to the practice of Dharma.

While he was most tolerant of people's shortcomings and
limitations, he always wanted his disciples to make as much effort
as they possibly could, simply for the goal of escaping from the
clutches of Mara, "the Evil One," who holds us prisoner in this
realm of suffering. He did not see this as something easily accomplished—"If practicing Dharma were easy, everyone would
be doing it," he often said—but as really the only thing worth
doing with a human life.

The worldly way of living generally involves filling life with
busyness, distractions, and amusements in an endless pursuit of
happiness and an effort to avoid boredom. But a constantly distracted and excited mind is a tired and worried mind. When a
person makes a commitment to undergo Buddhist training, he
or she is setting out to free the mind from all such dependence.
It can be an extremely painful and frustrating process, as accu-
mulated habits, hopes, and fears start to surface in the new open
space of nondistraction. Ajahn Chah pointed out that there are
people who think monastic life is some kind of escape, but when

it is actually undertaken, facing oneself for the first time with nowhere to hide can be like walking into a raging storm.

Ajahn Chah often speaks about heedlessness. By that term, he means a careless, unaware approach to living, and he notes that it is often compounded by comforts. But until one starts to do without such things, these links remain hidden. Soft living tends to make the mind soft. He spoke about the simple way of life in the not-too-distant past in Thailand: "Before, when the country was not developed, everyone built their toilet some distance from the house, often out in the forest. You had to walk out there to use it. But now the toilet has to be in the house. The city people even have to have it right there where they sleep." Such a concept struck him as funny. Laughing, he said, "People think that will make them more comfortable and happy, to have a toilet in their bedroom. But it doesn't really bring happiness, and it increases the habit of laziness . . ."

His way of training was not meant to be an endurance test, however. When he saw disciples making great efforts in a mindless, mechanical way, he would correct them. And he was never ambiguous about where the emphasis should lie. After the Buddha's years of fruitless asceticism, he came to realize the way to liberation lay in the mind. The body itself was just a material object incapable of enlightenment. It was also not something evil that hindered spiritual development and needed to be tortured or weakened; this is as much a deviation as trying to beautify the body and seeking happiness through sensual pleasure and social approval. So the role of asceticism is in creating simplicity and noninvolvement in confusion, not deprivation for its own sake. And statements such as "destroy your body!" or "destroy the world!" do not literally refer to suicide or nuclear weapons, but, in the context of meditation and Ajahn Chah's lively ways of teaching, to destroying attachment to these things.

One night, Ajahn Chah was welcoming a former lay patron who had just ordained and come to spend the rains retreat. He gave one of his informal rambling discourses, putting the Dharma across in recollections and personal observations. He spoke of traveling on *tudong*, the traditional ascetic practice of wandering in the countryside and wilderness, seeking solitude in forests and mountains and visiting spiritual teachers. "Sometimes I would walk forty kilometers in a day. It's not that I was strong, but I had energy of spirit. Even soldiers can't march like that. . . . Some days, I would go for alms and get nothing but rice. It was really interesting to watch my mind when I ate. I'd think, 'If only I had some salt!' Who would imagine that you could gain wisdom from eating plain rice?"

Ajahn Chah was not afraid to test the extremes in his own practice, and he saw this experience as instructional for himself. He sometimes pushed people to very difficult limits and beyond. Such methods can be painful to undergo, but one comes to see where the mind holds on and limits itself and to see that the real suffering comes from the mind's attachments, fears, and preconceptions.

He did not recommend fasting, vows of silence, or avoiding contact with others. He said, "We practice with our eyes open. If avoiding people and sense-contact were the way to enlightenment, the blind and the deaf should be enlightened." Wisdom is to be found in the realm of sense-contact. The world is transcended by knowing the world, not by avoiding it. Living at close quarters with others in the same routines day after day, which is the way of life in his monasteries, can reveal a lot about one's habits and the way one creates suffering for oneself. He often said, "If it's hot and difficult, that's it; that's the place of practice."

Teaching Dharma

AJAHN CHAH WAS ALWAYS AVAILABLE to his disciples for guidance, but he did not conduct frequent interviews to determine their progress. He urged people to self-reliance through knowing their own minds and not getting attached to or doubtful about whatever occurred in meditation. He often told the sangha that he was giving them a suitable environment in which to develop their own practice. He said, "It's like providing a pasture for your cows. If there's a pasture that's fenced in and has plenty of grass, the cows can eat grass and also be safe. If they are cows, they will eat. If they don't want to eat the grass, they aren't cows! Maybe they're pigs or dogs. . . ."

His meditation instructions were usually simple. Concentration and insight are generally not dealt with as separate topics. Mindfulness and insight are threaded through most of the teachings and are spoken of on different levels of refinement. Also, other standard meditations such as recollection of death and generation of lovingkindness (*metta*) were often not taught systematically or formally, but more as themes for contemplation and as attitudes to be kept constantly in mind. He would present these ideas in ways that pierce the heart. On his visit to the United States in 1979, he established the theme of facing the executioner. "Imagine there was a fortune-teller whose predictions were always right. You go to see him, and he tells you, 'Without question you are going to die in seven days.' Would you be able to sleep? You would let go of everything and meditate day and night. In truth, this is what we are all destined for, and we are facing the executioner every moment." And he recommended as homework thinking about one's own death three times a day at the very least.

Understanding the Teachings

THE STRUCTURE OF THIS BOOK follows Ajahn Chah's oft-repeated statement:

> First one learns Dharma, but does not yet understand it;
> then one understands, but has not yet practiced. One
> practices, but has not seen the truth of Dharma; then
> one sees Dharma, but one's being has not yet become
> Dharma.

The point of this classification is that until reaching the level of being Dharma, one still has suffering, and one's potential is not fully realized. Now that we are at a stage in the transmission of Buddhism to the West where many people have been sincerely studying and practicing the way of the Buddha for decades, this may be a concept that can be understood directly from experience. Ajahn Chah saw Dharma practice as a way of life and not merely a set of exercises or rituals, and the goal (though he rarely spoke of goals or attainments) as nothing less than the cessation of suffering, a state of clarity and peace in which the mind is no longer swayed by internal and external happenings. It might be helpful to keep this in mind when reading the teachings, which are full of repetition of basic themes and may at times appear to be too basic and simplistic. Ajahn Chah always urged his listeners to neither believe nor disbelieve his words, but rather to investigate the teachings to see how they related to personal experience.

Ajahn Chah was primarily a teacher of monks and nuns, people who have forsaken worldly ties and gone forth to a life of renunciation. While he was emphatic that Buddhist practice is not the exclusive province of monastics, he did emphasize the advantages offered by the discipline and simplicity of ordained life. Living in a monastery that is following the canonical discipline, one refrains from all harm. There is a community based on mutual helping, sharing, and respect. With minimal possessions, there is little to squabble over or covet. Dharma is something to be lived, an idea reflected in Thai words for spiritual practice. And living in this way for a number of years builds habits of attentiveness, restraint, and unselfishness; the result is often people who are strikingly happy.

Sometimes Ajahn Chah may sound moralistic to Western ears, in talking about things such as heedlessness or refraining from evil, for example. The Buddha explained evil as that which harms oneself and others, and he called heedlessness the way to death. Paying attention to the fine details of how one lives, in all situations, alone or with others, can refine the mind considerably and create a firm foundation for meditation practice. Talk of good and evil may rankle us due to habit—perhaps the result of too many joyless Sunday school lessons—but it may be worthwhile to think about the implications. Ajahn Chah speaks repeatedly of the need for moral conduct, but it is for the purpose of creating a relaxed mind and a harmonious living environment, not in response to commandments handed down from on high, the violation of which is met with punishment. As with all of his teachings, his instructions on morality and virtue have a practical purpose and do not involve taking anything on blind faith. He also speaks of the necessity of transcending both good and evil, but as in all schools of Buddhism, there is the need for close attention to them, not only at first, but most of the way through the path.

At other times he may seem to be speaking to Thai people and their cultural habits, such as when talking about the traditions of taking precepts, listening to teachings, making offerings, and having strange beliefs about what Buddhism is or what it can do for followers. With some reflection, however, similar patterns may be seen to exist in Western Judeo-Christian religious upbringings in general and among Western Buddhists in particular.

As in the original teachings of the Buddha, repetition is common in Ajahn Chah's words. The need to drive a point home cannot be underestimated, especially with the precious Dharma that contradicts habitual thinking so deeply rooted in worldly beings. Again, we can ask ourselves how thoroughly we have understood and assimilated into our being these seemingly simple ideas.

Ajahn Chah was something of a reformer in Thai Buddhism. Like the Buddha, he taught in the vernacular and cut through stultified traditions of his time. He was just as likely to use analogies to dogs, mangoes, chickens, rice fields, and buffaloes as he was to employ the classic Buddhist terminology he had studied before taking up the way of an ascetic meditation monk. In keeping with his view that Dharma teaching is a matter of skillful means to make people see, he often said that one who teaches needs to know what is appropriate for those who are listening. He also rejected the sectarianism that sometimes poisons relations between the two main monastic groups in Thailand.

Organization of the Teachings

ALTHOUGH THIS BOOK HAS BEEN DIVIDED into chapters with certain themes, the teachings themselves do not fit into such neat pigeonholes, and there is an overlapping of topics. Ajahn Chah generally did not limit his Dharma talks to one specific subject at a time, unless he was giving meditation instructions or perhaps explaining the monastic rules to the community. Some common elements are as follows.

The teachings return again and again to the themes of cause and effect, impermanence, nonattachment, moral living, avoiding extremes, and not taking things too seriously. Occasionally, Ajahn Chah offered glimpses of the other shore, of the experience of one who has gone beyond the mundane, but for the most part, he dealt with the problems we face and the ways the Buddha taught for dealing with and putting an end to them. He compared speaking extensively about nirvana, the deathless state of bliss, to explaining colors to a blind person, and noted that people in the Buddha's time complained that the World Honored One must be ignorant of nirvana, since he did not explain clearly what it was. Ajahn Chah often quotes the Pali term *paccatam*, which means the results of practice are to be experienced for oneself and cannot be given by another or understood through mere explanation.

Occasionally, Ajahn Chah spoke of the unconditioned, of original mind, of that which is beyond birth and death, and he seemed to get a great kick out of doing so. Hearing the Heart Sutra in rough translation from English to Thai, he remarked that it talks of deep wisdom beyond conventions, but this does not mean we can discard conventions; without conventions how could we teach, communicate, or explain anything? In the end, his concern was to train, not to entertain, to help purify people's obscurations so they could see directly, just as one tries to cure a blind person's malady rather than merely talking to him about colors. As the Buddha said, "I teach only two things, namely, suffering and the end of suffering."

Right view is mentioned repeatedly. Ajahn Chah called it the foundation of the path, along with *sila* (moral conduct), and it is indeed the first factor in the Buddha's Eightfold Path. It is meant in both an intellectual and an experiential sense, the latter being what is also called wisdom. Briefly, Ajahn Chah speaks of right view as understanding cause and effect; not holding things to be stable, sure, or permanent; seeing the unsatisfactory nature of conditioned existence (that is, everything that an ordinary, uninstructed person takes to be life); and not believing in the existence of a self. On the side of experience, it is a mode of being in which one does not react to internal and external phenomena with elation or depression, seeing them for what they actually are and thus not suffering. "Not suffering" is not a blank state, but one of peace, radiance, and joy—which is what most people who met him saw very strikingly in Ajahn Chah. This should be kept in mind when reading his description of wisdom and the state of peace as being beyond happiness or suffering. Obviously there is great happiness in liberation, but there is nothing in our ordinary experiences of happiness that remotely compares to it, nothing that can be conceived by the confused mind or found through the usual paths of seeking the pleasant and avoiding the unpleasant.

Although right view is the first path factor, it will pervade all the other aspects of the path if one is practicing correctly. It will be present and continuously amplified through the stages of understanding, practicing, seeing, and finally being Dharma. Another way to speak of right view is in terms of the two extremes, another common theme in the teachings.

When the Buddha gave his first sermon, the Discourse on Turning the Wheel of Dharma, he set out the Middle Way that avoids mistaken paths of spiritual practice, which he summarized as seeking gratification through sense pleasures and self-mortification. Ajahn Chah gives the two extremes a broader interpretation, describing them as the habits of reacting to whatever one encounters with elation and depression, joy and sorrow. One needn't wear a hair shirt and whip oneself to fall into the extreme of self-torment; rather, it can be understood as bringing needless pain upon oneself through various habitual reactions, such as guilt or suppression. Nor does one have to be a jaded pleasure seeker to suffer from the extreme of indulgence. Again, these are hard facts that can be seen in our own experience. The seeing leads to weariness with worldly ways. Weariness is not exhaustion or a sense of apathy or aversion, but a turning away from that which is recognized to be fruitless and meaninglessly painful. It also brings about detachment. One is then ready to seek refuge in something reliable and meaningful, to live with restraint and mindfulness, and to free the mind to find its natural condition of peace and happiness.

Understanding cause and effect and the correct and incorrect approaches to practice leads to another common theme, *silabbataparamasa*, usually translated as "attachment to rites and rituals." It is one of the three fetters of mind removed by attainment of stream entry, the first level of enlightenment, the other two fetters being skeptical doubt and mistaken belief in the existence of a self. It is another idea that bears explanation. Although Theravada Buddhism is known for its unelaborate modes of practice, there is still a fair amount of ritual involved in its traditional forms. It could also be argued that even keeping precepts or sitting down to meditate are rituals of a sort. Ajahn Chah's interpretation of silabbataparamasa has been translated here as *superstitious* attachment to rites and rituals, in other words, to any spiritual conventions. It is a belief that certain actions or modes of behavior by themselves will produce benefits, ranging from good health and riches to meditative states and enlightenment, without understanding or any change of habits being necessary. These actions can be the making of offerings; taking part in ceremonies, such as going for refuge or requesting precepts; or observing the outward disciplines of keeping rules and practicing formal meditation. Ajahn Chah often spoke of his own tribulations and mistaken attitudes in his earlier years. He told of one of his teachers, Ajahn Kinnaree: "Just sitting and sewing his robes, he was meditating much better than I was when I tried to sit and practice samadhi for long periods. If I sat all night, it only meant that I suffered all night . . . I would watch him do walking meditation. Sometimes he would just take a few steps and get tired, so he would go and lie down. But he was receiving more benefit than I did when I walked for hours."

Ajahn Chah also made constant references to doubt, as it is naturally present when one's views are not clear and when practice is falling away from the path. It can manifest in many ways, some of them quite subtle: doubts about the teachings, about one's own ability, about the teacher and spiritual companions, about the way of practice. Ajahn Chah repeatedly points out how doubt hampers one's commitment to spiritual practice and keeps one in a constant search for intellectual answers, and says that the antidote is looking directly at experience, including the experience of doubt itself.

Translation and Terminology

VARIATIONS IN STYLE AND TONE may be noticed in the different teachings. Apart from the limitations of the translator, there are a few reasons for this. First, two languages are being spoken. In Northeast Thailand, where Ajahn Chah lived and established his monasteries, the native language is the Isan dialect of Thai, similar to Lao. As years passed and people from other parts of Thailand, as well as Westerners who had learned or were learning Central Thai, came to study with him, he began to teach more in Thai. Lao is generally earthier, more informal, and even more a language of feeling than is Thai—especially in Ajahn Chah's case, as it was his mother tongue. Speaking to people he had known all his life, his words tended to be more informal, even blunt, sometimes scolding. He spoke Thai to people from all walks of life and corners of Thailand and the world. Sometimes his language was simple, a little slow and perhaps pedagogical, as when instructing a group of middle-class people from Bangkok; sometimes grandfatherly, as when teaching young foreigners; sometimes humorous and extremely relaxed. He mainly taught and trained monastics, but gave a wealth of teaching to laypeople as well.

As to which voice was that of the "real" Ajahn Chah, no one who met him would venture to guess. He was a supreme actor who responded to situations with wisdom and compassion and an extraordinary array of skillful means, and he displayed a wide range of personalities while doing so. He was able to be comforting, inspiring, or terrifying, yet could also exhibit the most polished comic talent, with a flawless timing and delivery that literally stopped people speechless in their tracks. Recollections of senior disciples were often startling to those who only knew Ajahn Chah in his later years and had fixed ideas about him. The former depicted him as tough and unsentimental, even ferocious, a man of mystery and a wielder of occult powers. But whoever he may have been, perhaps the most important fact is the great love that so many people came to feel for him over the years of his teaching activities.

Those who have studied other schools of Buddhism or even other Theravada teachings may find that Ajahn Chah's use of Buddhist terminology does not correspond exactly to usual and accepted interpretations. His teaching was mostly nontechnical and informal. Like most meditation teachers in Thailand, he did not teach from texts, and he often spoke of teaching as being only the appropriate use of skillful means to point out the correct way, to clear misconceptions, and to help avoid deviations in practice. Thus, some misunderstanding could occur if the words are taken too literally or as having a fixed meaning. He sometimes speaks of the mind in the classical terminology of the aggregates of form, feeling, perception, thinking, and consciousness, and at other times simply as feeling and thinking. The latter is also used to describe a person's basic outlook on life, or worldview. He often refers to "the one who knows," a common theme in Thai Buddhist teaching, sometimes in a neutral sense as mind itself, a basic awareness with the potential for delusion or wisdom; or he may speak of it as an awakened knowing, even as Buddha nature (a concept rarely broached in Theravada Buddhism).

There are also Thai Buddhist terms derived from the Pali language that may not have the same meaning and significance as the corresponding Sanskrit terms employed in Mahayana. Other terms are used informally and in a fluid way by Ajahn Chah, whereas in Mahayana they may always have a specific meaning. And there are common Thai words of Buddhist origin that have taken on a different flavor in the vernacular.

One recurring example is the Thai word *tammadah*, derived from the Sanskrit *Dharmata*, a term for ultimate reality, usually translated as "suchness," things as they really are. In Thai it simply means "ordinary," and is often used by Ajahn Chah in conjunction with *tammachaht*, "nature" or "natural." Nature is not meant to imply merely the physical environment, and statements that we should not try to alter nature don't mean that we can't pull weeds or create irrigation systems, but rather that we should avoid living in a constant struggle of not accepting the way things happen in the realm of cause and effect. The words for natural and ordinary would normally be taken in a mundane sense by Thai listeners, but Ajahn Chah expounds on them in a Dharma sense as "the way things are."

In translating from Pali and Thai, multiple renditions were often used to convey the range of meaning and flavor of the original. *Anicca* is generally understood as meaning "impermanence," but Ajahn Chah often spoke of this principle in terms of the uncertainty of existence. *Dukkha* has been translated as "suffering" and also as "unsatisfactoriness." The third of the three characteristics of insight meditation, the truth that there is nothing constituting a self or belonging to a self, has also been rendered in various ways: not self, absence of a self, selflessness. Ajahn Chah sometimes used the Pali word, *anatta*, and sometimes Thai equivalents, so it seemed appropriate to use different English terms to fit the context and the flow of the language itself.

Some readers may be familiar with certain translations of common Buddhist terminology, often depending on which tradition they have studied. The Pali word *kilesa* (Sanskrit *klesha*), for example, has usually been translated as "defilement" in Theravadin literature, and the actual meaning is something that stains the original purity of the mind. However, this translation tends to take on moralistic overtones in modern English. In Tibetan Buddhist books, it is usually rendered as "mental afflictions," "emotional afflictions," or "conflicting emotions." This variety was generally opted for here, to convey the sense of something afflicting the heart, but occasionally "defilement" is used.

Carrying on the Tradition

AJAHN CHAH LIVED in one of the more remote, unheard of, and inaccessible corners of Thailand, yet somehow a steady stream of Western seekers found their way to his monastery beginning in the late 1960s, and many ended up staying under his guidance for years. This "pot-bellied monk who looked more like a bullfrog than a saint"* had an appeal and a way of communicating truth that reached across cultural barriers and the strata of society. Over the years, he touched many hearts and shaped many lives for the better.

In Thailand, it was always striking to see the throngs of people who would turn up at even the most remote monastery when he visited. Watching adults come running from a village like children to meet his car, joyfully calling out "Luang Por!" was an unforgettable sight. His very being was a refuge to people, each receiving what they could at their own level. Through his vibrant, joyous presence, he instilled an absolute trust and sense of safety.

Today in the West, there are monastic communities in his lineage, including a number of monks who had the opportunity to live and train with Ajahn Chah. There are also many former monks and nuns, as well as laypeople, who spent time with him. Visiting from time to time, one is struck by the great regard in which he is still held, the love and gratitude people feel for him. From a simple remark such as, "Luang Por was good, wasn't he?" to the statement, "He was the most remarkable person I ever

---

*Batchelor, Stephen. "A Thai Forest Tradition Grows in England." *Tricycle*, Summer 1994.

met . . . and one of the greatest men Thailand has ever pro-
duced," it is obvious how he affected people's lives.

Yet this was no mere personality cult of blind devotion. He
was always on the alert for disciples who depended on him too
much, and he could make one's life miserable if he felt it was
needed to get someone out of his or her rut. As he repeats in his
teachings, the Buddha did not praise those who blindly follow
another without trying to discover the truth for themselves.

It would be possible to fill a whole volume with recollections
of Ajahn Chah and commentary on his teaching. At this point,
however, it feels appropriate to let the teachings speak for themselves.

NOTE ON PRONUNCIATION OF PALI TERMS: Generally, all
consonants are hard except for *c*, which is pronounced like *ch*;
otherwise *h* following a consonant is always aspirated, as in *hot-
house*. *A* is long, as in *ma* and *pa*. The following list of words that
appear frequently here shows syllable emphasis in capitals.

> bhikkhu: BHIK-khu (like *sick*)
> dukkha: DUK-kha (like *spook*)
> neyya: NAY-ya
> pacceka: pac-CEYK-ka
> samatha: SAM-a-tha
> sasana: SAH-sa-na
> sila: SEE-la
> songkran: SONG-krahn
> tathagata: ta-THAH-ga-ta
> upaya: u-PAH-ya
> vipassana: vi-PAS-sa-nah

ACKNOWLEDGMENTS

———

MANY THANKS ARE DUE the sangha of Ajahn Chah's ordained disciples, especially the Council of Elders for granting
their permission to translate the teachings for commercial publi-
cation. It has long been the custom in Thailand to print books
for free distribution, but this allowance was made in the hope of
making the teachings available to a wider readership. Ajahn
Jayasaro of Bung Wai International Forest Monastery (Wat
Nanachat) was instrumental in helping to clearly present the
facts to the elders and make the case for this book, following a
translation of the book proposal by Venerable Bhikkhu Kongrit.

Ajahn Pasanno of Abhayagiri Monastery in Redwood Valley,
California, helped with vocabulary questions and painstakingly
checked every translation, line by line, often from barely audible
tapes. He and Ajahn Amaro offered valuable editing suggestions,
as did Ajahn Jayasaro and Jack Kornfield. The Venerable Bhikkhu
Pasukho helped us when we were stumped by phrases in the Lao
language. Most of the translations were done from tapes col-

lected and remastered by Mr. Paiboon Jongsuwat of Ubon-rachathani, Thailand. These tapes were of talks given from the late 1960s to the early 1980s, and it is something of a miracle that they could be preserved in tropical conditions.

"Mindfulness of Breathing" and "The Path to Peace" in Chapter III were excerpted from *The Path to Peace*, translated and published by the sangha of Wat Nanachat.

Special thanks to Peter Turner of Shambhala Publications, who had the idea to create such a book, and who nurtured it through to completion with infinite patience, even as he was assuming additional responsibilities as president of the company; to Emily Bower, my editor, who is a real professional and a joy to work with; and to my wife, Lili, who saw mostly my back for the year and a half that I was at work on this project.

INTRODUCTION

THE BUDDHA SAID, "That one who sees emptiness, the Lord of Death cannot follow." When an awakened being passes away, what happens next? There are only the elements breaking up. There is no person, or self, so how could there be death or rebirth? There are only earth, water, fire, and air dispersing. The Lord of Death can then only follow after earth, water, fire, and air. There is no person to follow. Likewise, if you are looking for a solution to problems, there will always be problems because there is "you." When there is no person, there are no problems. There is no need for solutions, because there are no problems to solve anymore and no one to solve them. But if you believe that you die, you are going to be reborn.

Today I am speaking a little about the Dharma for grown-ups. When those of childish intelligence hear that there is no self, when they hear that nothing is truly theirs, not even the body, they may wonder, Should I stick a knife in my flesh? Should I smash all the cups and plates and be done with it because nothing is mine? It's not that way. It is thick obscuration that can lead people to have such absurd ideas.

How can we make the mind incline to and enter the Dharma? The *sotapanna*, or "stream enterer," is one whose mind has entered the stream to nirvana and does not return. Even if such people have anger, they do not return to the cycle of suffering and attachment. Even though there are desires in their minds, they will not return, because of the power of knowing these things as they are.

The sotapanna enters the Dharma and sees the Dharma, but his being is not yet Dharma. Sometimes there will be anger or desire and he will know them yet still follow after them, because although he knows and sees Dharma, his being is not yet Dharma. The mind has not become Dharma. So he may study Dharma, understand Dharma, practice Dharma, and see Dharma, but to actually *be* Dharma is something quite difficult. It is a place for each individual to reach, a point where there is no falsehood.

We are all like birds in a cage. No matter how fine the conditions in the cage, the bird cannot be content. It will always be restlessly hopping about, wanting to be free. The wealthy and the privileged are no better off—we could say they are doves in gilded cages.

From hearing the Dharma all the way to seeing it, you will still have suffering, and you won't be free of unsatisfactory experience until you *are* Dharma. Until you are Dharma, your happiness still depends on external factors. You lean on them: you lean on pleasure, on reputation, on wealth and material things. You may have all sorts of knowledge, but this knowledge is tainted by worldliness and cannot release you from suffering; you are still like a bird in a cage.

The correct practice of Dharma is derived from a teacher, who received it from another teacher, and it has come down in a long lineage this way. Actually it is just the truth. It doesn't reside with any particular person. If we respect the person of the teacher and only act out of deference to him or her, this is not Dharma.

Ajahn Chah, circa 1973.

We will practice as if doing a chore or fulfilling our duties because we see the teacher around, and when he or she is gone we slacken.

It's like working in a factory. We work for the company that owns it. We don't really like the job, but we do it to get money. We take it easy at every opportunity we get. That is the way people tend to be. Relying on a teacher out of respect is one level of practice. But then we ask, "When will we see the real Dharma?"

The teaching of the Buddha is something that clarifies. It enables humans to enter the stream and see themselves. When we see ourselves, we see Dharma. Seeing Dharma, we see the Buddha. Then we have entered the stream.

I've said this before: if you reach the Dharma you cannot lie, you cannot steal. We think that lying is deceiving others. We think we can act wrongly without others knowing. But wherever you are, doing wrong and not letting anyone know is impossible if you have entered the stream. To think you can is only the thinking of the ignorant. Whether living in a group of people or alone, even if you live in the middle of the water or up in the air, to do wrong and not have anyone know is impossible. When you truly realize this fact, you enter the stream.

If you have not entered the stream, you think you can do wrong actions and no one sees. You are just belittling yourself, not seeing Dharma. Whoever sees Dharma will not deceive others or do anything harmful, no matter what the situation. If we stop and recollect the authentic teaching of the Buddha, he said that wherever there is Dharma, there is someone who sees: it is we ourselves. To think otherwise is a real loss. It is contradicting the intention of the Buddha when he talked about being a witness to yourself. If you bear witness to yourself, you will be unable to lie or do wrong, and your practice will always be direct and upright, just like a compass that always points out north and south.

With a compass, when you enter a deep forest you will always be able to know in which direction you are headed. You might start to think you are heading east, but the compass will show you are going south. Then you realize, "Oh, I was wrong. It was merely my mistaken thinking that I was going east." The compass will always show you the right direction, so you will stop relying on your own guesses. Like this, wherever you are, you have this sense that shows you the truth. Our thinking may lead us elsewhere, but we have the compass. We can let go of our ideas and feelings because we learn that they will lead us the wrong way.

It is the nature of people to enjoy doing wrong. We don't like the result that comes from it, but we are addicted to such actions. We don't want things to come out twisted and wrong, but we like to act in wrong ways. This isn't right view. Things don't just float up into existence by themselves; they are born of causes. We can't get the results without causes. We want to work a little and get rich. We want to realize Path, Fruit, and Nirvana, but we don't want to do strenuous practice. We want to gain knowledge, but we don't want to study. We want to pass tests without applying ourselves, so we go to get sprinkled by holy water from Luang Por. What's the purpose? What will the water do? It's necessary to work hard and hit the books. But people are like this.

Well, they may get a little inspiration from the old monk spraying them with water, but in the language of common folk it's called not reaching the Dharma. That is one level.

In practicing Dharma there must be causes and results. Those who really apply themselves can put an end to doubt and can resolve and finish with problems. Like the compass needle that always points true: we may enter the forest and think east is north because of our own confusion, but the compass is always pointing out the right direction. This is the nature of Dharma. We call it *sacca dharma*, or "truth."

So practicing according to the way of the Buddha, there is no wrong. There is no wrong in the cause, no wrong in the result.

There can be right view, or there can be wrong view. Whichever there is will be the root of your practice, firmly clung to. There are just these two kinds of path. But when you have wrong view, you do not realize that it is wrong, rather you will think it is right and good. You cannot see, and things will not go well.

Actually there is not a lot to learn about in the real Dharma. There are just the principles of practice that need to be applied. They concern things that already exist, and we only need to practice and gain direct experience. Those things we need to study are merely for knowing what to practice and how to go about the practice: we should understand such and such, we should practice such and such, we should go straight ahead in such and such direction. . . . That's all.

The explanations and instructions are one matter. As to the teachings, we can compare it to mangoes. All the stages and characteristics of mangoes, such as sourness and sweetness, being small and growing large, can be found in a single mango. Studying one, it is possible to know about all mangoes.

But meditation is different for various individuals. Some people need more study; if they don't study, they won't be able to understand anything. When we say that some people don't need study, actually they are studying, too: they study directly through practice. There are these two approaches. We can study from ABC on, or we can learn by following the model of the methods for practice.

If things are not clear, we can look at the appearance and actual existence of things, such as hair, nails, teeth, and skin. Their nature is that they are not stable or reliable, not clean or beautiful. This is one way. If we study, we will really take a serious look at them and consider this. Without this kind of study we are not likely to know. Even though we may read the words that hair and nails and the rest are not lovely, they still appear as beautiful and attractive to us. We don't know what is hidden there. The facts are already there, the aggregates and elements arising and passing away continuously. That is all. As for their being impure and uncertain, impermanent, suffering and not self, that is already present. They are filled to bursting with these characteristics.

We recite, "Form is impermanent, feelings are impermanent, perceptions are impermanent, thoughts are impermanent, consciousness is impermanent. . . ." Thus we can say that we know, in a way; that is indeed one kind of knowledge. But when we are put to the test, we don't really know. When the time comes that form really displays its impermanence, then we cannot claim to know. When we get sick and the body is suffering intense discomfort, we get very upset and ask why this is happening to us. That's our impermanence right there. But we recite, "Form is impermanent, feelings are impermanent. . . ." We know it because of this study, but as to the actual phenomenon of impermanence, our knowledge is not clear. We recite the words according to the scriptures, but we only know the formula. In spite of our melodious chanting, which we do so perfectly, we have missed the point.

Some might even contemplate the parts of the body, doing the meditation on impurity, and experience desire. When they say "liver, intestines, stomach," their minds run far afield and they are thinking of chicken livers and kidneys, pigs' intestines, and whatever they may have eaten before, and they start getting hungry. It can really take a long time before people understand.

Actually, the truth is inherent in these things in its entirety. It's not necessary to make an elaborate business out of it. The Buddha emphasized meditation. When we sit to meditate, we can see the truth. The word for meditation, *bhavana*, may be interpreted as causing things to come about. Whatever has not yet come about, make it come about. Whatever is not yet in existence, bring it into existence.

No matter where you are, no matter what your situation, it is possible for you to be practicing Dharma well. Even if you are young, it's something for you to do. Don't leave it to the old folks to do. Mostly, this is what everyone thinks now. "When I'm older I will start going to the monasteries and spend some time on Dharma. Now I can't do it. There are a lot of things to take care of first, so I have to wait until I'm older." They pass the buck to their elders.

I don't know how great it is to be old, actually. Are there any old folks where you live? What kind of shape are they in? Could they keep up with you in a footrace? Their teeth fall out, their sight is weak, their hearing is going. When they stand up, they groan. When they sit down, they groan again. Yet when we are young we like to think, When I'm older, I will do it. Somehow we get the idea that in old age we will be energetic and robust. Old Mr. Kiem in the village here used to carry big planks around when he was a young man; now he has to lean on a cane to walk. Life's like this. So don't get these funny ideas, please.

While we are still alive, let's pay attention to good and evil. Whatever is wrong and bad, let's try to avoid doing. Whatever is good, let's make efforts to do. That's all. These are things that anyone can practice. You don't need to leave it for old age. Come on—you've seen aged people, haven't you? Every move they make is accompanied by groans and creaking. Don't you know why? Yet even so, we close our eyes and ears and say, "Let me finish with this first; let me take care of that piece of business. Wait until I get older, then I'll go to the monastery." Can you understand this? When you are old it's hard to sit for long. Listening to teachings, you might not hear clearly or understand well. So don't wait for old age. Practice steadily and continuously. Before old age comes, you have youth. It's not like you are old and then you become young. It only goes one way.

The truth is that you've been aging from a long time back. You probably have the feeling that you are young people. But as soon as you were born, your aging began. You could say that it began even in your mother's womb. As you grew there, you became older than you were previously. Then birth occurred. If you hadn't aged, there would have been no birth—you would just have remained in the womb. Then as you grow bit by bit, from infant to child and on, it is more aging. So by the time you have reached this point, you can certainly say that you are old. You don't feel that you are old, you don't see it. But if you hadn't aged, you wouldn't be at this stage of your life now. It's better to think that you are old already, and then you will feel the importance of having real Dharma practice in your life. Then eventually nobility and virtue will result. You should begin with virtuous ways right from today, when you are relatively young, and later on you will certainly have well-being. Creating good karma in the present, there is no miserable result later on. That's a good principle to follow. Actions that bring distress later on are those you can avoid. These are good things to give careful consideration in your youth. But if you have the idea that you must deal with different pressing matters before you can practice Dharma, there will likely never come such a time.

In Buddhism, our actions should be aimed at making body and speech pure first. This is spoken of as *sila*, or "morality." That's a simple way to put it. If the body and speech are pure, then there will be calmness, and the mind will be firmly established. This is speaking in a simplified way.

What is this calmness about? If you haven't stolen anything, you are free of worry. When the police come looking for a thief, you can relax because you know it's not you they're after. If your mind is in this condition, free of anxiety, then when sense activity and thinking occur you are able to know them clearly. Briefly, this is called the progression of morality, concentration, and wisdom.

Earlier, we learned that to practice samadhi we need a teacher. I'll relate the following from my own studies. You had to have a teacher. You brought incense, candles, and flowers to the teacher. You began your recitation, making obeisance to him, and then you supplicated and prayed, "May this take effect in me, may sila that is not pure become pure, may samadhi come to reside in my mind. . . ." We studied the text, and then we did the complete recitation of the factors of concentration, the different types of joy and rapture and so on. We invited samadhi to come, and then we sat. But I never saw it come. I just sat there and got worked up because nothing was happening. So I started to think, "Eh, this is not the way to do it. If you could just invite virtue and concentration and they would come, that would certainly be easy. . . . But it seems it's up to us to invest some effort here to make it happen." This is how it started to look to me, so I discarded the way I had learned.

In practice, some come to see easily, some with difficulty. But whatever the case, never mind. Difficult or easy, the Buddha said not to be heedless. Just that—don't be heedless. Why? Because life is not certain. Wherever we start to think that things are certain, uncertainty is lurking right there. Heedlessness is just holding things as certain. It is grasping at certainty where there is no certainty and looking for truth in things that are not true. Be careful! They are likely to bite you sometime in the future!

So in dealing with things, true or false, good or bad, pleasing or displeasing, never mind—it's important to train the mind to accord with the path, which means establishing right view. Please don't be careless! Don't get carried away building anything up, making a big deal out of it to the point that you get lost. If there is disappointment and upset over things, know that there is unhappiness, but don't let the suffering exceed the truth of what it is. If you like things, don't get carried away. You can have the liking, but it should not become excessive. In the local idiom we say, "Don't get drunk!" When you meet unhappy situations, don't become drunk with unhappiness. When you experience happiness or pleasure, don't become drunk with that. We say, "Don't get drunk," but it just means not to let things go to excess. Have a sense of moderation. If things stay with us, that's OK. If things leave us, that is OK. But if we are intoxicated with things, we suffer when we lose them. Or if unpleasant phenomena stay and won't leave, we suffer. If we grasp them firmly, we exceed the truth of them and lose the path. This is not Dharma, and we are not practitioners of Dharma. This excess leads us to stray from the path.

This straying is wrong view, which is the cause of suffering. The explanations about practice are aimed at knowing the cessation of suffering. Practicing according to that understanding is simply practicing to realize the cessation of suffering. If we have this kind of view, we know suffering and how it arises. We know its cessation and the way to practice to bring about cessation. This is what is called knowledge in Buddhism. It doesn't refer to anything else. If we don't understand suffering, we are going to get involved in suffering without any moderation. If we like something, we are not likely to establish any limits, there will be no reflection on whether or not it is really beneficial, and we won't heed anyone's counsel. No one will be able to stop us. Someone may be gorging himself on his favorite delicacies, and no matter what you tell him he has no desire to control himself. "No problem, I assure you!" To him it's all good, simply because he likes it. He doesn't think about later in the day when he will feel sick and bloated; when it's too late, he is taken by surprise and gets upset.

So the Buddha wanted us to know, this is suffering, this is the cause of suffering, this is the ending of suffering, and this is the path to ending suffering. All practice can be summarized into these factors. This is really all there is. To put the Dharma into concise, succinct terms, there is suffering born and suffering passing away. Outside of this, there is nothing else. Suffering arises; suffering passes away.

Why are we suffering, lost in the cycle of *samsara*, or "conditioned existence"? Because we don't know these things according to the truth; we don't know suffering. So we pick up

10

suffering, thinking it will bring happiness, and it ends up biting us. Like a farmer who sees a cobra lying alone in the field and feels sorry for it. He thinks, We should have lovingkindness toward creatures and give them a little help and comfort. He doesn't know what it really is. He doesn't know this is a creature that will inflict terrible pain. So he picks it up and gently holds it to himself. When it feels the warmth and comfort, it bites him. This happens because of good intentions, but there is no knowledge. This is something that can kill; you should understand this. It is just the same for us when we don't understand suffering, its coming into existence, its cessation, and the way to cessation.

All suffering and unsatisfactory experience come from causes. When the causes end, the suffering ends. All dharmas, whether pleasant or unpleasant, arise from causes. Knowing the four aspects—suffering, its arising, cessation, and the path—is all we need. No other Dharma is necessary, because everything is naturally condensed into these aspects.

The points of contact, the receiving apparatus, are the eyes, ears, nose, tongue, body, and mind. When the mind is aware and recognizes that experience is suffering, it will let go. It actually lets go in a great hurry.

So you who practice, please know this clearly. Knowing this important fact will enable you to be decisive in your practice. There are many scholarly and scriptural approaches to elucidate and help people see this clearly. Some of you have no doubt studied the sutras and the abhidharma. They talk extensively about the mind, and you may have gotten the idea that you need to learn all of this. It seems like a good thing, but you can get stuck in the discussion without really knowing what it is pointing out. You merely learn to enumerate the things that the scriptures say.

An easy example is the study of arithmetic. Some people have to learn methodically, step by step, and then they are able to do things with numbers. But for some, this isn't necessary. They have a natural affinity for numbers, so they don't need to learn the method of adding, the method of subtracting, and so on. They merely use the method of thinking, and they can intuitively figure sums, knowing immediately the same things as the person who has studied laboriously and employs the learned methods. There are different approaches for different kinds of people. The results are of equal worth, but the ways of reaching them are different. You could say that the intuitive people have no brand name. They haven't undergone a standard course of study, they haven't learned methods, but they know just the same and can get the same results. Their knowledge is also valid and useful.

You can practice without much study and still know well. The pacceka buddhas, the "solitary enlightened ones" who become awakened without a teacher, are a good example of this. They can't teach anyone, but they can instruct themselves. Though they know within themselves, they cannot tell others. They are always peaceful and radiant, but they cannot teach anyone else. It's like being a mute. A mute can dream, and in the dream she sees fields, mountains, animals, and so on. When she wakes, she can't tell others about it. If an ordinary person dreams of snakes, he can tell others about the snakes he saw; if he dreams of cattle, he can tell others about the cattle. The pacceka buddhas are just like a mute who has dreamed about something. Still, they have no desire, anger, or delusion and are out of the cycle of birth and death. Their burden is small. The mute has the same knowledge and experience as the one who sees the various things in dreams and is able to speak about it. In their knowledge, they are equal.

So all these things are within. The Buddha wanted us to seek out the truth. This is where truth is. When something is dirty, there are those who will simply try to avoid it. Actually, the problem is how to clean it. When you wash and scrub it, you see cleanliness in the same place where there was dirt. But some will see the unclean and want to get away from it, thinking the clean must be somewhere else. Cleanliness and dirtiness are mixed together. The deluded sentient being and the enlightened one are mixed together. Knowing and not knowing are mixed together. When we can separate them out, we see clearly.

If we look at the life history of the Buddha, we see that he didn't take any shortcuts. He really did things right. But for us, there's no end to the story. With our minds, when something comes and we like it, in the end there will be sadness. Why is that? Something we don't like we can lose or discard without any sadness. Why is that? It is ordinary, an extremely ordinary occurrence for us.

Let all of us enter the practice with correct understanding. Then there will be no returning. Like the stream enterer, whose mind has inclined toward the Dharma. Then in living together there will be very few problems. If we all get to this point of inclining the mind to Dharma, we will be in harmony. Whatever anyone may say to us, we won't take our reactions as the standard. If we have a sense of responsibility, we will be honest with each other, without jealousy or strife. This is the way of people whose minds have bent to the stream. Where do such people come from? From those whose minds had not yet bent, literally called the "thick ones." Those who become virtuous people, and eventually awakened beings, are originally just this class of people, no other.

So to summarize what our practice is about, we can use the terms that traditionally describe the four virtuous qualities of the *sangha*, or "the community of genuine practitioners." Whoever practices well; who is upright; who practices to escape from samsara; who practices wisely by way of body, speech, and mind will find it all coming together at the one point of accomplishment.

I

HEARING
DHARMA

IN TEACHING THE DHARMA, things have to be repeated over
and over for people to gain real understanding. This is normal. It's
what has to be done in order to get the important points across.

The words of the Buddha are called "good speech," because
they lead people's minds to the truth. It is speech that is good and
reasonable and full of meaning. When it really touches the mind,
one desists from harming oneself and others and gives up the
three poisons of desire, anger, and delusion.

But some will hear it and call it wrong speech, because it
doesn't agree with their opinions and habits. Actually, the things
that agree with sentient beings' minds are not always good. In
our minds there are concepts of right and wrong, but those
things are uncertain. Good speech, however, is straight, direct,
and upright. It is neither profound nor shallow, rather it is the
speech of the Buddha, which has the purpose of reducing the
emotional afflictions and getting free of delusion.

Such words do not merely try to follow people's personal

preferences. Some will say, "If it disagrees with me, it isn't good speech, and it can't be Dharma." But it's not a matter of that which agrees being good and that which disagrees being bad. These are just preconceptions and biases, the listener's habitual likes and dislikes. If we try to have everything agree with us, there will be no end to difficulty. We won't want to do anything disagreeable. Whatever we like, we will wish to embrace and act on it, no matter how much grief it brings. Poisonous food may be tasty, but there is danger later on.

The speech of the Buddha and of his disciples is all good; it is Dharma. But when ordinary people hear it, they may not understand it easily if it is not presented in a way that can reach their minds. It is not easy to see or easy to practice.

Any language is a tool to help us understand. Language is only language. If someone says just one word of English to me, I don't have a clue what they're saying, and it has no value or meaning to me even though it's a popular language now. Wherever we live, in whatever country, let us speak things that help us understand right and wrong clearly. This kind of speech is useful; it is Dharma. But know that hearing Dharma is for the purpose of the mind seeing and being Dharma, not for mere knowledge or memorization. It should enable us to follow in the footsteps of the Buddha and practice according to what he taught. Even though we have not yet attained realization, we should put language to work and contemplate it.

It's easy, in a way. For example, the Buddha said laziness and negligence are not good. Having heard that, when you find them arising in your mind, as they will, you recognize and know them for what they are. Then you can escape from indolence and give rise to diligence. When laziness arises, it is nowhere but in the mind. When it comes, let it be a cause for practicing Dharma, which means going against, reducing, and transforming this laziness. We listen to Dharma to make our minds into Dharma, to let it arise in our minds; if it has not yet arisen, we strive to make it arise. It's not so difficult to practice. We just need to apply effort to make the mind pay attention and work like this. You want your mind to be Dharma, not merely the sounds that come from

*Ajahn Chah (fourth from left, standing)
with a group of senior monks, circa 1980.*

your mouth. Don't keep the knowledge in your brain or in your mouth. Make the gates of body, speech, and mind consistent in Dharma.

Listening to Dharma is for the purpose of knowing how to practice Dharma. So if we say, "Practice to make it Dharma," then what exactly is Dharma? Everything in this world. Something that is not Dharma does not exist. Forms that we can see with the eye are nothing but Dharma. Beings in the world are all Dharma. One meaning of Dharma is nature, which arises just as it is, and which nobody can fashion or alter. The nature of phenomena is Dharma. This refers to objects, the world of forms.

The Buddha said to see Dharma and enter Dharma, that is, to see all things as they really are. Living beings and material objects, as well as the inner phenomena of feeling and thinking—all this is Dharma. There are these two categories: objects that can be seen by the eye or known by the other senses, and mind, which cannot be seen in that way. It is nothing far away from us, just mind and body. But this Dharma, this nature, arises independent of our wishes, from causes and conditions. In the middle it changes, and in the end it breaks up and disappears. The Dharma of nature has power above all things. No one can request it to become greater or less. Natural things have their own mode of existing according to their causes.

The Dharma that we come to request, the precepts and teaching, is a tool to help us understand. The teaching is words. Dharma does not exist in the words, rather the words are a path, something to point out the way to people, catch their minds, and lead them to know and realize Dharma. So it is said that the teaching itself is not Dharma. We hear with the ear and speak with the tongue, but that is not of ultimate value. These words and concepts are not Dharma itself. If they were actually Dharma, they would have an independent existence of their own above all things. So coming to understand Dharma is just a matter of working to develop the wisdom to see things according to truth rather than destroying or changing anything.

Take the body as an illustration. It is born of causes and conditions. When it is born it has a certain power, a law, to exist in a certain way, and doesn't listen to anyone. We were born, we were little, and we grew to adulthood and got older, our bodies changing according to their nature. They grow and age, no matter what anyone says, thinks, or wants. It doesn't do any good to cry and moan, to ask it to stop for even a day. In the beginning it is born according to causes, it develops by conditions, and in the end it will break up, not depending on anyone's wishes or orders. This is the nature of life, existing by this unchanging law. So the Buddha taught us to look at this point; this is extremely important. Skin, teeth, hair, and the rest, what will you see there? Constant change. Having arisen, they seek their own end and go on decaying on their own. Having arisen, they do not depend on the power of beings, but on the power of the causes and conditions that brought them into existence. Having arisen, they decay in the same way. They don't need to ask permission or agreement of any of us to help them grow, age, wither, and die. This happens on its own. We don't have authority over them. This is form, the body, changing according to its own nature, dissolving in the end. This is *sabhava dharma*, or "natural conditions." In any direction or place, there will never come a day when we can argue with it or tell it, "Hey, listen to me. Pay attention to my cries. Don't get old. Do as I say." Nature is like this. It is part of the Dharma that the Buddha taught. We are not these things, nor are we their owners.

If our awareness of these truths is not clear, if instead we are deluded about nature, it is called the dharma of delusion. Then we see these things as self, as ours, and in terms of self and others. This is ignorance, and when there is ignorance, mental formations arise. We struggle with things. We want to control, to get this or avoid that, and fall prey to like and dislike. "This is something I like, please let me have more of it. That is something I can't stand, please don't let it come to me. This should be like this, that should be like that." Such thinking comes from delusion. You become like someone who tries to seize another's house and field, taking what is not really yours. The desires just keep on appearing in great heaps, and you won't even know where they came from or what they are leading you to do.

Teaching and listening to Dharma, that this is such and that is such, are not really Dharma. They are words to point something out so that you can enter and see. Speaking to help people see the truth is skillful means, or ways of teaching, the dharma of study. When it is only speech without actually seeing, when you merely want to learn the words to be able to repeat them, no benefit comes. When you apply the words and see that this is the way things are, the unchanging constant law arising according to causes and conditions without a self or essence, this is actually what the Buddha was teaching about. If you don't yet see, there is suffering. If you do see, you won't long for anything. There will be no more tears or laughter over things.

We have been crying and laughing without end since we were little children; we have been insane, without rest. Always trying to get something that is not ours, always in contention, desiring something we can never really get, we are always living in a state of dissatisfaction and suffering. If you listen in order to make the mind Dharma and practice so that you see Dharma, you will finish with the problems of this life. It can end here. Understand that things do not exist for you to be able to season, modify, or improve them. They are just unalterable nature, the way they are, arising and passing away. When you have studied and practiced Dharma, you understand that the Buddha did not teach to fix things but to see according to truth. If you want to change things, that is not Dharma, that is not truth; it is just the habit of someone who wants to create and manipulate. If you do not see the truth of the way things are, there is no path to practice, and you are outside of the noble truths of suffering, its cause, its cessation, and the path.

Since the very beginning of the Buddha's dispensation, for those who hear and practice there has not been any requirement to adjust or modify things, only to know and surrender. Wisdom is that which knows according to the truth of *sankhara*, or "conditioned phenomena." However sankhara are, that is what we need to know. Sankhara have their nature to arise and pass away. Any other view of things is impure dharma, the teaching of ignorance embedded in the heart. There will be no cessation, the wheel turning endlessly: no solution, no end, no way to stop.

It's like insects crawling on the rim of a water barrel. They are always moving, but they aren't going anywhere, only traveling around and around the rim. The thoughts of ordinary benighted beings are the same. There is no finish or resolution; they just remain in the same old place. We may think we are headed far away, but we are only going around in circles, always coming back to the same place. We don't see this cycle in the heart because there is no wisdom to see. We rely on delusion as our wisdom, and real wisdom is nowhere to be found. This ignorance becomes the manager, there is no standard to practice by, and things get out of hand. This is not Dharma. In Dharma we want to see, according to the Buddha's words. This means seeing that there is no solution, nothing to change or adjust, because Dharma is always complete as it is. So we give up trying to control.

We can't increase or decrease things. We tend to think that things aren't right, that they are too big or too small. Why are they too big or too small? Because of our perception. Such is merely the deluded desire of uninstructed people, and it is as foolish and tiring as someone boxing and wrestling with a tree. So the Buddha advised us to see according to Dharma.

Whatever we may perceive has its existence according to nature and merely that. If we have awareness that knows according to Dharma, then no matter what things arise, there is no unhappy result. Whatever may happen to the body will not affect us. We will see that there is no profit from compounded phenomena, and we will remain unshakable in our own place, all things pacified. The Buddha said to investigate this body and the other foundations of mindfulness. There is nothing to solve or undo; we just need to know according to the truth.

The body experiences birth, aging, and death. There is nothing stable in it. Know that this reality is Dharma. It is the truth, and there is nothing to change, destroy, or solve. When you get to this point there is nothing more to say. There is no more burden to carry. If you know according to truth, there is no heedlessness about what you are doing, wherever you may be. You just see things as they are, conditions arising and passing away. Then what will you seek? What will you get upset and cry about? What do you want to toil and suffer over? What do you want to have or be? When will you say things are big or small, long or short? In the end, what will you say about nature? There is this cycle of existence, and that is all. When you see this profound truth, you will be at peace, free, without sorrow, in conflict with no one.

Seeing natural conditions arising and changing is called studying Dharma. Having learned about this, you should then train in it. The person who still has cravings does not see. If you have anger and get upset with people, it is because you haven't penetrated the Dharma. You are still fooled by things and have no freedom. Learning counteracts this. Then there will be an end to problems. There are problems only because there is the belief that there is me and mine. When you believe things this way, when thoughts of me and mine arise, countless problems will come to you endlessly. Selfishness and all kinds of troubles appear.

When a traveler arrives at a hotel, he negotiates a price for a room and informs the staff of how long he will be staying. But as he gets comfortable there, he may begin to feel like the hotel is his home, and after a while he forgets about moving on. When the management tells him that he must give up the room, he refuses to leave. "This is where I live! Why should I leave?" There is some misunderstanding, and it leads to strife.

When we start to identify with our bodies and minds and think of this life as ours, then we are similar to the traveler who doesn't want to leave the hotel. We have a wrong idea about this temporary stopping place, and we find ourselves always in struggle and conflict. Children of the same parents end up fighting, people in the same village cannot get along, citizens of the same country are at odds with each other, all because of this attachment to what they think is a self and things belonging to the self.

So the Buddha said to come back and look at the body. That is one Dharma to study. There is nothing we should undo or change. We say, "One who sees sankhara and is purged of attachment has happiness." Mind is sankhara. Body is sankhara. Sankhara are not us or ours. Thus, those who see sankhara are at peace. They see the mind and body not as self, but only as sankhara.

If something arises into existence, it is just sankhara. There is no being or person, no one who is happy or suffering. It is only sankhara. It is purged of happiness or suffering. There is nobody who is affected. If you see sankhara like this, you see Dharma. Nobody is any sort of entity, not a person, an individual, or a being. There is no one who is elated or miserable, no one who gets angry or attached, no one who dies. Things arise. Sankhara are like that. Seeing Dharma is like that. Whatever arises in the minds of yogins, they will know the Dharma to that extent. If your view is like this, it is called merit. All merits come together here, at the point of peace.

If we try to adjust or change Dharma because of a lack of clear vision, there will be suffering. Take the breath, for example. It is continuously flowing in and out without break. The body depends on it for life. It is nourishment; like food, it enters the body and supports it. The air goes in and out so the sankhara can survive. In and not out, or out and not in—there is trouble. But having been born, we don't want to get old. We don't want to die. Being together, we don't wish to part. Having things, we don't want to lose them. But it can't turn out as we wish, because this is just the way things are.

All dharmas arise from causes and conditions. When the causes and conditions exist, the result occurs accordingly. Who has created this? It is just the law of nature. When it breaks up, that is also nature. This law is called Dharma.

Formal teaching to explain this is simply a matter of skillful language and speech. It is not genuine Dharma itself, but only the path to train people and point out the way to understand truth. Still, we think that we have Dharma, we understand Dharma, we are Dharma. Well, if this were really the case, we would not have craving, anger, or delusion. If we did know, see, and embody Dharma, we wouldn't have these things. So we are the slaves of the afflictions without any surcease. If we really see, these things just evaporate from us. The profound Dharma is like this. That is one matter.

Then there is the dharma of practicing a code of conduct, people living together with restraint and consideration. This too is Dharma, living together without quarrel or strife. It is called *siladharma*, or "the way of virtuous behavior." It is the Dharma that the populace at large needs to practice for happiness. But this happiness is just attained as the beginning of suffering.

It's a little better than people who have no knowledge or morality. But still, we make this happiness and keeping it leads to suffering. This alone does not get us beyond, but it is still better than not having it. Making the causes and conditions for going beyond is another matter.

So when you listen to the Dharma, don't think that's all there is to do. Take it to heart and practice. Make it the cause and condition for attainment of nirvana, the deathless, the cessation of suffering and true peace.

We who are Buddhists need to study this, learn it little by little, and put it into practice through meditation. Even if desire, negativity, and foolishness are in our hearts, let us know them. When they arise, we know them and we know Dharma. Know that they are our enemies. "Oh, when will they be removed?" Remove them step by step through consistent practice—not through consistent sleep. Practice sila and Dharma. There will still be some grasping attachment remaining, but you will know you have it. Even if you are suffering, don't let it get too great, but have a boundary and be aware of it. When you are tending cows and buffaloes, they may get into the field, so you have to control them. They may eat some grain, but don't let them eat a lot. They will only eat a little because you are on the job. If you sleep through the day, they will probably polish off your crop. So you can't be heedless.

Our aim in coming to study and practice is for our minds to see Dharma; when our minds see Dharma, we will end suffering. We don't need to wonder what we are practicing for. We have eyes and ears, legs that are not broken. If we have opened our eyes, we will do what needs to be done, without waiting for or depending on the blind ones. We are able to speak. We are not mute. When we see, we can speak before them. We wake up first, and we get going early in the morning, not waiting for the ones who still sleep.

Why? Because this is a place of danger, it is a place of turmoil and confusion, an imperfect realm full of faults. The Buddha taught that, if you know, you should just go and not wait for the benighted. If your legs can carry you, don't wait for the ones with broken legs. Why? Escape from the enemy little by little until you are free and clear. It means developing virtue and knowledge. Until the day you get free of evil, you make the causes of goodness little by little, and this becomes the cause that is dedicated to the aim of everyone getting free. Awaken yourself!

Lotuses in the same pond don't grow at the same pace. While

some are blooming, some are still in the water, and others are at the level of the water. You should do what you can according to your abilities. If you wait for the others, you might be eaten by fish and turtles.

When fire is flaring up and threatening to burn down your house, you can't ignore it and take a rest. You have possessions, and you have to grab them and get out. Desire, anger, and delusion scorch us just like that. Death follows us always, every day without cease. At the very least, we should reduce our becoming and birth in the round of existence. In all our merit-making and other spiritual activities, we recite, "May it be a cause for realizing nirvana." What should we do to make the causes for nirvana? Meditation is essential. You don't merely sit here and listen to the words; that doesn't become a cause. First you listen, then you have to contemplate the meaning. The things you are supposed to give up, give them up. "This guy hasn't got it yet . . . That one, I'm not sure about the way she practices. . . ." Don't entertain such thoughts; don't push it off on someone else. If a tiger is chasing you, you don't wait for the other person to run—how will you escape the tiger like this? This is a danger to *you*!

Nirvana is not a place to stay or go to. Or put another way, it is not going and not stopping. It doesn't have advancing, retreating, or stopping. Understand that. When you enter and see, the fruit will come on its own. See the Dharma, earn your profit, and then even if you haven't gotten to the end of the path, there will be no more doubting.

This is appropriate for those of us who come to study the Dharma. Outside of the Dharma of our Teacher, there is nothing that can bring us to live in harmony together, to go beyond suffering and unsatisfactory experience, and to realize happiness and tranquility.

Dharma is far superior to anything you can find in the home. The things we have at home generally only bring trouble. It's not like they are going to cause peace. In the realm of family and possessions, there are only things for worry, concern, and struggle, things that stab us. Dharma has more value than that.

But if we live among these things, we must have Dharma. We

can't do without it. If there is no Dharma to match these things, they are not complete. Don't be careless. If we really understand and contemplate Dharma, we will see value in it. The things at home will still be there, but if we see Dharma we will stop carrying them. Then there is still the busyness and involvement, but we know what it is all about and won't take it for something real. Like dealing with a child, who says, "Mom, this happened. Dad, I need that. Hey, look at me." The parent says, "Yes, sure, OK," but doesn't take it too seriously. You answer to make the child feel happy and secure, but your mind is not caught up in the story, because you don't think in that way. So you can remain with your family and worldly responsibilities, doing what you have to do, but you aren't following the stream of worldliness. You are acting for peace and detachment, not for slavery and involvement. This is called the accomplishment and enjoyment of wealth. Even though you have wealth and possessions, you know them for what they are, know how to use them and live above them.

If you can practice like this, you will come to know that Dharma really does have value. But it is necessary to understand, to contemplate and practice.

If you think things are real there is suffering and there is fear. You are afraid of the different ways things may turn out. Everywhere you look there is fear. Actually you just fear yourself. There is thinking, then fear follows immediately. It deceives you, creating a picture to mislead you. For people who are so fearful, whether they go into a house or a forest, there will immediately be ghosts haunting them. Even when they hear mice running around, they are frightened and think it's the sound of ghosts. Immediately they are afraid, but it is only consciousness making a picture to deceive.

Or maybe you have some problem at home. Just thinking about it makes you want to cry. People criticize each other. "This one doesn't care about me, and that one makes trouble for me." The mind runs away like that. Actually no one is doing anything to you, but you, making the pictures. If you make the pictures, you will get lost and eventually end up crying. If you get very happy, you are making a picture. It gets to the point of laughing or crying, but still it is just you doing it. "This is good; this is really good!" You are just forgetting yourself, lost in your joy and laughter. The mind picks up one thing and you feel fear; something else you may feel is repulsive, so you hate it. Then you love another thing, you become obsessed until you are actually insane and there is no end to your tears flowing. There is no end to it when you react like this, making pictures.

All this is just the carrying on of people. As to what is actually happening, there is nothing. There is nothing to cry or laugh over, nothing worthy of love or hate in itself. It is only your mind being tricked. So the Buddha said to work on your mind here, correct your mind at this point. The Dharma is genuine, it is certain; it is the truth. But we are not true. We laugh and we cry. We love and hate, reacting to things. Things are said to be good and bad, and off we go in pursuit. Because we believe that we exist as self-entities and that things belong to us. This is just being deluded.

So you should not take anything—the body in good or bad health, the mind in elation or depression—as being too real. You only destroy yourself by doing that. The Buddha said when happiness comes, don't believe it too much. It is not something to cry or laugh over. It isn't something out there. It is here within us where things are happening, results being born from causes. There is really nothing, only our grasping, that makes things appear like this. Not seeing Dharma, we are always trying to make real these things that are not real.

But when we talk about things not being real, some will say there is nothing we can do. It doesn't mean being totally passive and defeated. Without going to extremes and believing too much in things as real, you take care of things as is appropriate. While objects are not yet broken, while the body is not yet sick, take care of them so you can make good use of them. When things break, you let go without tears—don't end up crying over these internal and external phenomena for no purpose. We have the habit of seeing body and mind as self. We call them "us" and "ours." But when we are involved in such grasping, we are outside of the Dharma, and the only result is that we suffer.

You should understand that all the things we practice are for leading the mind to see Dharma and to be Dharma. If you see Dharma, then although you have had the habit of anger, even if it returns it will come with decreasing energy. The same is true of desires, and this is because of the understanding and sensitivity born in the mind from correct practice and understanding. It will change you for the better. You don't need to change or improve on the Dharma. Don't try to resolve things that are done already. Resolve the things that are not yet accomplished facts. If you are trying to plane a piece of wood that is full of knots and hard like a rock, you should know when to give up. Or will you just sit there and cry over it? And if another piece is already smooth and varnished, you don't need to plane it further. Instead of trying to adjust the Dharma to fit you, adjust yourself to fit the Dharma.

Dharma is truth. If you reach the truth, there is no big or small, no happiness or suffering. There is peace. Even if there is thinking, the mind must be peaceful. If you experience phenomena, they will be just right, with nothing to try to increase or decrease. The characteristics of the mind will be such that when the mind meets objects and conditions, it has this truth.

It's like having only one chair in a room. You sit there, and when others come, they have nowhere to sit. Mind is like this. The mental afflictions may come, but because Dharma is in the mind they have nowhere to sit down, so they will have to go on their way. If you have mindful awareness of yourself, then when sense-contact and mental activity give rise to the habits of desire, anger, and delusion, there is no place for them to stay in the mind. There is one seat and you are occupying it already, so the habits cannot sit. They will leave the room. They can't move you from Dharma. The path and the afflictions fight it out in the mind. If there is no one sitting there, the afflictions can sit down and become the owners. This means you don't have presence of mind. You don't understand Dharma, so delusion can take the seat. Then there is no end to suffering.

The path and defilements fight each other in this way. If the path is brought to fullness, then when things happen in the mind, we meet the Dharma. This takes a person with energy; one who is not energetic will retreat at this point. The factors involved here are simply mind and its internal and external objects. If the mind is not fooled by these objects, what is the problem? Objects are objects, mind is mind. This is listening to Dharma to make it reach the mind. When that happens and Dharma enters the mind, there is no problem—the path kills the afflictions with this meditation practice.

If there is no one home, unwanted guests can come and make themselves comfortable. They sit down and eat and make a mess. Is that the result you want? Because you don't understand Dharma, and don't know right and wrong, good and bad, and don't recognize the way the mind contacts objects and reacts, they push you all over the place. If things appear to be good, you will smile and laugh. If they are bad, they make you upset and you may come to tears. It is the same as the house with its owner absent. Spinning around like that, unable to separate things, this is a Dharma practitioner who doesn't really know Dharma. It is someone who is operating at a loss. So you have to meditate to get the Dharma to enter your mind. This is why we listen to the Dharma on every lunar observance day and other holidays.

So in all activities and postures, learn to do this. When sense-objects come, get a handle on them by remembering they are one thing and the mind is another. Separate them out. Otherwise you don't know them. You follow what you perceive as good and bad, and this brings suffering. Not satisfied with them, you suffer. The mind is deluded by objects; the mind lacks discernment. So set up mindful recollection and awareness of yourself.

We say that in all postures, you should keep the meditation on Buddho in mind. *Buddho* means that "the one who knows," is arising continuously. When objects come, you know them. You can resolve things and can expound the truth. This is the fruit of Buddho. Let there be the one who knows; practice Buddho just for this. This is called hearing Dharma and realizing fruition, knowing Dharma and practicing it. You should be practicing and seeing it so you become it in your mind. This is called one who understands and sees. This is the way that the Buddha's teaching bears fruit.

2

UNDERSTANDING
DHARMA

The Here and Now Dharma

WE PRACTICE DHARMA BECAUSE we see the value of noble treasure, the wealth that is within. We have attachment to material wealth, but now we try to exchange it for inner wealth. This kind of wealth will be free from the dangers of the elements, such as flood and fire, as well as that of thieves. It is something that they cannot find. No external threats can touch this happiness of mind. This is what the Buddha meant when he spoke about merit. Making offerings is one source of such happiness, because we are overcoming the tendencies toward greed and miserliness.

Whatever Dharma practice we are doing, whether it is giving, keeping moral precepts, or meditating on lovingkindness toward all beings, the Lord Buddha has taught that they should all come to a single point, the pursuit of peace. So *Paccupana Dharma*, the "here and now truth," is something extremely important. We practice various activities we call Dharma, such as making offerings to support the Buddhist religion, but we should know just what this is. Merely seeking merits may not bring us to the *Buddhasasana*, the "dispensation of the Buddha." We need to distinguish between merit and skillfulness. Merit on its own is lacking in wisdom, and without wisdom we will never be free of suffering. Merit without skillfulness is like carrying something and not being able to put it down; it ultimately gets heavy enough to crush us. Skillfulness knows when to let go. Together they support the Buddhasasana. We listen to Dharma to increase our skillfulness and happiness, and then to reflect on these things to create benefit for ourselves and others. We learn to let go, because holding on to things leads only to suffering. *Dukkha*, the "pervasive unsatisfactoriness of life," is not the way it has to be. But do you know the causes? Suffering is in the present; we don't have to look to the past. Dharmas all come from a cause. They don't just mysteriously float up into existence. Nothing in this world can make people suffer but a lack of knowledge. Is a boulder heavy? If we just walk by it, where is the heaviness? But if we try to lift it, that's another story.

So birth, youth, aging, poverty, riches, and so forth are all suffering if we don't know them. The Buddha said that we should know dukkha and the other Noble Truths, the cause, cessation, and path. If we do know, there is nothing to suffer over.

Some people say that suffering is a fixed part of the mind, that it has been there forever. I was talking to someone about this just today. I tried to explain that suffering is not intrinsic to the mind. It arises in the present moment. You have a mood of aversion in the mind and you experience suffering now. Think about a lemon. If you leave it alone, is it sour? Where is the sourness then? It's when the lemon contacts the tongue that sourness occurs. If you aren't experiencing it, it's as if it isn't there. When there is contact with the tongue it arises at that moment. And from there arise dislike and afflictions. These afflictions are not intrinsic to the mind, but are momentary arisings.

When the mind has attained peace, that is the end of the path.

Ajahn Chah, circa 1977.

This is the goal the Buddha wished everyone to realize. But before we reach the end, we need to know how to practice in order to attain a peaceful mind. Our minds are not peaceful because they have not realized the genuine Dharma. The mind is still unskilled and unreliable, lacking the wisdom that knows things as they are, that sees the truth of all phenomena or sabhava dharma (natural conditions). Sabhava means "existing like that," existing just as it is. Whether or not a Buddha appears in the world, phenomena exist as they are. They do not change into some other mode of existence.

We are taught to begin with right understanding. Then there are right thought, right action, right speech, right livelihood, right effort, right mindfulness, and right meditation. We say there are eight, but they are really factors of the one path upon which each individual must travel. When understanding is correct, thinking will be correct, and so will speech and all the other factors. When the mind is established in what is correct, the entire progression of the path must be correct. Nothing will be wrong, and walking the path will lead to peace.

The Buddha taught about letting go. When there is pleasurable experience, he said to recognize that it is merely pleasure. When there is painful experience, he said to recognize that it is merely pain. There is no one experiencing pleasure or pain, happiness or suffering. These things appear as a result of previous causes, but when we are practicing correctly we won't find any owner of them. The Buddha taught us to see that it is merely happiness, merely suffering—not a self, a being, a person, or an individual entity. This is right view. There is no self or owner of these conditions.

We think in terms of *my* leg, *my* arm, *my* friends. Thus we see self. But according to Dharma, this is not seeing self. Understanding that these are not self is seeing self. You see it but don't carry it. If you see a snake but don't pick it up, there's no poisonous bite. It's still a snake, but the poison doesn't get you. So the Buddha said to see self. This is difficult to hear and understand. The world has its conventions. The teachings of the world, when they reach the mind of the Buddha, are all false.

The teachings of the enlightened ones, when they reach the minds of worldly beings, are false.

When people feel they are the owners of good and bad experience or that these things happen to their selves, they are at the mercy of impermanence. Because all things are subject to change, being attached to them can only produce experience that is unsatisfactory. You are sometimes pleased and sometimes upset as things come and go and keep changing. There is turmoil because wrong view has invaded your mind and given you mistaken ideas. You end up carrying happiness and suffering, and they get heavy for you.

If there is right view, then feeling is merely feeling. Pleasure is merely pleasure. Pain is merely pain. There is no owner of either pleasure or pain. The Buddha wanted us to contemplate in this way. If we contemplate for some time, there comes about that quality of the Dharma that calls the mind to look and see what is going on. What exactly is this happiness we experience? What is this suffering we have? Are they something stable or permanent? Or how exactly are they? We are certainly able to look at things we have experienced before. Happiness we've had—did it end? Have we ever had unhappiness? Did it last forever? When we come to know about phenomena and don't get so involved with them, the mind becomes peaceful because we are no longer trying to own anything. But still we can enjoy our lives and make use of things in this world. The household items we have— kitchen goods, furniture, and so on—are not really ours. We use them, but it is in order to gain the realization that they are not ours. We can use them freely and comfortably without having to suffer over them. We use them with a knowledge that is comprehensive and transcends ordinary ways. If we cannot be above all these things, we are under them, carrying them with the attachment that says, "This is mine," bearing their weight. This wrong view can only lead to suffering because things will never work out exactly as we desire.

Why do things break? Because they exist. Seeing things as already broken, you don't need to cry if they break. If the cup is not mine, then without this involvement, whether it breaks or not there is no problem. You have things in your house, so you'd better think about this. Still, you have to teach your kids to take care of things. If you just say, "It's not ours," you'll end up with no plates to eat off of. You speak in one way but see in another way; if you use adult concepts for children, no one cleans the dishes.

Living in the world there will always be things we must do, but we do them with letting go, and the mind is peaceful, without distress. So we can work at ease. This is right livelihood. Even if we have hard, grueling work, it's OK.

The Buddha wants us to escape from birth, but we want birth. What are we going to get? We don't see the liability yet. We still don't see the way the Buddha sees. His teaching talked of the conceit that says, "I am better than others; I am equal to others; I am worse than others." If we think in any of these ways, it is not accurate. If we don't have this conceit, there is no obstruction.

People want happiness, riches, and so forth. They are attached to merit, only wanting tangible benefits but not making real spiritual progress. In arithmetic there are adding, subtracting, multiplying, and dividing, but we only want addition and multiplication. This is just self-cherishing. People will practice their meritorious activities but still experience sickness and other problems, and they begin to wonder, Why does this happen? Where is the merit? But that isn't the point of merit and virtue. You don't seek merit to cause a cat to become a dog; it isn't something to change the nature of sankhara (conditioned phenomena). They are, by nature, unreliable. Whatever happens, you needn't get overly concerned or upset.

What we call skillfulness or wholesomeness is translated in our language as cleverness, a circumspect quality with which we can live our lives in the world. It is necessary to have merit and skillful means working together. Merit is like raw meat, which will go bad after a while. Wisdom is the salt that preserves it. Or you can put it in the refrigerator! It is said, there is no light like wisdom, no river like *tanha*, or "craving." So the Buddha advised, in acting, eating, and seeing, don't let them become tanha. Live in the world but know the world clearly, not letting the heart become flooded by craving; that is, keep letting go.

The Buddha's teaching is for the purpose of helping every being to escape from the cycle of samsara. But we who have such coarse defilements of mind and feeble wisdom have different ideas. When we hear the Dharma that says nothing is ours, we become afraid that we won't get anything; it just makes us uncomfortable.

Actually, we *can* say that these are our selves and things are ours, but that is only a conventional reality. It is not on the level of liberation. We need to learn about the way we use conventions in all aspects of our lives. For example, our names. When we were born, we didn't bring a name with us. After we came into this world, we were given a name. There wasn't any old name to be replaced—it was empty there. In the space that is empty, you can put anything. People are born empty like this, and a name is put on them, a designation for this existence. So we can call the person John or Mary or whatever, and they come to be so according to conventional understanding. They are not really John or Mary. They are a supposed John or Mary, not an ultimately true John or Mary. Really there is no one there, just natural conditions. But if we want John to come we have to say, "John." If we want to call Mary, we have to use the name she was given. It is a convenience for communicating and functioning in this world, that's all.

Having been born, things pass away. Having passed away, things are born again. Birth and passing away: all conditions are like this. When we look clearly, we will come to realize that what the Buddha taught is the truth. When we see the reality of this, it is not something that will bring suffering or impoverish us. Seeing that there is no self and that nothing belongs to us will make us much more comfortable than before. We will be able to use things at ease and live in the world at ease.

Some people will think about this and lose the desire to do anything. They think that, since they can't get anything that will be theirs, what's the use? Actually it is those who relate to things as their own and work in order to get things for themselves who suffer so greatly. It's better if we can do work for the sake of doing it, all the while realizing that there is no self involved and nothing belonging to us and training our minds to let go. Working and performing actions we will also be letting go and giving up, in accordance with the truth.

This is called right view, or right understanding. We know conventional reality as conventional reality and see how things appear to be and how we designate them as being such and such. The Buddha said that all these designations are empty. When he was teaching the Brahmin Mogharaja, he said, "Mogharaja! You should view this world as empty." These words can cause an ordinary person to lose heart. "Seeing this world as empty, the Lord of Death will not be able to follow you. He will not see you." The Buddha taught his disciples in this way.

Saying that this world is empty might give us the idea that there is nothing in the world. When we look at a bowl or a spittoon, these things do exist. It is not that they don't exist, but they exist in the sphere of emptiness. They exist but are empty. We can call something a spittoon as a convention that we create through our designation. Or we can use another convention and call it a pot. Actually it is empty of these names from its own side, but we view it in a certain way and then have attachment to seeing it as such.

There might be two people, one a clever sort, the other kind of foolish. The latter goes to the market and buys something. He doesn't really know what it is—he has unwittingly bought a chamber pot. He takes it home and uses it as a serving bowl for his rice and feels that it does the job pretty well. He doesn't know what others use it for.

When the clever guy comes along and sees this, he is startled and wonders what is going on. "What is this person doing? It's repulsive, using a chamber pot to serve rice."

So one is called foolish, the other smart. Why is the latter disgusted? The pot is new. It's never been used as a chamber pot. It's clean, so why should anyone be disgusted by this? It is only attachment to an idea, and this attachment brings about revulsion and anger. "Hey, look at this idiot, he's using a chamber pot to serve rice!" Out of these two people, which one is actually the fool?

The chamber pot is not really anything in itself. An ordinary pot is not really anything. We designate something as a chamber pot, and then if someone uses it to serve rice or soup or curry, others will feel that is a disgusting thing to do. What is the meaning of these negative feelings? It's only because of attachment to the designation, to the convention that says, "This is a chamber pot." It is not really a chamber pot in any absolute and unalterable way. It just depends on our perceptions and how we wish to use it. If it's clean, we can use it for a lot of different purposes.

If we understand the truth like this, there isn't really anything to get worked up over. We are not the owners of anything. We can use serving dishes, chamber pots, and ordinary pots without any problem. These things don't name themselves. We could call them a number of things; whatever convention will work is fine.

So it is said that our speech should be one thing but the mind another. If others are calling something a spittoon, we can do that also. If they call something a chamber pot, we can do that, too. It means adjusting ourselves to speak in accordance with the world, matching ourselves to the ways of this world in which we live. The Buddha and his disciples lived with society at large. They lived together with every kind of person, good and bad, wise and foolish. They were able to fit in anywhere because they understood the facts of conventional reality and ultimate reality. When you have this understanding, the mind is comfortable, at peace. There will be no attachment or clinging; that is the natural result of right view. You know what is convention, what is liberation, and the mind is free of disturbance, letting go of things.

The Buddha wanted us to practice Dharma. But what is practicing Dharma? Dharma means all things. The forms that the eyes see, sounds heard by the ears, these are all Dharma, because dharma means conditions that are maintained in existence. Having come into being, they pass away. We don't need to expect too much from them, because that is the way they are. We should internalize this truth and see it in our minds and bodies; it is not something far away. The components of body and mind are not stable or permanent. They have no inherent reality. The Buddha advised us not to see them as real. Why would you want to see something that has no inherent reality as real? Appearing and disappearing, constantly in a state of change—where is the reality in that? The only reality is this insubstantiality itself. The Buddha wanted us to see this truth, the truth that things are impermanent, unsatisfactory in nature, and without self-essence. Not seeing this and grasping at things, the only result is suffering. Seeing and letting go leads to freedom.

Those who genuinely practice are respectful. Why? Because they see the Buddha. When they sit here, it is as if the Buddha were in front of them. Walking, standing, lying down, it is the same—they cannot get away from it! They witness this in their own minds, so they respect Buddha, Dharma, and Sangha. The Buddhasasana does not become weakened or diluted. It is not given up and cannot be lost, because it exists in their minds. Wherever they are, they are hearing the Dharma of the Buddha.

This concept almost made my head explode when I first encountered it. I went to listen to teachings from Ajahn Mun, and he said, "You! Practice along, and listen to the Dharma of the Buddha. When you sit under a tree, listen to the teaching of the Buddha. When you walk, listen to the Dharma of the Buddha. When you sleep, listen to the Dharma of the Buddha!" I couldn't get it. I just could not figure it out, because it doesn't come from figuring and thinking. This is something that has to come from a pure mind. I couldn't properly contemplate these words, because they are talking about really seeing Dharma. But this isn't something far away, because that which is not Dharma does not exist.

We think the Buddha entered final nirvana long ago. But in truth the one who sees the Dharma sees the Buddha. It's difficult to get this point. When you see Buddha, you see Dharma. When you see Buddha and Dharma, you see Sangha. They exist in the mind. But see them clearly; don't merely pick up the words to play with. Otherwise people will say things like, "Buddha is in my mind," but their behavior doesn't match, and they never practice or realize anything according to the Buddha's intention.

The mind is the one that knows the Dharma. The one who knows is Buddha. The Buddha taught Dharma. He was enlightened to Dharma, but he did not take the enlightenment away with him. For example, you might be a teacher. You weren't born as a teacher; you studied to accumulate knowledge and got experience at teaching people. You work at it for a number of years, and someday you will retire and then pass away. But we can say the teacher doesn't die, because the virtues that make you a teacher have not disappeared. The Dharma of ultimate reality, the truth that makes one a Buddha, does not disappear. So we can say there are two Buddhas, that of his physical form and that of his mind. The Buddha said, "Ananda, practice well, develop yourself well. You will blossom in the sasana. Whoever sees Dharma sees me, and the one who sees me sees Dharma."

We hear the words and don't really know what they are about. It gets confusing—Dharma is Buddha, Buddha is Dharma. But the truth is like this. At first, there was no Buddha. When he realized Dharma, he was given the title Buddha. Before that, he was Prince Siddhattha Gotama. We are the same. We are called Joe or Alice or perhaps Prince so-and-so, but if we realize the Dharma then we too are Buddha, no different from him. So understand that the Buddha is still living.

Where is the Buddha? Whatever we do, truth is there. We think we can do evil and it doesn't matter, no one sees. Watch out! The Buddha sees. The Buddha still exists to support us to walk the path properly and continuously, but we don't see, we don't know it. Those who practice won't doubt good and evil; they are their own witness. But we think we can act in unwholesome ways and no one sees. There is no such thing. *We* see. Wherever we are, whatever we do for good or bad, we don't go beyond it. That is called karma. Truth in actions exists. The Buddha taught according to that principle. If everyone in the world were to practice and realize truth, they would all be transformed and become Buddha, the one who teaches the path of virtue.

So the Buddha still exists. You should be happy about this. It's not something to feel sad about. But some people feel frustrated and say, "Oh man, if the Buddha were still here, I would have made it by now. I would be enlightened." But in truth he is really here, in the path of practice, the standard of right and wrong.

The Buddha called humans "special beings," those able to realize Dharma. Unlike animals, for example, we can understand concepts. When trained by a qualified teacher, we can practice and realize the truth. It is much easier for us than for other beings.

The teachings say that human birth is hard to attain. This is difficult to understand. We think, How can that be? People are being born constantly. Sometimes they are even born two together. We don't quite get it because we don't know what a real human is. We look around and see plenty of people. A person without virtue is one type of human, just barely human. He or she is another kind of animal, only having the name human.

We come into this world and as children don't know what this is all about. We don't know what to practice, don't know what is the true wealth and virtue of human existence. As we grow up, we learn from parents and teachers, gradually developing virtues, and become complete humans. Then we can say that a human is born.

As humans we have greater potential than animals. I've sometimes given the example of a dog sleeping on a pile of unthreshed rice. When he gets hungry, he has to go looking for food. No matter how big the pile of rice, he can't make use of it, because a dog can't thresh rice and cook it. He might go wandering all around and find nothing, only to return to the heap of rice. He will be lying there, his empty stomach growling. He is right at the source of food but could die of starvation.

So humans have this greater potential. It can be used for good or evil. An evil person, the type we can call a human animal, may even destroy a whole nation, but we never hear of a dog destroying a country. On the other hand, if a human being takes an interest in Dharma and practices sincerely, he or she can accomplish things that are impossible for an animal.

In truth, to practice virtuous Dharma is not easy. It is correct, but difficult to do. Consider an easy example: the five precepts.

We observe them all the time. They are the measure of worth for a real human. Refraining from killing or harming any living thing, as well as spreading goodwill to all; not stealing, respecting the rights of others; knowing restraint and moderation and what is proper in sexual relations; truthful speech; and refraining from intoxicants. If everyone observed them, there wouldn't be much trouble in the world. Even without realizing Dharma, there would be little conflict, and we would really have a human world. There's not a lot to it, but those who keep the five precepts will have well-being. Recollecting the past, we will be OK *too late?* because we have done no harm, and when death comes, there will be no regret. So we are studying for the purpose of becoming real humans

Supporting the sasana by making merit is good. It is the bark and the leaves, but it's still good. A tree needs its bark, doesn't it? When you make offerings and take part in ceremonies, do it with a good mind, not a greedy or deluded mind, but as a Buddhist who believes in cause and result. When you go home and people ask, "You went to the monastery. Did you get any merit?" you can explain what merit is all about. This kind of activity is _upaya_, or "skillful means." Teaching is also one upaya. Understand this. It is convention. The real Dharma is something that we cannot see with the eyes or hear with the ears.

When a teacher instructs her students, she uses an example, such as Mr. A. has this much money. In actuality, there is no Mr. A. She uses chalk to create this person on the blackboard. Is it Mr. A.? Yes, as a supposition, a convention, but he can't run around and do things. We can talk about this Mr. A. for the purpose of learning, but he can't get up and move. This is upaya. There is no Mr. A. We just use the letter A and suppose this person into existence for some purpose.

If we just have mindfulness and clear comprehension of ourselves, we can do the practice. Some will think, I have no time to meditate, I have to sell things. Hey, when you're doing business, do you breathe? If you have time to breathe, you have time to practice Dharma. Meditation is nothing but this awareness and sensitivity, but when you talk about meditating while you sell, people think it means to sit down in the market and close your eyes. Awareness means knowing what you are doing at the moment. Today did you speak, act, and think wrongly? If you have mindfulness, you must know.

So don't think that practicing Dharma means you have to ordain and live in a monastery. When you are doing business or housework, writing or whatever, it is the same as with the breath—you don't need to set aside time just to do that. Even when you sleep you breathe. Why? Breathing is critical to life. Actually breath is an extremely refined nutrient. We can't do without it for two minutes. The finest delicacy we can do without for two hours or two weeks. But how far can we go without breath? So the Buddha told us to contemplate the breath. In and out, in conjunction with the repetition of Buddho. All parts of the body depend on it. It is the supreme food. When you contemplate, you see how valuable and precious it is for you, better than money, gold, or diamonds. If it exits and doesn't enter, your life is over. If it enters and does not exit, you are dead.

Seeing the frailty of your life through seeing the breath is the meditation on the recollection of death. Just realizing this fact—that if the breath goes in but does not go out again, or goes out but does not come in again, your life is over—is enough to change the mind. It will startle you into being awake. Your outlook will be transformed, and your behavior will change accordingly. You will fear wrong actions and have a sense of shame toward them. You won't be so inclined to follow your impulses of craving or hatred. Mindfulness will naturally increase, and wisdom will come rushing to assist you, teaching you many things.

Take an interest in your breath, set mindfulness on it, and many kinds of wisdom will arise. It is easy, because we all have breath. When you lie down, you can fix attention on it until you fall asleep. This is truly easy. It will make the mind clean and peaceful, no matter if you are an ordained person or a layperson.

Meditation is something to help us get beyond suffering. We

can see what is right and wrong, but if we don't practice we don't see clearly. Whatever we do, we should do it with knowledge. This is how the Buddha wanted his disciples to live.

The Trapper's Snare

NO ACHES AND PAINS IN the body, no fever or sickness: can there be such a thing? We beings are caught, caught in the snares of Mara, the Evil One. If we are caught in the snare, Mara can do anything to us. He can afflict us in our eyes, our ears, our limbs, anywhere.

It is the same as when someone sets a snare for animals, digs a trapper's pit, or baits a hook. When a bird comes to eat and is caught, what can it do? The snare has it by the neck; where can it go? It tries to fly, but it can't get away. It struggles but can't break the snare. Then the hunter, the owner of the trap, arrives. He sees the bird caught in the snare, just as he had hoped.

He grabs the bird. It struggles, and if it tries to nip the hunter or peck at him, he can break its beak. It may try to fly, but he can break its wings. It frantically tries to run; he can break its legs. The owner of the snare has all the authority here. However the bird tries to get away, there is no escaping.

Likewise, we are caught in a trap. The Lord Buddha was one who saw and knew clearly according to the truth. He was a prince, an heir to the throne who enjoyed all the royal treasures and privileges. When he saw what things were really like, he renounced everything. He clearly and unmistakenly saw the nature of ordinary existence and, without any regrets, left it behind. Seeing it as danger, he fled. Having been born, caught by birth, he saw that he was like a bird caught in a snare. The noose was around his neck. He saw the liability, so he left it all, just walked away. Thus, after his enlightenment, he pointed this out, showing what is harmful and what is beneficial in this realm of uncertainty. He would not allow himself to be submerged and drown in it. He refused to die there. He would not agree to be caught in the noose, so he was able to renounce the world and remove himself from it. Having seen, having attained realization, he then taught us to know about these things.

Still, though he explained the faults and dangers, the obscurations of people prevent them from seeing. The mind is so thick, so dark! It just stays like that and keeps on accumulating afflictions and desires. In all these dharmas, if we investigate, we can see the liability and suffering in them. Just as it is said "birth is suffering." We are born into this world; do we suffer? We have contacted birth. We have arms and legs, eyes and ears. All these things coming into existence are just suffering coming into existence. Then we have to find a way to get by, struggle to support ourselves, raise a family, and so forth. We contact something and become stuck in attachment. We touch something else and get mired in that. There is headache and worry about ourselves, anxiety over children, concern over wealth and possessions.

Having been born, anything can degenerate at any time. The ears can degenerate into deafness. The eyes can lose their sight. Pain can afflict the limbs or any other parts of the body. We cannot soar away because we are caught in the snare, the snare of the trapper. It is up to the trapper now to do as he wishes. We are in the trap. He can take care of us and raise us, or he can break our beaks, break our wings. This trap represents the demon of the aggregates, or the demon of the afflictions.

Here, the mass of humans do not understand the Dharma and only want to escape from reality. They strive to avoid it and struggle to get away. They don't want it to be the way it is, but wish for it to be otherwise. So it leads to suffering, by way of sensual desire, desire for becoming, and desire not to be.

So the Buddha taught us to analyze the body to give rise to dispassion, detachment, and disenchantment, and to see that these conditions are not a being, an individual, or a self. It's like when we are working the fields. We put up a scarecrow when the rice is maturing so the birds won't alight to eat the crop. We gather grass and sticks, tie it all together, and cover it with a shirt and pants; then the birds are afraid. They won't eat the rice now. The scarecrow is helping us. Now the rice has a chance to ripen, then we can harvest it, and the job is done. But actually it was only a skeleton of grass and sticks. Once we've harvested the rice, we can discard the scarecrow there in the paddy. That's all there is to it.

We are just like this scarecrow. When consciousness leaves this body, there is nothing—no different from the skeleton of grass. The scarecrow in the field does not go anywhere, and ultimately it is just discarded there.

But now we can move, we can go places. We have all sorts of thoughts and feelings and desires to do things and travel about. We think about going and we go. We think about staying so we stay. We want to sing and dance and play according to the way of the world. To put it simply, it's just as if we are waiting for the day of death. The harvest time comes, the crop is reaped, the rice gathered and carted away, and the scarecrow is discarded in the field.

When the day of harvesting comes, we depart. Someone who doesn't know the beginning or end of things will feel elation and depression and go on spinning around. Not wanting to have illness when he gets sick, not wanting to get old when he gets old, not wanting to die when he dies, not wanting life to disappear. But things are like this.

We don't understand the law of nature, and we want things to be stable and permanent. "This is me, that is her"—everything is seen in terms of me and mine, and Dharma is never contemplated. The point is, when it gets to the end, everyone must leave it all behind. Material gain, reputation, praise, whatever happiness or suffering there is, it is all left here in the world. They are worldly accomplishments.

We people are no different than a bird confined in a cage or a fish in a tank. Whenever the owner wants to take them, he can do so. If he wants to kill them, he can do that, because they are trapped in his tank or his cage. This is suffering in the cycle of samsara. There is no way out, other than learning the Dharma to know things according to the truth.

Looking at Dharma, don't look far away. If you look far away, you won't see. If you have doubts about Dharma, look at yourself. Look at this body and this mind. What is there that is certain

47

or reliable? To what extent are they your self? How much essence do they have? How stable, how permanent or long lasting are they? There's no such part that is like this.

We have hair, and it will gray. We have teeth, and they will decay and fall out. The ears will lose their hearing, the vision will weaken. The skin will become dry and wrinkled. Why is it like this? Because we have no power to force things to be the way we want. They follow their own conditions and do not listen to the commands of anyone.

It's like a river that flows to the south. If we see it and want it to flow in the other direction, can that happen? There can only be frustration then. The water flows south, and we want it to flow north. When will this ever be resolved? Is the water wrong, or are we wrong? It is just a way to create frustration. Nature is like that, things following their laws. No matter how much we wish to force it to be otherwise, it just continues on in that way. What should we do? If we think like this, where can we find happiness? The river flows on in the same direction. Thinking, we cannot make it change; trying to do something about it, we find it is beyond our ability.

So the Buddha wanted us to practice meditation, to listen to the Dharma and investigate, and to see according to the truth, the truth of the river. If it flows south, let it flow that way. Don't fight it. If there is a person with the eye of wisdom who stands by the river, sees it flowing south, and can accept that because it is just the nature of things, there is no conflict or frustration. The water flows in its way, and that's all there is to it. That is Dharma, that is nature. There is aging, sickness, and death. In the beginning there is birth, in the middle aging, and in the end breaking up and disappearing. Those who can contemplate and see the truth of this will be at peace.

The Buddha taught about the wisdom that knows sankhara. Water is sankhara. This body that we suppose to be our self is merely composed of earth, water, fire, and air, and they are all flowing constantly. Since being born, since being in the womb and flowing out into the world, we have kept on flowing—formerly small children, growing to adulthood, getting older and heading for old age—flowing right up to the present day, flowing according to nature.

When we see this, we can see that it is not really a being, not a person, not self or other. It is just nature. Whoever will cry over it, it is still the same. Whoever may laugh over it, it is still just that. Whoever tries to impede it, it is still that. It does not endeavor to please anyone. The Buddha urged us to look into this. It is something that is not permanent or stable; if not known as it actually is, it is a source of suffering, because this nature is not a being or a person, self or other. There is merely earth, water, fire, and air. That's all. In the end, they separate and break up. This is the law of nature.

If we wish to practice Dharma and live according to Dharma, we should look at nature. Have you noticed trees? There are big ones and small ones, tall and short trees. When the dry season comes, the leaves fall. When the rains come, the leaves appear again. When the time comes to fall, they fall. When the time comes to grow, they grow. When the time comes to dissolve, they dissolve. Just like us. That is the nature of sankhara. We are born, we age and fall, then we take birth again. Like the trees, like the leaves—not different.

In the forest there are beautiful trees and ugly trees. Some are bent and gnarled, some straight and tall. There are trees with pith and those without. Just like people. There are bad and good people, crooked and straight people. This is also nature.

But in the case of the trees, what are the causes and conditions of their existence? It is the soil and the water that nourish them and enable them to grow and blossom. For us humans, it is karma. Karma means our actions, which cause us to be strong or weak, to have little or much wisdom. Trees have seasons—hot, cold, and wet—which occur according to nature. Humans appear according to karma, their actions.

Doing good actions, things become good; doing harm, the results are painful. Beautiful actions make life beautiful, while ugly actions bring ugliness. This truth of the existence of beings is called karma. Today, for instance, why did you come here? You came in search of a certain type of karma—you want to find peace, to be happy and at ease. Taking and observing the precepts today, practicing meditation and listening to teachings, is a root cause, creating the source, making positive karma.

Listening to Dharma, there needs to be understanding. If you have great understanding, there will be great fruit; if your understanding is little, the fruit will be little. If there is little right view, there will be a lot of suffering. With much right view suffering will vanish and tranquility will come about.

Coming here today you are seeking spiritual nourishment. We are trying to educate the mind by looking externally and internally; this is called coming to practice Dharma. Throughout this body Dharma exists. We can see it clearly, without having to look far away.

When we do see it clearly, there arise dispassion and detachment, there comes world-weariness; there is some fear, and the mind chews it over with concern. Thus the Buddha urged us to look into the realities of birth, aging, illness, and death, to see them according to the law of nature, which is Dharma.

If we see according to the law of nature, it can be said that we are practicing Dharma. We will see that we humans are not different. It does not matter which village or province or country we hail from. If we really look, we will not see differences. In the beginning, we are born; in the middle, there is change; and in the end, we disappear from this world. It is the same for absolutely everyone. So the Buddha wanted us to contemplate morality and Dharma, to see that they are the same as us, and we are the same as them. Then there can be understanding and forgiveness, because we are all the same; we are kinfolk in birth, aging, sickness, and death. We are all members of one clan. If we know this, there is a sobering urgency born within the heart. When we contemplate this body, we know that we are all the same. Someone else's child is like our child. Others' parents are like our parents. Our own existence is like that of someone else's; someone else is just like us. If the mind comes to see in this way, there is an end to harming, to envy and strife, to aggressiveness.

Seeing like this is right view. If there is right view, it is path. When view is right, then thinking is right, action is right, liveli-

hood is right, speech is right, effort in meditation is right—
everything is right, having entered the path through right view.
If we are doing this, there is always Dharma practice, no matter
where we are.

The Buddha taught us to look at ourselves. He did not point
up at the heavens or down to the earth, at the mountains, the
clouds, or the sky. The Dharma is something that is with us. If
we come to know ourselves, attachment and grasping start to
wither away and decrease, to back off. It is because of seeing that
this can happen. If there is no seeing, there is no decrease, no
breathing room.

Practitioners of Dharma should know how much fruit is born
of their efforts. It is not that one practices and has no idea; one
should definitely know, know what is going on with oneself,
whether one is practicing correctly or wrongly, and what kind of
results one is getting. If people do not know this yet, they are not
getting any fruit from their practice. There is nothing really
going on. It's just like they are doing things because someone
told them to, blindly following along with the group. Someone
told them so they do it, with nothing happening on their side.
The Buddha wanted us to have wise discernment, to be astute
and employ wisdom to see and know things in the present moment. It is not a matter of waiting for death so we can know. If
we don't see and know now, we will not know later on. We must
see now.

If we investigate the body until there is dispassion and detachment, we will see that we are like the bird in the trap or the
fish in the tank. The hunter or owner can take us out and destroy
us at any moment. Our limbs, senses, and organs—our bodies—
can break down on us any time. Such is the characteristic of
these things. We cannot stop it from happening. They will not
obey our commands. Why? Because they are not real; they are
not actually ourselves, nothing dependable. They are not really
and definitely *our* legs, *our* arms, *our* eyes or ears. That is conventional reality, mere designations. They are only spoken of as ours.

If we all contemplate these things; these heaps; the aggregates
of form, feeling, perceptions, thoughts, and consciousness—you

can call them the five aggregates, the dharmas of name and form, or simply mind and body, which is what it all comes down to—then it is not something else, something far away.

The Buddha said, "Bhikkhus, whoever watches over their minds, they shall escape the snares of Mara." But do we really know the mind? It tells us to cry and we cry, it says "Laugh" and we laugh. When it says to crave something, we crave it. These things are not so difficult to see; the mind should actually be easy to teach, but people don't teach it. If it gets angry, discipline it immediately—take up the stick and it will behave. But we don't train ourselves like this.

If we really did teach ourselves, oh! How could we sleep like we do? When we sleep, it would not just be a matter of falling into a stupor every night. Teach yourself this every day. When you put your head on the pillow, contemplate the in and out breath. Think to yourself, How about that—tonight I am still breathing! Tell yourself this every day. You needn't do a lot of chanting and recitation. "Am I still breathing?" You wake up in the morning and think, Hey, I'm still alive! The day passes, the night comes again, and you ask yourself once more. Ask yourself, "If I lie down, will I get up again?" Rest for a little while and get up; when you get tired again, ask yourself again. Day after day, you have to do this. If you keep at it, things will come together and you will see. You will see the truth of what is taken to be self and others. You will see what is convention and supposition. You will understand what all these things really are. Then that which is heavy becomes light, that which is long becomes short, and that which is difficult becomes easy. But you have to generate enthusiasm. Then it can be done. If you are one of the lazy ones who just wants to sleep, what will you get from that?

If you look outside, you won't see. We have it already, if we look. Having been born, it is all here. As soon as things arise, we can see immediately that they are impermanent, leading to suffering, and not our selves. We see this, and we recognize that we are like this and that others are like this. This is the first step in contemplating Dharma. This is the path that has an end. This is the path to ending birth. This is the path to ending death.

If we pay attention, we will know. Just like when we are working in the fields. Is the sun high yet? Is evening coming? Just by looking at the sun, we know. When dusk is coming, there is no more we can do, and it is time to return home.

When we work, we have to know the time and occasion. If we pay attention throughout the day, then we know. Is it time to go to the fields? Is it time to return home from the fields? If we are looking, we will necessarily see and know. If we are continuously looking at mind and body, we will likewise know. Was it like this before? How is it now? Is it like a small child? If we think like this and investigate, the mind will turn. The heart will become forlorn; it will feel the insecure desolation and loneliness that result from a life of delusion. Continuing to look here will cause the mind to turn over. If it does not turn over, we cannot see the Dharma.

There must be causes. Things arise from causes. When we make efforts to practice Dharma, we are creating causes. For example, a husband and wife live together. They experience love as well as disagreements and quarrels. If one of them dies, leaving the other alone, where there was a loving couple, now there is only one. That person will most probably go to find a monastery. Like people who are sick—when an illness happens, they will immediately think about finding a doctor. If they are not sick, they don't have such an idea.

Things that happen thus are called the cause. The feelings of people work like this. If we are living comfortably and happily, we don't think about these things, and the mind will not turn. Likewise, in practicing Dharma we are supposed to contemplate to the point where we develop world-weariness and detachment, but we can't do it. We listen to the teachings; the venerable teachers use different approaches and similes to instruct us, to help us see clearly. What is the hair like? What is the truth of the teeth, skin, nails? Look! Are they fresh and youthful as before? Are they aging? Are they changing? So the Buddha told us to contemplate our bodies. See within your own body. If you see, it is just as if you have an infection, a disease, or some unbearable pain. You will only think about finding a cure for it. You will naturally want a doctor and medicine. That's natural. If the fever or pain increases and won't go away, this will be your only thought, to find a doctor. But previously, before you were ill, such thoughts weren't relevant. If someone had told you to go to a doctor, you would have had no interest. Now there is a cause.

Our meditation is similar. Why are we told to contemplate the hair, skin, and so on, these things that we already have? This is where the cause lies, the cause for dispassion, weariness, and detachment. There can be knowledge here. There can be delusion here. If there is knowledge, delusion ceases. If there is delusion, knowledge ceases. If there is seeing, blindness ceases. The Buddha constantly talked about contemplating birth, aging, illness, and death. What was that all about? The causes are right here.

Speaking about death leads to detachment and dispassion in regard to this life. If you keep on investigating this point, entering deeper and deeper into it, weariness with the world and detachment will come. Investigating Dharma, you will eventually see Dharma, meaning the truth, and when you see Dharma, you will be able to find peace. Where else would it take you?

This is the cause, the meditation called establishing mindfulness on the body, or contemplating the body. From the top of the head to the soles of the feet, back again from the feet to the top of the head, over and over again. Meditate like this to give rise to weariness and dispassion, to make the mind turn over.

For example, you have a family, a home, and ample possessions. When everything is going well, the mind is not likely to turn, because you are happy and comfortable. Just as when you are sailing in a boat, if the boat is well built and the water is smooth, who is thinking about swimming? But if the boat starts sinking, swimming becomes important—or could you remain indifferent? Some people ask, "What's the deal, always telling us to meditate on these body parts?" Well, this is how it is for us. If you are sailing along, you might not be thinking that you need to be able to swim, but you're really much better off if you've already learned how. If the boat starts sinking, will you have any concern other than swimming?

When we meditate on this and really see the truth of it, the result will come by itself. When you really make up your mind through having seen impermanence, suffering, and absence of a self in this body, you are called one who has contemplated the Dharma, who is practicing Dharma.

When you know this one point, you will know many things. Having mastered this point, your practice will roll along unimpeded, seeing instability, unsatisfactoriness, and lack of self in your own body and the bodies of others, internally and externally. The source of virtue is here; this is where you have to look. This is what the Buddha taught. He did not talk about things that are extraneous, about places people do not go or things people cannot see. He pointed out things that are facts of our own existence. When we sit, these things are sitting with us. When we walk, they are walking with us. When we lie down to sleep, they are lying down with us.

Yet having these things inherent within us even to this extent, we still do not see! It's like with the skeleton we keep in the meditation hall. Folks will talk about it, but they really don't see it. Some look at it and feel frightened. They flee the hall; they don't want to look. These are people who do not see. If they really saw, they would know no fear. If you are afraid, where will you run? The skeleton is always right here with you. Think about it. Even if you run away, it is running with you. Wherever you go, it stays with you. What else is it that you are afraid of? The places of escape are exhausted.

Recognizing this means you see. Then there is dispassion: "Oh! Things really are impermanent, suffering and not self!" When you see a skeleton, you know it is the same as yourself. Sitting there chewing your betel and smoking your tobacco, the skeleton is there. Coming and going, walking around, the skeleton is there. Chattering and gossiping, it is there. It is just like you. In the future you will be just like the skeleton in the hall. Everyone will become like this. Before, that skeleton was a living person, just like you. Later, we will become like it. Are you afraid? Is this true or not? Where can you run?

So you look at one person, and you know he is the same as any other person, the same as yourself. When you see one person in this way, you understand all people in the universe. We are all the same. There is no substantial difference; for the greater part, we are all just the same.

Please see the truth of this. Before, the skeleton was like us. Later, we will be just like it. The mind will change from this investigation. Keep up your investigation, and you will realize that things are not genuine or reliable. The only thing that is genuine is the accumulation of good or evil. In this life, good leads to good, bad leads to bad. Right thinking leads you in right paths, while wrong thinking leads you astray. This is occurring right now. This is the only thing that is real, and the results will always return to follow after you.

Even our own skeleton cannot follow us. We certainly don't need to consider family, friends, wealth, and possessions reliable; starting from our very own bones, there is nothing genuine. The only thing that is real is that which leads us to the various states of becoming and birth, meaning good and bad deeds of body, speech, and mind. Doing good brings good, and acting in unwholesome ways brings pain. This is what is really certain and true, and only this.

So the Buddha wanted us to look into this matter. We don't need to think about gaining anything in this life. Give up unwholesome ways and practice good while you are still living. Once you die, there is nothing you can do. The Buddha wanted us to see the urgency of the situation and hurry up and get to work. You still have eyes and ears that are functioning. Consciousness has not yet departed from your body, so you can understand things. Throw it away! If you throw it away while you are still living, it will bring lightness. What does throwing away mean? Strive to give up, to look, to investigate. When the consciousness departs and leaves a corpse behind, what can you accomplish? They will carry the body away to be cremated or buried, and that's the end of the story.

We have our traditions for honoring and supposedly helping the dead, and we employ all sorts of idioms in our language to describe how we gain merits from such practices. People may put out rice cakes, saying that the dearly departed will benefit. Then they sit there enjoying the cakes themselves; but where is the deceased at that time, and what benefit does he or she get?

It's better to train yourselves. The Buddha did not praise the dead. He praised the opportunity of this human birth. It's important to practice while you are alive. If there is wrong in you, give it up now. If there is something good, practice it now. These are your two friends, your refuge. In the present this is your refuge, and throughout your future lives it will be your place of refuge. The various material possessions are only what they are. Isn't that so? Do you see how young people fight over these things now, and how it leads them nowhere? We are old enough, so we should know to stop doing that and seek tranquility and relinquishment instead. We've done enough of the worldly business already—it's time to stop now, isn't it?

Even though you are living in a house, you should contemplate these things. You are not ordained, but let the mind be ordained, investigating the truth. Worldly accomplishments and possessions only go so far. They really do not lead to any ultimate kind of benefit. They exist within their limits. They will flow away, so let them flow. The Buddha wanted us to meditate and see. If we contemplate in this way, it will be what the scriptures call the preliminary training, the first step. It will destroy the attachment to our own bodies. Destroy our bodies! What does this mean? Through seeing the impermanence, suffering, and lack of self there, we realize weariness and dispassion, and real faith will arise.

Please contemplate this. The first result will be that, with the arising of world-weariness and dispassion, you will refrain from harmful actions. When you stop this, it is sila. If you don't understand these things, you don't know what is karma and what is wrongdoing. If you do know, you will stop. Whatever is not good or beautiful, you will stop doing by way of body and speech. That is morality. When you give up all wrongdoing, there is morality.

Having given up wrongdoing, the mind is composed and can attain samadhi. When the mind is composed in samadhi thus, wisdom will be born. When the Buddha began teaching, some disciples became enlightened in their seats just by hearing his words. Some attained the *arahant* stage, the end of the path, right there on that single occasion. So when did they keep precepts? When were they practicing meditation and developing samadhi? They realized weariness with samsara and dispassionate detachment, and they were able to stop. That condition is sila. Then, with no wrongdoing in the heart, but only coolness and tranquility, there was samadhi. From this state of calm, the mind was able to contemplate things and know them as they are.

Hearing Dharma, contemplating Dharma thus, pure morality and the rest arose, and this was the path. In that moment it happened. Now, people like us have a lot of doubt and uncertainty, and we think, Oh, they must have really had a lot of good karma behind them to do that. But it happens in the present also. It really can. If we listen and understand clearly, it can happen. The mind gives up; it lets go. If it can't let go right now, it can do so tomorrow or the day after, at another sitting in the near future. Not knowing clearly today, it will know tomorrow; not realizing tomorrow, it will realize the day after tomorrow. It must know, if we really take an interest in the Dharma.

When hearing the name of Dharma, don't get the idea that it is anything other than nature. We have it; we are it. Whatever you practice, strive to make it genuine. Strive to make the mind see—see impermanence, see unsatisfactoriness, see the absence of a self. See that nothing is permanent or lasting throughout this world of ours. That is all.

When your view is like this, whatever you look at becomes truth that makes you turn inward to see; external phenomena are no different from yourself. Keep turning inward continuously, and everything is Dharma. When you see animals, Dharma is there. Large creatures are Dharma; small creatures are Dharma.

Even when you see rocks, earth, or grass, it is all Dharma, because all of this is nature.

Seeing Dharma, you will practice Dharma accordingly. This is what the Buddha's teaching is about. It is not something else that is distant from us. We are speaking about the source of the path. If you have faith and seek the Dharma, where will you look for it? Seeking in one monastery, searching it out in some other monastery, going to forests here and there, it just remains the way it is. In the forest, the Dharma is in yourself—right there in your body. If you go to learn in a monastery, it is pointed out the same way, right there within yourself.

In listening to teachings, the principle is the same. It's not necessary to hear a lot. You should listen in order to understand and know what it is all about. What are the important points? What should be investigated? How should you practice? How do you want to train the mind? You want to liberate the mind from suffering, to go beyond conventional reality. Where is this conventional reality? Where is this suffering? How do you transcend it?

Happiness and suffering are the great teacher. Love and hate are your great teacher. This is where the path is. If you are attached to feelings of love, they will lead you to pain. Look into this. These feelings very directly point out the path. If you are attached to any of them, that is a mistake. Looking into this, you can really come to know.

Why is it that we are told to transcend the feelings of love and attachment? Take a good look. In your lives, at home or elsewhere, when you are very attached to someone, loving them more than others, it leads you to suffering. Think about it if you are skeptical. You have to know what this affection is about. Don't throw yourself away; don't fall asleep! Don't let your mind slumber. Love for people, attachment to possessions, these only bring suffering. Remember this! If it won't stick in your mind, write it down! Look at it! It is really the truth.

When you have feelings of love and hate, you need to look into them. They are teaching you, showing you not to fall into extreme ways. Impulses are trying to lead you into the left-or right-hand paths of indulgence or suppression. The teachings talk of the extremes of indulgence in sensual pleasure and self-torment. When the Buddha was first enlightened to the Dharma, this was what he taught about. These things were true in the Buddha's time, and they are true for us now.

Where can you look to understand the truth of this? Just in your own mind. The tendency we have is that when we love someone, we want to be with them all the time, and when we feel hatred toward someone, we don't even want to be near them. Do any of you have these feelings? Please look and teach yourselves. Do you see how they lead you to suffer? This is talking about the Noble Truths, suffering and its origin, which is love and attachment. You can see the fact of this if you look at your lives. Are your attachments and anxieties something good and beneficial? Don't let your minds get caught in unreasonable attachment. It's as if you eat a banana and toss the peel away, but when the chickens and other animals want to eat it, you still feel possessive and concerned over it, unable to relinquish attachment. With gain, you are elated. With loss, you are depressed. This is just what the Buddha talked about when he said to avoid the two extremes. Talk to your mind to make it capable of avoidance.

Therefore practitioners of Dharma, having heard the teachings, need to investigate these feelings of attachment and aversion toward people as they occur and continuously make efforts to train their minds. Looking at this and avoiding extreme reactions will support the mind and support the path. Don't fall in the ditch! Love is a ditch. Hatred is a ditch.

The Buddha really understood these things. Through his practice and enlightenment, he saw that they are truly impermanent, full of suffering, and without self-essence. When love comes, put it aside. When hatred comes, put it aside. If you are not able to put them down, train the mind to do so. These things by themselves are not going to bring peace to the mind.

This is the Dharma. This is what the Buddha's dispensation is. You have to look right here. You have to seek peace here. This is the path to nirvana. "You want to go running after those things?

You'll fall into the lower realms." Tell your mind that. Don't get attached and give meaning to such things.

Don't you go to work in the fields? You know how to shout at the buffalo so it will obey you and go where you want it to. So why can't you shout at yourself and get some control of where your mind goes?

We are talking about reaching the place where there are no causes, where causes are exhausted. If there is love or hate, it means causes exist. If there is a cause, there will be a result. If there is birth, there will be death. This is how it is for us. When there is love and attachment, there is going to be hatred and aversion. If we go to heavenly states, we will also end up going to hell. Going to hell, we then go to heaven. It's like this, the realm of becoming and birth. So the Buddha wanted us to investigate. It is not something that only applies to certain people; these principles are universally true. So where should you practice your samadhi? What will you meditate on? When you see, you let go immediately.

Make your efforts here. Train the mind with skillful means to make it pliable, just as a blacksmith heats metal to soften it and can then shape it into any useful tool he desires. Just so, we soften our minds with training in precepts, with restraint, with the practice of meditation, and with investigation. Our minds will then soften and surrender to become peaceful.

3

PRACTICING
DHARMA

The Path to Peace

OUR PRACTICE IS TO WORK AT removing desire, aversion, and delusion, the mental afflictions that can be found within each and every one of us. They are what hold us in the round of becoming and birth and prevent us from achieving peace of mind.

Realizing peace involves working not only with the mind, but with the body and speech as well. Before you can practice with your body and speech, you must be practicing with your mind; but if you only practice with your mind and neglect your body and speech, that won't work either. Practicing with the mind until it's smooth, refined, and beautiful is similar to producing a finished wooden pillar or plank. Before you can have an attractive varnished pillar, you must first cut a tree. Then you cut off the rough parts—the roots and branches—before you split it, saw it, and work it. Practicing with the mind is the same. You have to work with the coarse things first; you work through the rough to reach the smooth.

In Dharma practice you aim to pacify and purify the mind, but it's difficult to do. So you have to begin with externals, body and speech, working your way inward until you reach that which is smooth and resplendent. You can compare it with a finished piece of furniture, such as a chair or a table. They may be attractive now, but once they were just rough bits of wood with branches and leaves that had to be planed and worked. This is the way you obtain furniture that is beautiful or a mind that is perfect and pure.

Therefore the right path to peace, the way the Buddha showed for attaining true happiness, is sila (morality), samadhi (meditative concentration), and wisdom. This is the path of practice. It is the way to complete abandonment of craving attachment, aversion, and confusion. This path involves going against our habitual tendencies of taking it easy and wanting enjoyment and comfort, so we have to be ready to endure some difficulty and put forth effort.

The Buddha taught that this is the way the practice is for all of us. All of his disciples who finished their work and became fully enlightened had previously been ordinary worldly beings like us. They had arms and legs, eyes and ears, greed and anger, just like us. They didn't have any special characteristics that made them particularly different from us. They practiced and brought forth enlightenment from the unenlightened, beauty from ugliness, and great benefit from that which was useless. You must understand that you have the same potential. You are made up of the five aggregates, just as they were. You have a body, pleasant and unpleasant feelings, memory and perception, thought formations and consciousness, as well as a wandering and proliferating mind. You can be aware of good and evil. Everything's the same. Those who became enlightened in the Buddha's time were no different from us. They all started out as ordinary, unenlightened beings. Some had even been gangsters and murderers. The Buddha inspired them to practice for the attainment of path and fruition,

Photographer unknown

Ajahn Chah, circa 1975.

and these days, in similar fashion, people like you are inspired to take up the practice of morality, meditation, and wisdom.

If the mind is able to look after itself, it is not so difficult to guard speech and bodily actions, since they are motivated and supervised by the mind. Mind is where the intentions for all your actions originate. You learn to look after yourself with mindfulness, the one who knows, who is the same one who formerly motivated you to perform unrestrained and harmful actions. Then, through restraint and caution, your speech and actions become graceful and pleasing to the eye and ear, while you yourself remain comfortable and at ease within this restraint.

Continuous restraint, where you consistently take care with your actions and speech and take responsibility for your behavior, is sila. Being unwavering in the practice of mindfulness and restraint is samadhi. This is samadhi as an external factor in the practice, used in keeping sila. However, it also has an inner, deeper side.

Once the mind is intent in the practice and sila and samadhi are firmly established, you will be able to investigate and reflect on your experience of different inner and outer phenomena. When the mind makes contact with different sights, sounds, smells, tastes, tactile sensations, or ideas, the one who knows will arise and establish awareness of like and dislike, happiness and suffering, and the different kinds of mental objects and conditions that you experience.

If you are mindful, you will see the objects that pass into the mind and your reactions to them. The one who knows will automatically take them up as objects of contemplation. That aspect of discerning the good from the bad and the right from the wrong from among all the phenomena in your field of awareness is wisdom. This is wisdom in its initial stages, and it matures as the practice progresses. This is the way morality, meditation, and wisdom are practiced in the beginning.

As you continue the practice, fresh attachments and new kinds of delusion begin to arise in the mind. This means you start clinging to that which is good or wholesome. You become fearful of any blemishes or faults in the mind, anxious that your samadhi will be harmed by them. At the same time, you begin to be diligent and hardworking, and to love and nurture the practice. Whenever the mind makes contact with phenomena you become fearful and tense. You become aware of other people's faults as well, down to the slightest things they seem to be doing wrong. This is because you are concerned for your practice. This is practicing on one level, based on having established your views in accord with the essential foundations of practice taught by the Buddha.

You continue to practice like this as much as possible; you might even reach a point where you are constantly judging and finding fault with everyone you meet. You are constantly reacting with attraction and aversion to the world around you, becoming full of all kinds of uncertainty and continually attaching to views about how to practice. It's as if you've become obsessed with the practice. But don't worry about this yet—at this point, it's better to practice too much than too little. Practice a lot and dedicate yourself to looking after body, speech, and mind. You can never really do too much of this.

Once you have a foundation, there will be a strong sense of shame and fear of wrongdoing established in the heart. Whatever the time or place, in public or in private, you will not want to do anything that is harmful to yourself or others. The practice of mindfulness and restraint with body, speech, and mind and the consistent distinguishing between right and wrong is what you hold as the focus. You become concentrated in this way and by unshakably sticking to this way of practice, the mind actually becomes sila, samadhi, and wisdom.

As you continue to develop your practice, these different qualities are perfected together. However, practicing at this level is still not enough to produce the factors of *jhana*, or "meditative absorption"; the practice is still too coarse. However, the mind is already quite refined—on the refined side of coarse. For an ordinary unenlightened person who hasn't been looking after the mind or practicing meditation and mindfulness, just this much is already something quite refined. It's like a poor person, to whom having a few hundred dollars can mean a lot, though for a millionaire it's almost nothing. A few hundred can be a lot when you're hard up; in the same way, even though in the early stages of practice you might only be able to let go of the coarser mental afflictions, this can still seem quite profound if you are unenlightened and have never practiced and let go before. At this level, you can feel some satisfaction at being able to practice to the full extent of your ability.

If this is the case, it means that you have entered the correct path. You are traveling along the very first stage, which is something quite difficult to sustain. As you deepen and refine it, sila, samadhi, and wisdom will mature together from the same place, from the same raw material. It's like the coconut palms. They absorb water from the earth and pull it up through their trunks. By the time the water reaches the coconut itself, it has become clean and sweet, even though it is derived from that plain water in the ground. The palm is nourished by what are essentially the coarse earth and water elements, which it absorbs and purifies, and these are transformed into something far sweeter and purer than before. In the same way, the practice has coarse beginnings, but by refining the mind through meditation and reflection, it becomes increasingly subtle.

As the mind becomes more refined, mindfulness becomes more focused. The practice actually becomes easier as the mind turns more and more inward to focus on itself. You no longer make big mistakes or deviate wildly. When doubts occur in different situations, such as whether acting or speaking in certain ways are right or wrong, you simply halt the proliferation of mental activity and through intensifying your effort turn your attention deeper inside. Samadhi becomes progressively firmer, and wisdom is enhanced so you can see things more clearly and with increasing ease.

The end result is that you can clearly see the mind and its objects without having to make any distinction between mind, body, and speech. You see that the body depends on the mind in order to function. However, the mind itself is constantly subject to different objects contacting and conditioning it. As you continue to turn inward and wisdom matures, eventually you are left contemplating the mind and its objects—which means you start to experience the body as something immaterial. The body's physicality is experienced as formless objects that come into contact with the mind.

Now, examining the nature of the mind, you can observe that in its natural state it has no preoccupations. It's like a flag on the end of a pole or like a leaf on a tree. By itself, it remains still; if it flutters, that is because of the wind, an external force. In its natural state, the mind is the same, without attraction or aversion, without ascribing characteristics to things or finding fault with people. It is independent, existing in a state of purity that is clear, radiant, and stainless. In its natural state the mind is peaceful, without happiness or suffering. This is the true state of the mind.

So the purpose of practice is to seek inwardly, investigating until you reach the original mind. Original mind is also known as pure mind. It is the mind without attachment. It isn't affected by mental objects and doesn't chase after pleasant and unpleasant phenomena. Rather, it is in a state of continuous wakefulness, thoroughly aware of all it experiences.

When the mind is like this, it does not become anything, and nothing can shake it. Why? Because there is awareness. The mind knows itself as pure. It has reached its original state of independence. This has come about through the faculty of mindfulness together with wise reflection, seeing that all things are merely conditions arising out of the confluence of the elements, without any individual controlling them.

In the past, because the roots of desire, aversion, and delusion already existed in the mind, whenever you caught sight of the slightest pleasant or unpleasant thing, the mind would react immediately. You would take hold of it and have to experience either happiness or suffering, and you would be constantly involved in these mental states. Through wise reflection, you can see that you are subject to old habits and conditioning. The mind itself is actually free, but you have to suffer because of your attachments. That's how it is as long as the mind doesn't know itself, as long as it is not illumined. It is not free; it is influenced by whatever phenomena it experiences. In other words, it is without a refuge, unable to truly depend on itself.

In contrast to this, the original mind is beyond good and bad.

But when you separate from original mind, everything becomes uncertain, and there is unending birth and death, insecurity, anxiety, and hardship, without any way of bringing it to cessation.

Ordinarily, if someone criticizes you, you will feel upset. Accepting sense-impressions without full mindfulness in this way causes an experience like being stabbed. This is clinging. Once you have been stabbed, there is becoming, change, and this is the cause for birth into some further state. But if you train yourself not to attach importance to phenomena, nothing is created in the mind. It would be like someone scolding you in a foreign language—the words would have no meaning for you, so you wouldn't absorb that information and create suffering for yourself.

Samadhi means a mind that is firmly concentrated, and the more you practice the firmer it becomes. The more you contemplate, the more confident you become. It becomes easier to know the arising and passing away of consciousness from moment to moment. The mind becomes truly stable to the point where it can't be swayed by anything at all, and you are absolutely confident that no phenomena whatsoever have the power to shake it. The mind experiences good and bad mental states, happiness and suffering, because it is deluded by its objects. The objects of mind are the objects of mind, and the mind is the mind. If the mind is not deluded by them, there is no suffering. The undeluded mind can't be shaken. This is a state of awareness in which all phenomena are viewed entirely as elements arising and passing away.

It might be possible to have this experience yet still be unable to fully let go. Whether you can or cannot let go, don't let this bother you. Before anything else you must at least develop and sustain this level of awareness and fixed determination. You have to keep at it and destroy the afflictions through determined effort, penetrating ever deeper into the practice.

Having discerned the Dharma in this way, the mind will withdraw to a less intense level of practice, which the scriptures describe as the mind undergoing "change of lineage." This refers to the mind that has experienced a transcending of the boundaries of the ordinary human mind. It is the mind of the ordinary un-enlightened person breaking through to the realm of the noble awakened being. But this is still taking place within the mind of the ordinary unawakened person. Such an individual is someone who, having progressed in his practice until he gains temporary experience of nirvana, withdraws from it and continues practicing on another level because he has not yet completely cut off all afflictions. It's like someone in the middle of stepping across a stream. She knows for certain that there are two sides to the stream, but she is unable to cross over it completely, so she steps back.

The understanding that there are two sides to the stream is similar to the change of lineage. It means that you know the way to go beyond the mental afflictions but are still unable to go there; thus, you step back. Once you know for yourself that the state of transcendence truly exists, this knowledge remains with you constantly as you continue to practice meditation and de-velop your spiritual perfections. You are certain of both the goal and the most direct way to it.

Simply speaking, this state that has arisen is the mind itself. If you contemplate according to the truth of the way things are, you will see that only one path exists and there is nothing else to do in life but follow it. You understand that states of happiness and suffering are not the path to follow. Attaching to either will cause suffering to arise. You understand this and are mindful with this right view, but at the same time you are not yet able to fully let go of your attachments.

So you must walk the middle path, which means being aware of the various states of happiness and suffering, while at the same time keeping them at a distance. Whenever the mind at-taches to states of happiness and suffering, awareness of the at-tachment is always there. You don't encourage or give value to the positive states even as you are holding on to them, and you don't despise or fear the negative states. This way you can ob-serve the mind as it actually is, and at all times you take the Middle Way of equanimity as the object of mind. Equanimity will necessarily arise as the path to follow, and you must move along that path little by little.

When eventually the mind is fully aware of the various positive and negative states, it is able to lay aside the happiness and suffering, the pleasure and sadness, to lay aside all that is the world and so become the knower of the world. The mind in full knowing can then let go and settle down, for the reason that you have done the practice and followed the path to this point. You know what you must do to reach the end of the path, and you keep striving to uproot and dislodge your attachments.

Focusing on the conditions of mind from moment to moment, it's not necessary to be interviewed by a teacher about your state of mind or to do anything special. When there is attachment to happy or unhappy states of mind, there must be the clear and unwavering understanding that any such attachment is delusion. Such attachment is attachment to the world, being stuck in the world. What is it that creates the world? The world is created and established through ignorance, because we are not aware that the mind gives importance to things, fashioning and creating sankhara (mental formations) all the time.

It's here that the practice really becomes interesting. Wherever you have attachment, you keep working at that point. You are in the process of finishing the job; the mind doesn't let a single experience slip by. Nothing can withstand the power of your mindfulness and wisdom. Even if the mind is caught in some unwholesome state, you know it as such and are not heedless. It's like stepping on thorns. Of course, you don't try to step on thorns, you try to avoid them, but nevertheless sometimes you step on one. When you do, how does it feel? Once you know the path of practice, you know that which is the world, that which is suffering, and that which binds us to the endless cycle of birth and death. Even though you know this, you are unable to stop stepping on those thorns. The mind still follows various states of joy and sorrow, but doesn't get completely lost in them. You sustain a continuous effort to destroy any attachment in the mind, to clear from the mind all that is the world.

Everything external has been set aside at this point, and from here on you just watch body and mind, observing mind and its objects arising and passing away, understanding that having arisen they pass away. With passing away there is further arising—birth and death, death and birth, cessation followed by arising, arising followed by cessation. Ultimately, you are merely watching the act of cessation.

Once the mind is practicing and experiencing this, it doesn't have to go following up on or searching for anything else. Instead, it will be aware of whatever arises with full mindfulness. Seeing is just seeing. Knowing is just knowing. The mind and phenomena are just as they are. The mind isn't creating anything additional.

So keep practicing, calming the mind little by little. If you start thinking, it doesn't matter; if you're not thinking, it doesn't matter. The important thing is to develop this understanding of the mind.

Morality Brings Happiness: A Talk Given on Songkran, the Traditional New Year

Morality is the vehicle for happiness,
Morality is wealth and treasure.
Morality is the vehicle for dispassion;
Thus may morality be purified.

We who have come here to seek refuge in the Buddha, Dharma, and Sangha today find ourselves in this moment in time, which is passing by right before our eyes, as we sit here. It is as the Buddha taught: days and nights are relentlessly passing; how well are we spending our time? This is the speech of the Buddha, his very serious admonition to us to watch over ourselves. Still, some Buddhists let the days and nights pass without recollecting what they are doing that day, what they have done in the day past, or what they will do on the morrow. It is a mistake to let the time pass without employing mindfulness, to pay attention to whether we are doing good or causing harm, knowing whether our intentions and behavior are good or bad. Yet it is indeed rare to find individuals who think about this and have this kind of sensitivity.

Today we have completed another year according to the old calendar. Actually, we don't have to take so much interest in what we have completed, and we don't need to think in terms of Sunday, Monday, Tuesday, and so on. We can consider that we are starting from today, whatever the day is. Twelve months make a year, no matter when we start. It disagrees with worldly convention, that is all.

So we have come to this season of the year when we meet according to tradition. It is the end of another year in which we have been trying to practice the Dharma. We will have happiness and harmonious living because of honesty and morality. Living in a group or in the larger society, we will experience happiness and well-being because of morality and Dharma, the practice of virtue.

When I was a child, on this day the village elders would lead us together to other districts for what was called communing over water. We would drink from the same water, make vows over the same water, proclaiming our intention to be honest and straightforward toward each other. For example, in this district, in this township, in this province, we would say, "Although we live in different villages and have different concerns, let us have a common outlook for the purpose of bringing happiness to everyone; let us all live firmly established in virtue and spirituality." We would vow in this way to establish truthfulness in order to have integrity in our dealings with our superiors, toward the village, the nation, religion, and royalty. It was in order to instill respect and caution, to be aware, to be modest and humble toward each other. Then our villages and our nation would be able to live in peace and happiness, because of siladharma, noble behavior by way of body, speech, and mind. In this way there could be harmony.

If we are without honesty and integrity—well, just look at the way things are all around us these days. If you take a look, you will probably be able to see. Within one village, people quarrel with each other. Children of the same parents dispute with each other. Citizens of the same country are fighting with each other. It's because of delusion. I'm not pointing a finger at anyone; it's only because of our delusion that this happens. Those who are, in actuality, brothers and sisters are quarreling and fighting and killing each other, all to no purpose. Why is this? Because of wrong understanding. People who don't understand correctly do not think about the meaning of virtue and spirituality.

So our Supreme Teacher established what is called the Buddhist religion. It can be called Buddhist science, which is a body of knowledge superior to all other disciplines. Those subjects we study in the world, even when studied to the doctoral level, are disciplines with no end to learning. They are disciplines that have limits, which exist in the realm of desire and attachment and which lead to suffering. They do not help us to let go of suffering. This kind of knowledge is called science, but it is not the same as Buddhist science. In Buddhist study, if we have learned properly, we learn to let go, put down, stop. If there is harm in something, we learn to see the harm. Instead of holding tightly to things, we learn how to loosen our grip and let go. We learn about giving up. This is Buddhist science.

The teachings of the Buddha are a body of knowledge that is true and correct in all ways. They had to be taught, because these things do not come naturally for us. This knowledge does not change into some other set of concepts, but its validity remains the same. For example, the Buddha taught that doing good brings good results and doing evil brings evil results. This is a fixed law. It is certain. It is knowledge that comes from pure wisdom that is certain and reliable; thus, it can be called truth. Still, there are those who say that doing good is not certain to bring good results. They may have practiced virtue but not seen any good come from it. "I practiced virtue, so why can't I see any benefit? We can see plenty of people doing bad things and getting good results, and plenty of people doing good yet still experiencing suffering."

This is true, but only in the way of wrong understanding, insofar as it is wrong view. It does not actually accord with the truth. If we really see according to the truth, we realize that the Buddha's teaching is not something that changes. Whatever happens, the truth that the Buddha awakened to is something fixed and certain. The truth is always the truth. When it appears as untruth that is because of the wrong understanding of human beings.

For example, Mr. A. might be arrested and accused of some crime. He is perfectly innocent of the charges, but he doesn't have any witnesses on his side. The police may bring forth a parade of witnesses to testify against him, while his only witness is his own awareness and integrity. In this case, he can't win. Because he can't prove the other witnesses wrong, he ends up going to jail. Still, he is in the right, and it will only be his body that is incarcerated; his mind will not be locked up. *Mandela, Jews*

If this happened to most of us, we would probably feel wronged and get pretty depressed. But according to the Buddha there is never any valid cause for feeling wronged. If such things happen to us, if we have not done anything wrong yet must pay a price and experience suffering, we have to place the blame on karma, our actions. Though we haven't done anything wrong today, we may have done so yesterday; if we didn't do it yesterday, we may have done it some time in the past. We can conclude that we did something previously and thus have this experience in the present because of the principle that nothing happens without a cause. If there is no cause, phenomena do not arise. All phenomena appear due to causes—if we can always contemplate this principle and consider things in this way, our lives will be joyous. *Don't take karma personally.*

To find people who really trust the Buddha's teachings like this is very rare. For example, I established this monastery together with the lay supporters and monastic disciples more than twenty years ago. You may have heard the history of Wat Pah Pong. We were able to create a monastery here and bear many hardships over the years because people had appreciation for the truth and were not afraid. This is not just talk. Many of us had malaria for three years, and there was no way to get treatment. We often had no candles, flashlight batteries, or oil for lamps.

There were even more snakes and other poisonous creatures than there are now, so when we walked at night we recited verses of lovingkindness and protection. If we died, we died; if we lived, we lived. We could have this attitude because we were following a virtuous way, and we could trust our own minds.

So the Buddha taught to look into yourself, know yourself, and train yourself. Don't be too eager to train others. You should be looking at yourself. If others say we are good, that's not our standard to measure by. If others say we aren't good, that is not to be taken as a standard, either. Don't get too happy or depressed by what others say. Turn inward and seek out the truth of the matter within yourself. When they are saying we are not good, where is it that we aren't good? Is there such a deficiency? If there's something amiss, correct that. Give up what is wrong. Don't get upset with others for speaking. If what they say isn't true, never mind; they are just seeing things incorrectly, and you can have confidence in what you are doing. You should trust yourself, not reacting to praise or criticism with enchantment or unhappiness. Whether others' speech is right or wrong, never mind. If it's right, what is there to be upset and argue about? If it is wrong, why should you want to contend with them? In this way there is no loss or wrong for yourself. The mind remains happy and satisfied within the practice. So it is said: "Morality is the vehicle for happiness, morality is wealth and treasure; morality leads to dispassion, thus may your morality be pure."

We should think about this and realize that the five precepts are the moral standard of a genuine human being. All of you who are laypeople within the Buddhist fold, have you ever really vowed to maintain these five precepts purely? Have any of you made that determination? Think about it. This is something good and true, but there are probably those who will respond, "I can't do it. The world insists that I behave contrary to the precepts. Society forces me to act in certain ways that violate the precepts, and I have to go along with society's ways."

From what I have seen, among all the groups of people I encounter, if people have happy lives they will not be very interested in these things. It's usually only the old and infirm with whom I can really communicate. They're the old-fashioned ones who come here and want to keep precepts. Modern-minded people don't see anything of value here. They don't feel it necessary to have any standards or principles to go by. Thus in our society we have increased trouble, conflict, and distress. It's like a burning charcoal. We somehow get the idea that it isn't hot. If we pick it up, however, will it be hot or cool? There's some wrong understanding here. Of course, it is really hot. So the populace today is very hot and troubled. Take a look around you. Look at ajahns and their disciples. Look at parents and children. Look at our leaders and the people. There is not much harmony. Why is this? No one can figure it out. It is just because we lack morality. There is no honesty or integrity, and when everyone becomes like this there can be only heat and torment. This heat is hellfire. Living in a hellish environment, people do all sorts of wrong actions and become hell-realm beings. It's called going to hell while still alive.

Honesty and integrity are being lost—we could say they are about half gone—so we can see there is a lot of turmoil and strife in many places. The reason for this is only that morality and Dharma are lost to people, and the pursuit of pleasure and excitement has taken their place. Virtue is constantly declining these days, and the only result is the increase of misery and trouble. Unhappy conditions appear, and we can't figure out any solution. What can we do? What's going on? It happens like this.

Morality and Dharma are true and correct. There is nothing incorrect in them. A poor person can practice; a rich person can practice; any type of person can practice the path of good. This good is like the backbone for all humans. A life that is established on a foundation of goodness will shine brilliant and supreme. We needn't worry that any good we do will be wasted. Even after we die, the virtue we have created will remain in the world. This is something we can observe. Virtue does not die. Our children can carry it on, and when others meet our children or see anything that was connected with us, they will think about us and feel happy. In this way we are still giving refuge and assistance to others in the world.

The *Brahmaviharas*, or "divine abidings," of lovingkindness,
compassion, joy, and equanimity, should be the foundation of
our awareness. We should have love and compassion equally toward all people we meet. We can't just think, this one is not a
friend or a relative, so therefore we don't need to have any concern for her. Actually, we are all friends and relatives in birth.
There are no "other people." Even though we are from different
townships or provinces, we are like grains of rice. They grow
from one plant or in one field, and as they grow and increase,
they are spread around and planted in other places. One grain
makes a plant, one plant makes many grains that seed new plants.
But it is still rice from the same plant spreading the species far
and wide.

We people are the same. From a common ancestry, we end up
following our predilections and spreading out in the four direc-
tions. When we have scattered far enough, we start to forget ourselves. So we encounter different people and think, This is no
relation of mine. When we travel to another village, we think,
This is not my home village. The truth is that we are relatives in
birth, aging, illness, and death. So our Supreme Teacher instructed us to turn our minds to Dharma and establish Dharma
as the foundation of our lives. This means helping each other,
without exception. Whoever is suffering, whoever is in difficulty, we should try to help as well as we can. Please think about
this and try to have this attitude. Living in this world together, we
should think of each other as parents, relatives, and children. But
it's as if we've been separated for many years, so we forget who
we are, and we begin to fight and cause all sorts of strife with
each other, becoming like animals just because of this forgetful-
ness. Forgetting becomes the cause of fighting, struggling, and
even killing each other. Yet we really are one people; we are all
relatives, brothers and sisters.

Let's try to be people with Dharma in our hearts, meaning
metta, or "lovingkindness." When you meet a female elder, you
should have the attitude that this is your mother. When you
meet a male elder, you should think, this is my father. If someone is older than you, think of him or her as your older sibling.

Like this, everyone is your sibling, your child, your parent. Please make an effort to have this kind of attitude and give equal help to all those in difficulty.

Metta is love. There are two types of love. In one we love selectively, as suits our own purposes. The other is all-inclusive love. In the first way, we love ourselves and those close to us. We won't care about anyone outside of our own family; we just won't have any interest. Caring about our own is good, but it's too limited. It's narrow-minded thinking. It is love, also, but it isn't the love of Brahmavihara. The Buddha wanted us to have measureless, all-inclusive metta. No matter where anyone comes from, we should have the same caring attitude. Whether someone is close to us or distant, we have the same love toward them. In this way, our tranquil mind is said to be all-inclusive, a boundless Dharma. This should become our natural habit.

We people, whatever our station in life, have been born together into this world, so when someone else is suffering it is impossible for us to enjoy happiness by ourselves. For example, if someone is going hungry, we won't hoard all the food for ourselves. We are different from animals. If you throw a big lump of rice to some dogs, they won't think about sharing it. They will just run at it and bite each other over it, because they are hungry and that's all they know. The stronger ones bite the weaker ones, and the losers limp away yelping. If you want each one to get a share, you have to break it up into smaller balls and scatter them around. Then when each dog is eating in its own little territory, they might not fight. People have these tendencies, too.

Why is it that society is deteriorating today? Because metta is not all-inclusive. I've seen the elders in a village where the kids are troublemakers. The youngsters go around robbing houses in the neighboring villages, and eventually they end up stealing in their own village. So the old folks round them up and try to teach them. "Hey, you guys, don't go stealing in our village or our township. If you're going to steal, do it somewhere far away. The other towns and villages are OK to rob. Just don't do it here." This is how they teach the kids. Well, elders are pretty important. We look up to them for their wisdom, but they say things like this. Actually, they are being thoroughly selfish. If the elders in the other villages are telling their youngsters the same thing and sending them to rob this first village, how will things turn out? "This is our home; don't do that here." We think of older folks as having wisdom, but this is dark wisdom. It doesn't have anything to do with Dharma. There is a narrow metta for only a few. But people tend to be this way.

If we don't have Dharma in our lives, we are no different from animals. Maybe like chickens. What does a chicken do besides eat, sleep, and breed? When someone is raising a chicken, he keeps on feeding it, but for only one purpose. The chicken has no idea; it's just happy to be fed. The owner keeps feeding it and picking it up to weigh it every day: "Is it two kilos yet? Is it three kilos yet?" The chicken gets to feel that its owner loves it, always picking it up like that. Finally, market day arrives. Still, the chicken doesn't have a clue. It's easy to catch because it's used to being picked up. The owner puts it in the back of the truck—hey, what fun to ride in a truck, never done that before! Even when it's been sold and its head is on the chopping block, the butcher stretching out its neck to make a clean cut, the chicken is enjoying the pleasant sensation of a massage.

If we don't have Dharma, but live by envy and ill will, society will have no peace or happiness. Children born into such an environment will be hard to teach. Communication within a family will be difficult and strained. This is only because there is no Dharma. But foolish people ask, "Can you eat Dharma? You go to the monasteries, but what do you get from that? What do you bring back? Where is the Dharma you got? Is it anything you can feed your family with?" Actually, when we don't eat Dharma we are just asking for trouble. Whoever does eat Dharma only for the purpose of having Dharma, and lives according to Dharma, will naturally be a person of integrity and will enjoy happiness. That way is correct. There is no misery or turmoil in the aftermath. This is called eating Dharma. If we don't eat Dharma, there is no peace in society, only conflict and struggle.

Wherever you go, you should not be proud or stuck in your ways. In some places, you may not be familiar with the dialect or customs. Don't put on airs and be pretentious. Not knowing others' ways and holding on to your inflated self-esteem will not work out very well.

I'll relate something about Ajahn Mun. He was practicing meditation in the mountains in Pak To, among the hill tribe people. One day after his sitting, a villager came and asked him, "Where did you come from, kid?"

He answered, "I came from Ubon."

"So, Junior, have you eaten yet?"

"Yes, sir, I ate already."

The villager spoke in this informal way, with forms of address used when speaking to an inferior, something which we usually think of as impolite—especially so when talking to an ordained person. But those villagers considered it the best way to speak. If we weren't aware of their custom, it would make us angry. If the villager asked us, "Where have you come from, kid?" we would feel insulted and wouldn't want to answer. Our throats would get all stiff. But this was not the way of Ajahn Mun. He understood the minds of people. But we don't understand people like this. When others use forms of address for a superior in talking to an inferior, it doesn't go down well. In their circle, they considered this the best way to speak, but for us, not understanding the custom, we would probably only get angry.

These days I have been considering things. I go to various places to give lectures, and groups of people come here as well, yet in a gathering of a hundred or a thousand people, there might be four or five who really make an effort to practice the Dharma. So I prefer speaking to small groups. It's easier to instruct and admonish those who really have faith and devotion. If there are a thousand people and only fifty or so are really being mindful of themselves and making some sincere effort, there's no way to accomplish anything. It's the same thing when you do your work. When you're working in the fields, you might go out and work really hard for a few days, transplanting the seedlings for the next rice crop. But someone follows after you, pulling them up after you put them in the ground. No matter how long you keep at it, she just keeps following behind, pulling up all the seedlings. Who could manage like this? Tomorrow you plant again, and she is walking after you to undo what you have done. Can you succeed in your work? Does it create any benefit? When you look back, you see the other person destroying your work, pulling up the seedlings and throwing them into the paddy. What should you do? What are you laboring for? Before too many more days pass, we are going to die, so why should we bother with ignorant people like that?

The Buddha said that whatever actions bring no benefit we need not do. "Morality leads to happiness" is the truth, but people don't have happiness. If we try to talk about morality and virtue, people become afraid. It seems it has become very difficult to be a moral and spiritual person in society these days. But if people really have an accumulation of merit, if they have faith and mature minds, they will think about things deeply and have the wisdom to disengage themselves and find time to practice Dharma to the best of their ability.

"Morality is a treasure." All wealth and enjoyment is born of morality. There is the treasure of wealth; the treasure of eyes, ears, of nose, tongue, body, and mind. All these things that we possess as we sit here are treasures and accomplishments, and they are born of past moral conduct, the treasure of morality.

When we think of treasure, we only think about the kinds of wealth that can be seen by the eye, such as money, possessions, jewels, and gold. We don't consider our own eyes and ears themselves, our nose or our body. Think about it. If these limbs and sense organs are not whole, how will we enjoy material riches? We should be taking care of ourselves. Our eyes, ears, and limbs are things we should take care of. If someone were to try to buy an arm from you, offering many thousands of dollars, would you want to cut it off and sell it to him? Would tens of thousands of dollars to pluck out one of your eyes interest you? What is their value to you? That you are whole and enjoy these kinds of wealth because of morality is something you don't think about. The inner wealth that is born of morality is like this, but we don't see it as wealth.

Please make some effort to consider this. Sitting in this gathering there might be some half-people, and quarter-people as well. Days and nights keep passing. They don't stop but keep passing by. Ask yourselves, "Today, what have I done? Have I been living mindfully or heedlessly? Just how have I been doing things? What's the story here?" All of us need to look at ourselves in this way. Doing this, we will be able to solve our problems. Don't be too keen on solving others' problems; work out your own issues first. If you can't fix yourself, you won't be able to do anything for others. If you can solve your own problems, and then you do your best to help others but they aren't able to make use of your help, you needn't get upset over that. You remain in a state of normalcy, not feeling you've lost anything. There is no harm done to you.

The Buddha taught this. Thus, we can say that morality is the parent of all Dharma. Just like the breath is the progenitor of all our limbs and organs: if the breath stopped, could we continue to function? Sila is like this. It means purifying the actions of body and speech. We could say that morality is fifty percent of the path. Of course, there is more to do; for example, a person can speak nicely, yet still have a black heart. But in order for there to be Path, Fruit, and Nirvana, when it comes down to it, there must be morality first. So we have the verses beginning with "Morality leads to happiness . . ." The Lord Buddha urged all his followers to practice pure morality. Just as all of us were born of a mother and a father, so all Dharma, meaning all that is good and noble in the world, is born of morality. Every week on the lunar holiday we talk about this, because it is the parent that will give birth to the child of goodness and excellence from the womb of this existence. But people don't have much trust in it.

If people were to practice and realize this for themselves so the truth of it penetrated their hearts, that would be the most excellent sort of merit. I would really rejoice to see people genuinely come to understand the Dharma like that, and I would feel that the opportunity of being born as a human and meeting the Buddhist religion has not been wasted. But if one has all the conceptual knowledge, as many of us do now, but doesn't practice, what's the point? What will come of that?

Please understand this. We have only this one gathering this year. Next year at this time we will meet together again to do the traditional water ceremonies of the New Year once more. But it isn't certain, is it? We can't really be sure that the people who are here now celebrating the New Year will be here again next year. Put simply, we can't really entertain any hopes for anyone. We may not be able to do the sprinkling of water with some people next time. Why is this? Because things keep passing. These days, impermanence is in hot pursuit, out to destroy us. Sometimes people come and ask, "Luang Por, aren't you afraid of the communist guerillas?" Hey, why should we be worrying about communists? Have they been out to kill us from the day we were born? I'm not so afraid of communists. There are many things that are inherent in this life and in this body that are much more frightening. So don't go thinking about too many extraneous matters, things that are far away.

Thus, let all of us who are Buddhists disengage ourselves from meaningless activities and make serious efforts to practice goodness. If we don't yet have virtue, we should strive to develop it. If we have a little virtue, we should strive to increase it. If we have great virtue, we should continue on until we can be released from the cycle of samsara. And by the blessings of the Three Jewels may all of you be protected and supported in your practice of this morality and Dharma. May you have happiness and long life; may your practice lead to the end of suffering and bring you to the place of peace and happiness. Please don't be heedless.

Today, I have spoken for an appropriate length of time. I only wish to remind you now to practice Dharma. Whatever precepts and actions we have established here at Wat Pah Pong, you should determine in your minds to practice them and make yourselves good examples for your families and loved ones. This would really be something auspicious. Now I will make the wish that all your pure aspirations be fulfilled.

Meditation Practice

MINDFULNESS OF BREATHING: LECTURE AT A RETREAT AT THE INSIGHT MEDITATION SOCIETY*

I would like to ask you about your practice. You've all been practicing meditation for a while. Are you sure about the practice yet? These days, there are all sorts of meditation teachers around, and I'm afraid it might cause you to have some uncertainty about what you should be doing. Actually, there is nothing greater than the Buddha's teachings on concentration and insight meditation that you are practicing. If you have a clear understanding of them, it will bring about unwavering peace in your hearts.

Making the mind peaceful is known as samadhi (concentration meditation). The mind is extremely changeable and unreliable. Have you noticed this? Some days, you sit down to meditate and in no time at all the mind is calm. Other days, you sit and no matter what you do there's no calm. The mind constantly struggles to get away. Some days, it goes well; some days, it's awful. The mind displays these different conditions for you to see.

You should understand that the eight factors of the Noble Eightfold Path come together in sila (virtue or moral conduct), samadhi, and wisdom. There is nowhere else to look for them. This means that in order to have a successful practice, there must be morality, there must be mental collectedness, and there must be wisdom present in the mind. So in practicing meditation you are creating the causes for the path to arise in a very direct way.

You are usually taught to close your eyes in sitting meditation so you aren't busy looking at external things. With eyes closed, your attention is naturally turned inward toward the mind, the

---

*Retreat held in Barre, Massachusetts, 1979.

source of many different kinds of knowledge. Sitting with the eyes not focused on any external objects, establish awareness on the breath. Make awareness of the breath more important than anything else. By keeping with it, you will come to know the place that is the focal point of awareness. When the factors of the path are at work together, you will be able to see your breath, feelings, mind, and mental objects as they are in the present moment. Ultimately, you will know that place that is both the focal point of samadhi and the unification of the path factors.

When developing samadhi, fix your attention on the breath and imagine that you are sitting alone with no other people and nothing else around to bother you. Develop this perception, sustaining it until the mind completely lets go of the world outside, and all that is left is simply the awareness of the breath entering and leaving. The mind must set aside the external world. Don't allow yourself to start thinking about the people sitting around you. Don't give opportunity to any thoughts that will stir the mind. It's better to throw them out and be done with them. There is no one else here—you are sitting all alone. Develop this perception until all memories and thoughts concerning people and things subside, and you are no longer taking an interest in such externals. Then you can fix your attention solely on the in and out breaths. Breathe normally. Allow the inhalations and exhalations to continue naturally, without forcing them to be longer or shorter, stronger or weaker than normal. Allow the breath to continue normally and smoothly, and observe it entering and leaving the body.

Once the mind has let go of external objects, you will no longer feel disturbed by the sound of traffic or other noises. You won't feel irritated with anything outside. Whether it's forms, sounds, or whatever, they won't be a source of disturbance because the mind won't be paying attention to them as it becomes centered upon the breath.

If the mind is agitated by different things and you can't concentrate, try taking an extra-deep breath until the lungs are completely full, and then release all the air until there is none left inside. Do this several times, then reestablish awareness and continue to develop concentration. Having reestablished mindfulness, it's normal that for a period the mind will be calm; then it will become distracted again. When this happens, bring it back, take another deep breath, and expel all the air from your lungs. Fill the lungs to capacity again for a moment, then reestablish mindfulness on the breath. Fix your mindfulness on the inhalations and exhalations once more.

The practice tends to go like this, so it may take many sittings and a lot of effort before you become proficient. Once you are, the mind will let go of the external world and remain undisturbed. External phenomena will be unable to penetrate inside and disturb the mind. When they cannot penetrate, you will see the mind. You will see the mind as one object of awareness, the breath as another, and mental objects as yet another. They will all be present within the field of awareness, centered at the tip of your nose, where mindfulness is set up on the inhalations and exhalations. Then you continue to practice at your ease. As the mind becomes calm, the breath, which was originally coarse, correspondingly becomes lighter and more refined. The body feels lighter, and the mind becomes progressively lighter and unburdened, letting go of external phenomena.

From this point onward your awareness will be turned away from the world outside and directed inward to focus on the mind. Once the mind has become concentrated, maintain awareness at that point where it is focused. You will see the breath clearly as it enters and leaves. Mindfulness will be sharp, and awareness of mental objects and mental activity will be clearer. At that point, you will see the characteristics of sila, samadhi, and wisdom and the way they merge together. Once this unification of the path factors occurs, your mind will be free from all forms of turbulence. It will become one-pointed, and this is samadhi. When you focus attention in just one place—in this case, the breath—you gain clarity and awareness because of the uninterrupted presence of mindfulness. As you continue to see the breath clearly, mindfulness will become stronger, and the mind becomes more sensitive in many different ways. You will see the mind one-pointed in the center of the breath. The external world gradually disappears from your awareness, and the mind will no longer perform any work on the outside.

It's as if you've come inside your own house. All your sense faculties have come together to form one unit. You are at your ease, and the mind is free from all external objects. Awareness remains with the breath, and over time it will penetrate deeper and deeper inside, becoming more and more refined. Ultimately, awareness of the breath becomes so refined that the sensation of it seems to disappear. You could say either that awareness of the sensation of the breath has disappeared, or that the breath itself has disappeared. In other words, awareness of the breath becomes so subtle that it's difficult to define it.

Really, there is still breath, but it has become so refined that it seems to have disappeared. Why? Because the mind is at its most refined, with a special kind of knowing present. All that remains is the knowing, even though the breath seems to have vanished. Take this very knowing as the meditation object and sustain that.

At this point you might begin to doubt, because it is here that the visionary meditation experiences called *nimitta* can occur. These can be of many kinds, including forms and sounds. It is here that all sorts of unexpected things can happen in the course of the practice. If nimitta do arise—some people have them, some don't—understand them for what they are, meaning impermanent phenomena. Don't doubt or allow yourself to become alarmed.

At this stage, you should make the mind unshakable in its concentration and be especially mindful. Some people become startled when they notice the breath has disappeared. When it appears the breath has gone, you might panic or become afraid you're going to die. So you need to understand it's just the nature of the practice to progress in this way. Observe this feeling that there is no breath, and sustain it as the object of awareness as you continue to meditate. The Buddha described this as the firmest, most unshakable form of samadhi. There is just one firm and unwavering object of mind. When your practice of samadhi reaches this point, you will be aware of many unusual and subtle changes and transformations taking place within the mind. The body will feel extremely light or might even disappear altogether. You might feel like you are floating in midair and seem to be completely weightless. It might be like you are in the middle of space, and wherever you direct your sense faculties they don't seem to register anything at all.

As you continue to practice, you should understand there is nothing to worry about. Establish this feeling of being relaxed and unworried securely in the mind. Once the mind is concentrated and one-pointed, nothing will be able to penetrate or disturb it, and you will be able to sit like this for as long as you wish. You will be able to sustain concentration without any feelings of pain or discomfort.

Having developed samadhi to this level, you will be able to enter or leave it at will. When you do leave, it's at your ease and convenience, rather than because you're feeling lazy or tired. This is samadhi, relaxed and comfortable. You enter and leave it without any hindrance. If you genuinely have samadhi like this, sitting to meditate for just thirty minutes or an hour will enable you to remain cool and peaceful for many days. Receiving the results of samadhi like this has a purifying effect on the mind. Whatever you experience will become an object of contemplation. This is where the practice really begins. It's the fruit that comes as samadhi matures.

Samadhi performs the function of calming the mind. Samadhi has one function, sila has its function, and wisdom performs another function. These aspects you are developing in your practice are linked, forming a cycle. Once the mind is calm, it will become progressively more restrained and composed due to the presence of wisdom and the power of samadhi. As this occurs, it gives rise to an energy that acts to purify conduct. Greater purity of conduct facilitates the development of stronger and more refined samadhi, and this in turn supports the maturing of wisdom. They assist each other in this way. Each aspect of the practice acts as a supporting factor for the other two, and in the end these terms become synonymous.

As these three factors continue to mature together, they form one complete circle, giving rise to magga, or "the path." Magga is the synthesis of these three functions of practice working smoothly and consistently together. Preserve this energy. It is the energy that will give rise to *vipassana*, or "special insight." Having reached this stage, where wisdom is funtioning in the mind independent of whether the mind is tranquil or not, wisdom will provide a consistent energy in your practice. You see that whenever the mind isn't tranquil, you shouldn't have any attachment to that; even when it is tranquil, you shouldn't have any attachment. Having let go of the burden of such concerns, the heart will feel much lighter. Whether you experience pleasant or unpleasant phenomena, you will remain at ease. The mind remains peaceful in this way.

It's also important to recognize that when you end a session of formal meditation, if wisdom is not functioning, you will give up the practice altogether without any further contemplation, development of awareness, or consideration of the work that still has to be done. When you withdraw from samadhi, you should know clearly that you have withdrawn. Then continue to conduct yourself in a normal manner, maintaining mindfulness at all times. It isn't that you only practice meditation in the sitting posture; samadhi means a mind that is firm and unwavering. As you go about your activities, make the mind firm and steady, and maintain this steadiness as your state of mind at all times, with continuous mindfulness and self-recollection. As you experience phenomena that cause like and dislike, consistently be aware of the fact that such mental states are impermanent and uncertain. In this way, the mind remains calm and in a state of normalcy.

There are two kinds of peacefulness. One is the peace that comes through samadhi. The other is the peace that comes through wisdom. The mind that is peaceful through samadhi is still deluded. Such peace is dependent on the mind being separated from phenomena. When it's not experiencing any contact or activity, there is calm, and consequently you get attached to the happiness that comes with that calm state. But as soon as there is impingement through the senses, the mind gives in right away. It gets to be afraid of phenomena. It will be afraid of happiness and suffering, of praise and criticism, afraid of forms, sounds, smells, and tastes. People who are peaceful through samadhi alone are afraid of everything and don't want to get involved with anybody or anything, because they are afraid their state of mind will be disturbed. People practicing in this way just want to stay in isolation to experience the bliss of samadhi without having to leave it. They want to hide themselves away in a quiet place.

This kind of samadhi can involve a lot of suffering. People find it difficult to come out of it and be with others. They don't want to see or hear anything. They don't want to experience anything at all! They have to live in some specially preserved, very quiet place where no one will come and disturb them with conversation.

This kind of peacefulness alone can't do the job. If you have reached the necessary level of calm, then withdraw and use that calm as a basis for contemplation. Contemplate the peace of concentration itself, and use it to connect the mind with and reflect upon the different phenomena it experiences. Use the calm of samadhi to contemplate sights, sounds, smells, tastes, tactile sensations, and thoughts in light of the three characteristics of impermanence, suffering, and lack of self.

When you have contemplated sufficiently, it's all right to reestablish samadhi. You can reenter it through sitting meditation and then, with calm reestablished, continue with the contemplation. Use the state of calm to train and purify the mind, as well as to challenge it. As you gain knowledge, use it to combat the mental afflictions. If you simply enter samadhi and stay there, you don't gain any insight; you are only making the mind calm, that's all. However, if you use the calm mind to reflect, beginning with your external experience, this calm will gradually penetrate deeper and deeper inward until the mind experiences the most profound peace of all.

The peace that comes from wisdom is distinctive, because when the mind withdraws from tranquility, the presence of wisdom makes it unafraid of sights, sounds, smells, tastes, physical sensations, and thoughts. It means that as soon as there is sense-contact, the mind is immediately aware of what is happening. When there is contact, you lay it aside because your mindfulness is sharp enough to let go right away.

When you are training the mind like this, it becomes considerably more refined than when you develop samadhi alone. The mind becomes very powerful and no longer tries to avoid anything. With such energy, you become fearless. In the past, you were scared to experience anything, but now you know phenomena as they are and are no longer afraid. You know your own strength of mind and are unafraid. When you see a form, you contemplate it. When you hear a sound, you contemplate it. You become proficient at contemplating mental objects. You are established in the practice with a new boldness that will prevail no matter what the conditions. Whether it be sights, sounds, or whatever, you recognize them and let go of them as soon as they occur. Whatever it is, you can let go of it. You see happiness clearly and let go. You see suffering clearly and let go. Wherever you see them, you let go of them right there. Keep letting them go, casting them aside as they arise. No phenomena will be able to maintain a hold over your mind. You leave them behind and remain secure in your place of abiding. All phenomena lose their value and are no longer able to sway you. This is the power of vipassana. When such a quality of awareness arises within your mind, the practice can be called vipassana, clear knowing in accordance with the truth. This is peace at the highest level.

Practicing here this evening we have meditated together for an hour and now stopped. It might be that your mind has stopped practicing completely and hasn't continued with the reflection. That's not the right way to do it. When we stop, all that should stop is the formal sitting meditation.

Keep a state of meditation and reflection going at all times. Just taking a walk and seeing dead leaves on the ground can provide an opportunity to contemplate impermanence. We are no different from the leaves: when we get old, we are going to shrivel up and die. Other people are the same. We should make efforts to raise the mind to the level of constant contemplation and awareness like this, whether walking, standing, sitting, or lying down. This is practicing meditation correctly, following the mind carefully at all times.

I've often said that if you don't practice consistently, it's like drops of water. The practice is not a continuous, uninterrupted flow. Mindfulness is not sustained evenly. The important point is that the mind does the practice and nothing else. The body doesn't do it; the mind does the work. If you understand this clearly, you will see that you don't always have to be in formal meditation for the mind to know samadhi.

Once you recognize this, you will be developing awareness at all times and in all postures. If you are maintaining mindfulness as an even and unbroken flow, it's as if the drops of water have joined to form a smooth and continuous stream. Mindfulness is present from moment to moment, and accordingly there will be awareness of mental objects at all times. If the mind is restrained and composed with uninterrupted mindfulness, you will know the wholesome and unwholesome mental states that arise. You will know the mind that is calm and the mind that is confused and agitated. Wherever you go, you will be practicing. If you train the mind in this way, your meditation will mature quickly and successfully.

Please don't misunderstand. These days, it's common for people to go on retreats for several days where they don't have to speak or do anything but meditate. Maybe you have been on a silent retreat for a week or two, afterward returning to your normal life. You might leave thinking you've "done vipassana," and because you feel you know what it's all about, you return to old habits of sensual indulgence. When you do this, what happens? Before long, none of the fruits of vipassana will be left. If you do a lot of unskillful things that disturb and upset the mind, wasting everything, then next year you go back, do another retreat for several days or weeks, come out, and carry on partying and drinking, that isn't the path to progress.

So you need to contemplate until you see the harmful effects of such behavior; this is what is meant by renunciation. See the harm in drinking and going out on the town. Reflect and see the harm inherent in all the different kinds of unskillful behavior you are accustomed to indulging in until that harm becomes fully apparent. This will provide the impetus for you to take a step back and change your ways. Then you will find some real peace. To realize peace of mind, you have to see clearly the disadvantages and pitfalls in such forms of behavior. This is practicing in the correct way. If you do a silent retreat for seven days, where you don't have to speak or get involved with anyone, and then are chatting, gossiping, and indulging all over for another seven months, how will you gain any real or lasting benefit from those seven days of meditation?

I would encourage all of you to try to understand this point. It's necessary to speak in this way so habits that are faulty become clear to you, and thus you will be able to give them up. You could say the reason you came here is to learn how to avoid doing the wrong things in the future. What happens when you do the wrong things? It leads you to a state of agitation and suffering where there is no goodness in the mind. It's not the way to peace. This is how it is, but many places where meditation is taught don't come to grips with it. Really, you have to conduct your daily life in a consistently calm and restrained way.

This is a form of reminder to you all, so I will ask your forgiveness. Some of you might just feel I'm scolding you— "The old monk is telling us off!"—but it's not like that. It's just that you may need reminders, because in meditation you have to be constantly turning your attention to the practice. Please try to practice consistently. See the disadvantages of practicing inconsistently and insincerely, and try to sustain a dedicated and continuous effort in the practice. It can then become a realistic possibility that you might put an end to the mental afflictions.

CONTEMPLATING THE BODY:
A TALK TO CANDIDATES FOR ORDINATION

These robes are the banner of the Buddha. Think about it. Tomorrow you will go to the village for alms. People will happily offer you their food and show respect. Even old people, their heads white and their backs bent, will show you respect. Why? Because of the power of the ocher robes. These robes are of the ultimate power. If you don't use them correctly, the people in the villages will feel that you have lost your minds. "Crazy" will be their only verdict.

When ordaining, going forth in the Buddhist religion, many instructions can be given. But today I will not say too much. I will follow the way of the ancient teachers, who urged us to learn and practice meditation, specifically the fivefold meditation on hair of the head, bodily hair, nails, teeth, and skin. Just talking about them, it can seem like a game or a joke. But if they are carefully considered, they are extremely profound.

We are here to learn meditation, and meditation is these five objects. "Venerable hair, venerable nails . . ." They are called the root meditations. These five meditations were born with us and have always been with us, but we haven't recognized them. So it's necessary to study the five root meditations as a basis for entering the path to nirvana. You can establish right view when you study a root meditation and contemplate its meaning. Some people will say they already know it and ask why they need to study such a thing. In fact, they don't know. They don't really know their own hair, their own nails, and the rest. They don't see them according to the truth. Meditation monks always hear such talk but are not moved by it.

Hair of the head is born from the scalp, nourished by the body's fluids. Bodily hair and nails are the same. They are nothing to get obsessed with. When people dress themselves up, they are not really doing it in accordance with the true path. They are dressing up and adorning something that we don't see as being beautiful. Did you see how they dressed up the corpse in the meditation hall for the funeral recently? In such a case, we can observe very clearly that people are trying to make beautiful something that is really not beautiful or clean.

In truth, this body is not a clean thing. It is a matter of delusion, such as thinking that hair is beautiful. Actually, how could hair be beautiful? Is it something clean? There is nothing natu-rally clean or beautiful about hair. Put one beautiful hair in someone's food, and how much will they appreciate it? Who will want to eat it?

Put some hair on the ground, and who will want to pick it up? If you see some skin or hair on the path to the village when you are going for alms, will you feel attracted to pick them up for any reason? This is the truth of them, but people are always making efforts to adorn and beautify them, which only serves to delude all of us.

We are easily deluded. We don't know the truth of hair, nails, and the rest. So when we are ordained, these five things are taken up and the nature of them pointed out: hair is not beautiful, nails are not beautiful, teeth are not beautiful, skin is not beautiful. They are pointed out as unclean and unattractive. But people in-sist on trying to beautify them, so we are fooled. Not seeing the truth of them, we don't see the Buddha. These things conceal the Buddha from our sight. So we are taught to make our vision pure and clear in regard to these things. Think about them, con-template. You can sit and repeat the words and think about them. "Skin, hmm. The skin envelops the body and everything in it. If we were to peel off the skin, what would we see? Who could stay near us? If we peeled off the skin, leaving only the flesh on the bones, the little novices would dash out of the hall; they couldn't stay. So where is the beauty?" Look and examine these five objects completely, and you will see they are not really beau-tiful; you will exhaust your interest in them. Rely on these five objects of meditation.

But people like to be misled. We are misled by the adornment and beautification the world lives by. Style the hair, make up the skin, polish the nails, whiten the teeth. Make up everything, make the things that are not really beautiful into objects of at-traction, and then there are causes for delusion. When you don't see clearly, you get fooled. Like a fish. Fish swallow hooks, have you seen? In truth, the fish doesn't eat the hook; it eats the bait. If it just saw the hook, it wouldn't bite. It doesn't think it's going to be swallowing a hook, but that's what happens because it's lured by the bait. When it bites, the hook catches its mouth and it can't get free.

We people are the same, being lured by hair, nails, and the rest. We shouldn't want them. Why do you want to carry these impermanent, uncertain things? Those who get attached to these things are deluded, thinking they are great, beautiful, and wonderful, like a fish who swallows the bait.

The fish doesn't know what it's doing; it eats bait but ends up caught on the hook. Then, however much it wants to escape, it can't. It is caught. Hair, nails, skin, and teeth catch us in the same way. Once we get attached to them, ow! When finally we come to realize what is going on, it's difficult to get out. We might think about getting out of the world then, but we worry about our children, our possessions, all the sorts of things that fill up a life. We can end up bound by them, staying just where we are until death.

This is being deluded, like the fish that is deluded by the bait. We are caught in the world because we think the five objects are attractive and wonderful, and we are absorbed by them our whole lives. In truth, it's a small thing, not a great matter, just the matter of a hook catching the fish's mouth. Please consider this.

So when you ordain and study Dharma in this way, you can be at ease. Even if you disrobe because of some previous commitment or pressing matter, you should recall this and be careful, thinking about the hook. This can bring you peace, whether you are ordained or a layperson. The time may be short now, but never mind. Don't be heedless. Contemplate these things. This is a meditation that you should learn and come to know, and it should instill some caution. People have no fear or caution because they don't know the truth of this. This is a brief meditation all of you should learn.

MEDITATION EXPERIENCES

I had problems in meditation. I remember one time when I kept coming up against an obstacle. It was as if I were walking somewhere. I got to a certain point, and there was nowhere else to go. Another time was like walking and bumping into something, so I stopped. I would go again, but I kept bumping into it, again and again, and kept retreating. Finally, I became afraid and gave up.

In the first example, there's nothing to bump into, but still there is an obstruction. In the second, when you come to this obstacle, you become afraid and turn back. The mind wonders, What is this? In your sitting and walking meditation, you keep on coming to this point and wondering what it is. But whatever it is, never mind. After some time, it will cease. Then it can return, and there is the same wondering, What is going on here? This kind of uncertainty can really plague you.

This happens in samadhi. It is actually a matter of having attachment in the experience of samadhi. These feelings and experiences come, and we become bewildered as to what is going on. It means that our understanding doesn't yet reach the level of letting go.

I once went to see a meditation master named Ajahn Wang. He was living on a hilltop with one other monk and two novices. I hadn't met him, but had come to feel there must be something special about someone living like that. When I did finally meet him, he was happy. He knew. He knew that a sincere practitioner was going to be arriving at his dwelling. He understood about meditation monks, and he was happy to meet someone who was practicing.

In the evening, he spoke to us about practice. He was a disciple of Ajahn Mun, in the generation of Ajahn Lee. These were really serious practitioners.

I said to him, "Venerable Ajahn, this seems like an appropriate occasion for me to ask you for some guidance. I want to know what meditation is really all about." I then spoke of the difficulty I had experienced.

He said, "Oh, that's not all there is to the matter. That's a very small part of it." He spoke from his own experience.

Once when he was doing walking meditation, he stopped and fixed his attention, and his body sank into the ground. He was aware of this—why wouldn't he know what was taking place?—and he saw his body sinking further and further into the earth. With awareness, he could just let it keep sinking, let it do what it would. Finally, it got to the end. He didn't know where or what this end was, but he was aware that his body had reached it. Then his body started rising up. It rose up to the surface of the earth, but it didn't stop there. It kept on going, rising up and up.

He was aware of all this, and he was also really astonished at how such things could happen. His body kept on floating until it came to a tree, and then it exploded, boom! His intestines were hanging from the branches of trees like garlands. I asked, "Ajahn, was this a dream?"

It wasn't a dream. Well, this was certainly strange to hear about. But these things really happen. When you experience such things, you will know they really do happen.

If this were to happen to you, your body exploding and guts hanging in the trees, what would you feel? If your awareness is steady, you can just watch it all happening. If the body explodes, you simply know that it explodes. If the intestines go flying out, you know they are flying out. You just need the firm conviction that this is nimitta (a sign or mental image occurring in meditation), and you come to have a deep conviction that nothing can harm you. Fixing your attention, the nimitta will appear to the mind and then disappear. Still, after it is gone, it might leave you wondering what it was that happened.

I further inquired of the Ajahn, "I am at my wit's end. I didn't have this experience you spoke about, but there's something else that happened to me. It's like being on a bridge. I'm trying to cross a river on the bridge, but I get to a certain point and can't go any farther. There's nowhere to proceed, so I go back. Then I try again, but I always have to stop. This is something that happens in samadhi, not just in an ordinary state. I watch what is going on, and sometimes I see something blocking me. I wonder who is going to help me. So I have my doubts about what I should do when this happens. What is this, Ajahn?"

"This is reaching the limits of perception," was his answer. "When you get to the limit, just stand right there. Take note of what is happening. Stay there. If you are aware of it, the perception will resolve itself. It will change by itself without any need to force it. You just note that it is occurring, and you are aware of your state of mind when it occurs. It will change.

"It is like the perceptions of a child being transformed into the perceptions of an adult. A child is fascinated by things and always wants to play with them. When the child grows up and sees those same things, she will not be interested in playing. She will be looking to 'play' elsewhere. There has been a transformation of perception."

I gained some understanding from his explanation.

Then he said, "Don't talk too much! Don't have so many issues! There are so many issues, but all you need to do is be aware that anything can happen in samadhi. That's enough. Anything is possible, but never mind. Don't have any doubts about whatever occurs. When you have this perspective, these experiences will just arise and pass without causing you any hindrance. They are impermanent mental functions. There is no inherent reality in them. If you follow after what appears, then when you see a duck, it can become a chicken, and the chicken can turn into a dog. This could make you very confused, and there will be no end to it.

"Fix your attention on whatever arises and watch it pass away. But don't then get the idea that it's finished. Don't think you are done with everything," he warned. "Soon enough, there will be more. But if you have the attitude of not being taken in, not believing in these things, you keep on letting go of them. Then they pose no danger to you.

"Watching like this gives you a foundation. Don't run after these things! Keep on noting. When you meditate, you will gain familiarity, and you will be able to turn these experiences inward for your mind to know them. Dealing with them in this way, undoing the confusion of appearances, some wisdom will gradually come, and your ability to deal with these things will naturally increase; they will be resolving themselves."

The Ajahn said, "In the future, it will be just as it was in the past, and you should practice in the same way. Your experiences may be greater or lesser, but no matter what you experience, no matter how extraordinary, you need to keep this understanding in mind.

"Be careful!" he said. "Some people seem to practice very comfortably. They don't have obstructions. There is no suffering for them. This is previous karma coming to fruition in the present. When the mind becomes concentrated, this karma rushes in and invades. To say that things invade the mind doesn't necessarily mean bad experiences are occurring. There can be happy experiences also, making the mind bright and clear. Harmful things can be fearsome, but they can also appear in attractive forms. However, all experiences are a peril to the mind. Don't get fixated on them at all!"

I studied with him like this for three nights. Then I took my leave, went down the mountain, and practiced as he had advised. For many days, I meditated and looked into this, contemplating many different things. It was very good. It led me to believe that it is possible for people to practice on their own, but that way can be very slow. Without someone to point out the way to deal with the mind, the path can become circuitous. It is generally like this for people. When they get stuck, they're stuck deep.

In matters of the mind, if we go to extremes, it leads to madness. Problems of the mind are not so easy to resolve. There was an abbot in this area who had a novice ordained with him. He didn't know what was happening—he wasn't a meditator—but his novice practiced meditation.

After a few months of practicing, this novice started talking a lot. He would give Dharma talks on many subjects. It was certainly interesting. He'd never studied the texts, but he could speak about these things. It seemed quite marvelous. The abbot listened to him, and it all sounded correct. So he started thinking this could be an arahant.

The novice was able to explain all facets of the Dharma correctly, speaking in an extremely elaborate and skillful way. His ajahn didn't have experience in meditation and couldn't really understand these explanations, so he became convinced that his novice had realized deep wisdom. He thought the novice had overcome the defilements and so was able to teach like this.

Then one day, they found the novice's body hanging from a tree. He had actually been insane, and finally he had killed himself. Then the ajahn was able to realize the novice had been mad, not an arahant. This is what it can be like when a meditator doesn't know how to practice properly and hasn't been shown the way to deal with problems and obstacles.

What happens is a weariness with life. One sees no point in living and doesn't wish to go on. But it is weariness in the way of emotional affliction, not in the way of wisdom. One sees no meaning in being alive and feels it would be better to die.

Things like this happen because people believe their own thinking. Trusting your mind can even lead you to take your own life. When it falls into wrong ways, it can be very wrong.

The way I see it—this is just my opinion—you shouldn't be interested in magical powers at all. When the mind becomes tranquil, contemplate the physical body. Place the attention here for an appropriate time. Develop insight rather than looking for miraculous occurrences. Enter the correct path and practice insight meditation to develop the wisdom that sees arising and passing away. This will be helpful to you.

Some people don't think like that. They want to practice tranquility meditation to the very limit. They want their practice of morality and meditative concentration to reach the limit. Where this limit might be, or where it can be finished, they don't really have any idea. The fact is, a wise person needn't be too forceful about anything. What is important is to uproot conventional reality, the seeming appearance of things, to make an end of them and be liberated. Liberation is transcendence and voiding of conventional reality, the apparent. In the apparent, things are determined as really existing and having certain characteristics, being a certain way. When you do away with these suppositions, you attain transcendence and are liberated from all these phenomena. This is knowing your own mind. It's really not necessary to get too infatuated with anything. This is enough.

But this can become a vexing problem. Practice gets very difficult for some people because they get caught up in their thinking. They go overboard and deviate from the path, thinking they are going to do a lot, practice really hard to get some great result. Just what "doing a lot" means, or what "great" is, they are unclear about.

QUESTIONS AND ANSWERS

STUDENT: As to what you were saying about investigating sankhara after the mind has reached an appropriate level of tranquility, we have heard this mentioned many times, such as in the instructions for meditating on the thirty-two parts of the body. By employing concepts and recollection to investigate like this, is one able to come to genuine insight?

AJAHN CHAH: You do need to use the concepts at first. Actually, the truth can never be reached by thinking and perceiving. Any kind of concept, negative or positive, will not make an end of things. But it's the only way to instruct people. We are talking for the children to understand, to show them that they must do this and this and this. When you get to the end, there will be nothing left. You don't want to be following any mental formations. If you believe that your conceptions are wisdom, then you are constantly led around by them. They are merely sankhara, conditioned phenomena. And the knowing is not a self and also should be let go. Consciousness is merely consciousness, not a being, a person, an individual, or a self. Put it down! Let it be finished with.

S: How much tranquility should one develop?

AC: Enough to be able to contemplate things, to have the mindfulness to make this investigation.

S: So this means remaining in the present, not thinking of the past or the future?

AC: You can think of past and future, but don't get caught up taking any of it as real. The mind has to think of all kinds of things, but don't believe it. Understand what thoughts are and that they're only thoughts. The point is not to get caught by thinking and follow after it.

If you follow your thinking, you will always have issues and problems. It's better to end this kind of involvement with appearances. Mind is merely mind. It is not a being, an individual, a person, or a self. This is called awareness of the mind. It is not yours. Pleasure is merely pleasure; pain is merely pain. When you see things in this way, there are no doubts.

What is called investigating or contemplating uses the faculty of thought to look at things, but eventually it comes to see something beyond thought, because as you practice, you learn not to fixate on or believe in these perceptions. Thoughts and feelings are merely thoughts and feelings.

That which we are talking about does not arise and does not cease. It abides as it is. Or to put it simply, it is not born and does not die.

Let's take this mind. We call it mind in order to have some idea about it, to know its activities. But talking about the *real* mind—well, what is beyond the mind? Where does the mind come from? When we look at it, we see arising and ceasing. What is arising and ceasing is not actually the mind itself, but some sort of feeling, meaning mental impressions and conceptual activity. The ultimate truth is not something that comes into existence and disappears in that way. But these things that appear and disappear are called mind in the way of designation and convention.

In the way of conventional reality, we believe in our mental activity as being what it appears to be and call it our mind. But where does this mind come from? Having had the habit of believing in mind for such a long time, we are not very happy right now. Isn't that so?

At first we have to see impermanence, unsatisfactoriness, and selflessness as the nature of the mind. But the truth is that there is really nothing there. It is empty. We see arising and passing away, but actually nothing is arising and passing away. We see the arising and ceasing by relying on perception and conceptualization. But then we take this perception to be wisdom; we grasp the mental activity as wisdom. This is not genuine wisdom. If it is wisdom, everything is finished with. There is no more involvement. We are aware of perceptions and feelings but don't get involved with them. We realize that following after them is not the path.

S: How should we practice to reach this point, the true mind?

AC: First you become aware of this apparent mind, realizing that it is uncertain and impermanent. Seeing that clearly, there is nothing you will want to take hold of, and you will let go. From knowing, you let go, and there is no more cause for conceptualizing over things. Then there will be no doubt.

The names we give to things are all conventions and designations in the realm of appearances. It is to help people recognize things. Nature just exists as it is. For example, in this building we have the foundation and the upper stories. The basis on which things exist is not born and does not die. The things that are born and die are running around upstairs. Sometimes we call it mind, or perception, or conceptualization, or whatever. But to put it simply and directly, there is no form, feeling, perception, or thought. They only exist in the way of designation. The aggregates appear and disappear. They don't really exist.

Have you read the story of Sariputta teaching his disciple Punamantani? I read this story when I was a novice, and it has stayed in my mind ever since.

A monk was going to take up the practice of ascetic wandering, so Sariputta, as his teacher, gave him some instruction. Sariputta asked, "Punamantani, when you are doing your ascetic wandering, what if someone were to ask you, 'What happens when the enlightened one passes away?' How would you answer him?"

The monk answered, "If this question is asked of me, I will answer that form, feeling, perception, conceptualization, and consciousness appear and then cease to be."

That is all. That was the correct answer. Sariputta was examining his disciple before letting him go to practice the ascetic ways. He had the correct view: the aggregates, having come into existence, then pass away. This finished the matter.

When you understand this, you should contemplate it further and develop wisdom to see it very clearly. It is not merely arising and passing away. The result will be recognition of your true mind. You will still experience arising and ceasing, but you won't be drawn to happiness, and suffering cannot follow you then. Attachment and clinging will be done with.

S: From what you were saying, it sounds like there is something else outside of the five aggregates. Is it called original mind or...?

AC: It's not called anything. All of that is finished. Someone may want to call it original something or other, but it is all done with, exhausted. The original things are exhausted.

S: So it's not called original mind?

AC: As a convention, we can say that. If we don't have any conventions, there is nothing to talk about, no original or old or new or whatever. Anything we speak about, all those designations such as old or new, are just convention. Without convention, there is no way to gain understanding. But you should know the limits of it.

S: How much samadhi is necessary to reach this kind of understanding?

AC: Enough to have control of the mind. Without samadhi, what will you be able to do? Without a well-focused mind, you won't reach this point.

It should be enough to be able to see, enough for wisdom to arise. I don't know how to measure how much. What degree of tranquility does the mind need to attain? Let's say to the degree where you no longer have any doubt. That's enough. If you ask, I have to answer like this.

S: Are "the one who knows" and "original mind" the same?

AC: No, no. The one who knows is something that can change. It is our awareness . . . Everyone has this.

S: So not everyone has original mind?

AC: The original mind is in every person. Everyone has the one who knows. But the one who knows is something you can never reach conclusion with. Original mind exists in everyone, but not everyone can see it.

S: Is the one who knows a self?

AC: It isn't—it's only an awareness arising.

Questioning like this only leads to endless confusion. You won't come to clear knowledge just from hearing another's words. Thinking that if you ask the right questions about all the fine details you can find out the truth is not how it works. It is really something to be realized for yourself. But take the words and investigate what they point to.

S: You often teach us about meditating on the thirty-two parts of the body when the mind has been calmed. Should we investigate the thirty-two parts according to the formula?

AC: It's not like that. When the mind is in a state of tranquility, investigation occurs on its own. This is investigation within samadhi. It is not thinking, This is like this, that is like that. That is ordinary mental activity, investigation outside of samadhi. But when the mind is concentrated, there is no thinking; contemplation arises within tranquility. The discursive mind that thinks about things during ordinary activities and tries to specify how things are is coarse. It is coarse, but still compatible with samadhi.

The important point is to have mindfulness in all situations, mindfulness which is aware of the way things are. Why is it that the Buddha did not have aversion or delusion? It is because he had this kind of awareness. There is no cause for anger coming about. There is no cause for delusion coming about. Where could they come from? There is this awareness ruling your experience. There is nothing more to be done. You have reached an end of doing. You can put it all aside with the mind in full awareness. You don't need to place your attention on anything, because the mind is doing it on its own; it occurs naturally.

At this point, you don't need to practice samadhi because it is already present. Things can still appear as right and wrong, there can still be feelings of like and dislike, but you just keep letting them go. Whatever things like this appear to you, let them go, with the recognition that they are impermanent. You come to know the source of things and reach the place that is called original mind, where nothing is permanent, where nothing is anything at all. That is truth.

Whatever comes flowing down the stream, when it gets stuck you cut it loose and let it flow away. What is it that comes flowing by? You don't know, but when it gets stuck, you release it and let it flow on; it is the phenomena of sense objects and mental activity. When phenomena are appearing, you keep on sweeping them out. When nothing appears you remain in equanimity.

Just saying the words is easy, isn't it?

This is similar to the business of morality, meditation, and wisdom. The way it's usually presented in Buddhism is that you teach about morality in the beginning, with meditative stability in the middle, and wisdom in the end. This is a classification you can remember. But really, with some people, it isn't necessary to begin by teaching morality. Like Americans. They come to meditate and immediately settle down into pacifying the mind. You don't need to say anything yet about the usual explanation of sila first, samadhi second, and wisdom third. First, just let them sit to develop a tranquil mind. Then some sensitivity will be born. It's as if there were a poisonous snake in a basket with a lid on it. Even if someone were to walk right next to it, they wouldn't be worried because they wouldn't know it was there. They are not yet aware of the danger.

Trying to teach morality is like that. You have to be aware of the habits and dispositions of people in different places. For a Westerner, you can just teach tranquil sitting meditation first. Then when the mind is calmed, some change will take place and the person will see things differently. At first, even if there is a poisonous creature about, the person is unconcerned, because she isn't aware it is there. Sila is like that. It's not necessary to go through the precepts one by one; morality isn't just a matter of reciting, "I vow to refrain from taking life. I vow to refrain from stealing". . . . It's too slow that way. It doesn't get to the point. Like a stick of wood. It has a beginning, a middle, and an end. If you pick up the end, the beginning comes along with it, and you can get to the beginning by starting from the end. Or you can start at the beginning and get the end. You can't insist on telling someone that this is the beginning and that is the end. If people are attracted to samadhi practice, let them develop a peaceful mind through that. Then sensitivity will arise, and they will be able to see things in a new light. Picking up the end, they will get to the beginning, because the beginning and the end are one piece. The changes that come about in the mind through samadhi will enable them to see things, and wisdom will start to permeate the mind. A feeling for what is right and what is wrong will gradually develop.

These three aspects [sila, samadhi, and wisdom] rotate and develop by turns. Wherever you take up practice, that is fine. The traditional way is to talk about morality, meditation, and wisdom. It is useful and shouldn't be discarded, but you can't cling to it as the only way. Whatever clarifies the mind so it can be aware of the poisonous snake is useful. Then when there is awareness, there is caution. You will get to the same place either way. Someone who will teach others has to use whatever skillful means are appropriate.

When a child from the city goes to the countryside for the first time, he will see all kinds of things he hasn't seen before and doesn't know about. He will see a duck and ask, "Dad, what is that?" He sees a buffalo and cries out, "Mom, look at that big animal!" He carries on like this over everything he sees, until his parents are tired of answering. No matter what they explain, the child keeps on asking because he's never seen these things before and is fascinated. Finally, they just grunt in reply. The child doesn't get tired of it though. "What's this? What's that thing? What could this animal be?" There's no end to his curiosity and his questions. But when he grows up he will know all about these things and they won't be a mystery to him anymore.

It's like this in meditation. I used to be this way, too. But when real understanding came, the questions stopped. Through gaining some maturity in practice and inclining the mind toward investigation, one is able to resolve the questions by oneself.

So you have to observe yourself constantly. Each of you has to look carefully to see how honest you are with yourselves and know when you are deceiving yourselves.

Thinking is only a matter of conceptualization and creation. If we are not fully aware, we start to believe it is a matter of wisdom. So we follow after it and end up with dissatisfaction and suffering. If it were really wisdom, would it bring any suffering?

Still, this is something that can lead to wisdom, something that can cause us to see and to know. Don't get the idea they are far apart. Wherever conceptualization exists, wisdom is there. Wherever there is the created, the uncreated is also there. The uncreated is freedom from conceptualization. The created is conceptualization.

This is pointed out through many different methods by different teachers. In Zen, for example, they have their ways for imparting wisdom. You are asked a question, and when you answer, they beat you. Bam! They ask again, so you don't answer this time, but they hit you again. "Hmm. . . . What's really going on here? I might lose my life over this; how should I respond? What should I do?" These methods can bring about wisdom. What to do? Going forward is not right. Retreating is not right. Standing still and giving no answer is not right either. Whatever you try, you only get a beating. Some feeling comes about, and you start to seek more deeply for the answer. This is the method of Zen that I read about. It's curious, isn't it? It can really cause people to gain wisdom. However you answer or don't answer, you are beaten. You lose all your ideas about what is right and wrong. You can't move, you can't stand still. What do you do? You come to the end of your tether, but still there is something more to go through. So the mind keeps on investigating to find a way. Their methods are pretty good, I think. It's mysterious. But for us, it's just a lot of thinking and guessing about the way things are. We know something, but what we know is only what someone else has said. So there will always be more things to ask about and learn, and there are always more doubts. The more things are explained, the further we are from understanding. Why is it like this? What is blocking us? This knowledge itself is blocking us.

So you really need to search inwardly. When you keep looking, your understanding will become more subtle. This refined awareness will seem like something very good. But the Zen master doesn't accept it. "Get rid of the subtle! I have no use for it!" And you get another beating. When the subtle still remains, you have to drive it out. You don't know what to do, where to abide or to go, and you run out of options. It's better just to throw it all away.

It is taught that all of our thoughts and feelings are just the fantasy world of mental concoction. It is not real knowledge. It is the creation of fantasy, but we feel it is genuine knowledge. It is knowing without letting go. With real knowledge, one lets go.

Samadhi has its difficulties. People can get sidetracked. "When I sit, I have so many experiences. I see lights. I see colors . . ." They really get caught up in all this. When they tell me about their samadhi, there's not much I can say. It's just more childish stuff. It really is like the child fascinated by the animals and asking endless questions. That's what a child has to do, because it doesn't know what things are. When it grows up it will know for itself and won't have to ask anymore.

When the factor of rapture arises in meditation, there is a happiness of mind that cannot be described; but one who has reached this will know it. Happiness arises, rapture, one-pointedness, discursiveness, and investigation. These five things come together at a single point. They have five distinct characteristics, but they are unified, and they are all experienced together. It's like different fruits in a basket; although they are different, we see them together in one place. The factors of jhana (meditative absorption) come together and are experienced in the mind. To describe them is impossible—what is the joy like? how does bliss happen? what is discursiveness like?—but if they are developed and experienced, they fill the mind and you will know. At this point, practice is something different. Your meditation becomes different and even strange. It's necessary to have mindfulness and clear comprehension. Don't get confused about what is going on. It is only a mental experience, a mind moment, the nature of mind displaying its potential.

Don't have any doubt about these things that occur in practice. If it goes up into the air or is submerged under the ground, if it seems to be dying, never mind. Just look directly at what your state of mind is and abide with that awareness. That's all. You will have your foundation right there. With mindfulness and clear comprehension, knowing yourself in all four postures of standing, walking, sitting, and lying down, you are not grasping at whatever appears in your field of experience. When you are constantly aware of all that occurs, whether there is attraction or aversion, happiness or displeasure, doubt or certainty, there is investigating and knowing, getting the essence of practice and experiencing the fruit. Don't go fixating on the way things appear to be. Recognize whatever appears to the mind as merely so— merely a moment of sensation and awareness, something impermanent that arises and passes away. There is nothing more than that. There is no self or other, no essence, nothing that should be grasped.

When body and mind are seen thus with wisdom, we are aware of all the old habits and patterns. Seeing the impermanence of mind and body, seeing the impermanence of the totality of all feelings of happiness and suffering, of love and hate, we realize there is only so much to them, they are merely what they are, and the mind turns. It turns away and becomes weary of it all. It becomes weary of mind and body, these things that appear and pass away and are unreliable. Wherever we may be, we see this. When the mind becomes weary, its only concern will be to find a way out. We no longer want to live as before because we see the imperfections and liabilities of the worldly way. We see the liability of this life we have been born into. With this per-spective, wherever we go, we will see the facts of the imperma-nent, unsatisfactory, and selfless nature of phenomena, and there will be nothing we wish to get or grasp hold of. Sitting beneath a tree, we hear the teaching of the Buddha. Sitting atop a moun-tain, we hear the teaching of the Buddha. Sitting on a plain, we hear the teaching of the Buddha. We will see this world much more clearly. We will see body and mind more clearly. The realms of form and formlessness we will see more clearly. They become clearer in the light of impermanence, in the light of the unsatis-factory nature of things, in the light of the absence of a self.

Whenever we humans hold on to things as being permanent and real, suffering comes immediately. But when we realize the truth of body and mind, suffering is not born. Without attach-ment, there is no way for suffering to take hold. In all situations, wisdom will arise. Even seeing a tree, wisdom arises through this contemplation. Seeing plants in the fields, seeing insects, wisdom arises. They all end up at the same point to become Dharma—the point of not being certain. This is the truth. They are things that are not permanent. In what way are they permanent? The only permanence or certainty is that, having arisen, they are tran-sitory and unreliable. They cannot change into something that will not undergo transformation and then cease to be. That's all. If you truly realize this, you have traveled your path to the end.

According to the Buddhist way, if you think, I am better than others, this is not correct. I am worse than others, is still not cor-rect. I am equal to others, is also not correct, because there is re-ally no such thing as I. Uprooting the conceit that says, "I am," you become the knower of the world, knowing clearly accord-ing to the truth. If your vision is true thus, then the mind is true, with complete knowledge of the actual way of things. The causes are cut off. With no causes, nothing is born.

So the practice must proceed like that. The foundations one needs to develop when starting out are first, being an honest per-son, one who is straightforward; second, having fear of wrong-doing and being ashamed of bad actions; and third, having a humble mind, being of few wishes and easily contented. Those of few wishes, who are restrained in speech and actions, will know themselves and be free of distraction.

These elements are the foundation, and when they are complete, there will only be virtue, meditative stability, and wisdom in the mind. They will fill the mind, and there will be nothing else there. Such a mind will live wholly in morality, meditation, and wisdom.

So we practitioners should not be heedless. These words are not often heard, yet this admonition applies to everything. Even when something is good, when you seem to be in the right, don't be heedless. Don't be heedless in regard to what is wrong, to what is good, or to happiness or suffering. The Buddha taught us not to be heedless about anything. Why? Because all these things are uncertain.

Relate to your own mind in this way as well. If it becomes tranquil, don't grasp that state. Just let it be. It's a natural reaction to be gladdened by it, but just be aware of what is happening. Whether there are good or evil states, be aware of them.

A teacher can explain the methods for training the mind, but it is only you who can do it for yourself. You can know everything in your own mind. Who else can know for you? If you rely on what is correct like this, you can reach the point of ease no matter where you are or what you are doing. But this means really practicing. Efforts that are not genuine or sincere will not help. Genuine practice is not something tiring because it is done by way of mind. If you have mindful awareness of yourself, you know what is going on. You know what is right and what is wrong, and you know the way to practice. There isn't really a lot you need.

Relating to your friends in Dharma, there are two things to consider, what are called in the vernacular the example and the essence. It is taught not to take the example, rather to take the essence. Ajahn Tongrat, a master of the last generation, was a case in point. People who weren't smart could not get his Dharma, because they would only look at his example. His speech wasn't restrained—this was his example. He would make requests of laypeople all the time, and when he scolded someone in the assembly, he would really lay into them. His example was like this, but in his essence, there was nothing—really nothing. It was merely speaking, and his speech was all Dharma. In truth, whatever he said was aimed at Dharma, but people didn't have any idea what he was doing. His intention was to give Dharma, not to give harm, and no harm was done, no loss was incurred by anyone. But in his comings and goings, his words and actions, he did not seem to be restrained; his example was like this. Some monks tried to follow it, and the result was only their own undoing.

When Ajahn Tongrat and his monks would go for alms, there was one house where the people were kind of stingy. They didn't like to give food, but of course almost everyone in the village would at least offer a little rice, so they had to come up with some excuse, such as that they didn't know the monks were coming. So when Ajahn Tongrat would get to their house, he would shout in a booming voice, "Hey! Is the rice cooked yet?" and wait in front of the house. Then the people would have no choice but to come out and put some rice in the monks' alms bowls.

The other monks would see Ajahn Tongrat do this every day, and later on one old fellow started doing it, too. Wherever he went on alms round, he would shout at every house, "Hey! Is the rice cooked yet?"

This eventually came to Ajahn Tongrat's attention. One day, in the assembly, he singled out this monk and scolded him for soliciting donations of food.

"What do you mean, Ajahn?" asked the old guy in all innocence.

"People are telling me that when you go for alms you are shouting out, 'Hey, is the rice cooked yet?' This is completely inappropriate for a bhikkhu."

Of course, the old monk thought he was doing the right thing, following his teacher's example. But he didn't know the reason Ajahn Tongrat displayed such behavior, and he didn't have the same mind of detachment. The ajahn prodded the

stingy laypeople out of the wish for them to develop generous
hearts, not merely for the sake of filling his stomach.

The different types of beings who come to the Dharma may be
classified by the ease or difficulty with which they practice and
gain realization. Previous accumulation of merit and the development of *parami*, the "spiritual perfections" that prepare one for
enlightenment, isn't really something we can have a competition
in, the way we do to measure bodily strength and abilities. Some
say, "I have good intentions. I want to develop, but I just can't do
it." Well, you have to try to do it, push it along.

For some, practice is difficult. There are obstructions and
troubles in everything they do, and realization comes ever so
slowly. It means they've created only a small store of parami in
the past. So now, in the present, they have to create a lot of it.
They can't just give up and turn back. If a poor person thinks—
OK, I'm poor, that's how it is, so I needn't try to work and
change things—then he's really in trouble. He's got to think, I am
poor, so I should work hard or at least work like others do. It's
the same here. If we practice a lot, work hard, and develop the
path energetically, we can progress, too.

Then there are those for whom practice is difficult, but realization comes fast. Their practice may even bring them close to
death—they will have to struggle and fight—but they can realize the truth quickly. If they experience a lot of pain, it doesn't
matter. The pain will soon be gone.

For the third type of person, practice is easy, but knowledge
comes with difficulty. They don't have much struggle or obstruction, and they can keep on practicing smoothly, but it takes
a long time. Maybe not until the time of death will they see.

With the fourth group, practice is pleasant and easy. Their path
is one of happiness, and realization comes easily. There are people like this, too.

Whatever the case, whether results come fast or slow, whether
we seem to have a lot of ability or not very much, making efforts

to practice virtue is always worthwhile. Whatever we do will not be lost. Virtue accomplished will undo nonvirtue; that which is correct will remove that which is wrong. At the present moment, the fruit may not have come, but later on it will. This is karma. When one karma is giving its result, another karma cannot. We are receiving the results of past actions now, not yet the results of the actions we do in the present. But nothing is lost. When one karma is finished, another will follow. So we do our practice now, and there will be benefit when the time is right.

Lay Practice: Don't Let the Monkey Burn Down Your House

BUDDHISM TEACHES US TO make earnest efforts in the things we do, but our actions should not be mixed with desire. They should be performed with the aim of letting go and realizing nonattachment. We do what we need to do, but with letting go. The Buddha taught this.

But this is tiring. There is no great enthusiasm for it. People in the world do whatever they do to get something—like the people who come to see you in your capacities as doctors and administrators. It's because they want something. Generally, whatever is done is done because of a wish to get something, and attachment and clinging to things becomes a way of life. But we do our own work according to our responsibilities. If we act like this, doing work that is correct with right understanding, we can be at ease.

When planting a tree, if you want to do it the right way and get fruit from it, how should you go about it in order to have a relaxed mind? You do that which is your responsibility. Getting hold of the sapling is your job; digging the hole is your job; planting it, fertilizing and watering it, and keeping the insects off it is your job. That's it. Stop here. How fast or slow it grows isn't your job. Let go of this part. You make the causes in planting and taking care of the tree, but you don't think, When will it be fully grown? When will there be fruit? That isn't your business, it's the plant's. If you think, I've watered it and all the rest, now how can I force it to grow faster? that won't help. It isn't your responsibility, but there's a connection: if you've done your work properly, the tree is bound to grow according to nature. If you think like this, you will be OK. If you want it to grow in a day or two after all your hard work, that's mistaken. There's no happiness that way. Don't think about it too much at this point.

It's a matter of making causes. If the causes are good, the result is bound to be good, because all things are born of causes. We have our duties, so we do them to the full. But we act without attachment, taking care of our own responsibilities. If we try to take care of the tree's responsibilities, we will get upset. The important thing is to make the causes good. Then the result will be good. If we think like this, there will be lightness of mind. Otherwise, we are doing the other's work, watching the tree today, going back to watch it tomorrow, trying to see it grow.

This is called right livelihood, but there are lots of ordinary things that will bother us. Insects pester the person taking care of the tree and upset him. When there are a lot of tasks and a lot of people, there can be many issues—friction between people and so forth—to trouble our minds when we are trying to do our best.

This is normal. For example, blame and praise are paired judgments. Without criticism there is no praise, and without praise there is no criticism. We have to be able to contend with both. We should realize that these things are helping us, waking us. That's all they are, wake-up calls. But we don't see it like that. If someone disparages us, we are immediately angry and heavy-hearted, and if we are praised, we give a sigh of contentment. It is like this, but we don't realize that they're a pair. We can do our work well now, but before we didn't know how to do things right. One comes from the other. From knowing what is wrong, we come to know what is right. This is really very natural. If we have such understanding, then letting go will follow. This is something for all of you to make efforts at, to think about and practice.

The Buddha taught that certain actions are good. But a few

people will practice, while others have no interest or knowledge and behave in contrary ways. This might disturb you. You should just view it as the way things are in this world. It has to be like this. Now, when people criticize or slander us, we can't bear it. Yet soon enough it will happen again. If there is praise, there will be blame; they are a pair. Understanding this, we come back to resolve them. We cannot have only one. That's impossible. They occur continuously in this life; they are obstacles we must face.

When we work, we have to experience obstacles. If there are no obstacles, there is no suffering. If there is no suffering, we don't think about things, isn't that so? Thus the Buddha spoke of the truth of suffering.

If you think according to Dharma, you can come to have ease of mind, gradually teaching yourselves. Think about this a little. You plant a mango tree with the desire to get fruit. But will every single mango be edible? When you're enjoying ripe mangoes, do you ever consider how many were lost or rejected?

If you get discouraged by considering this, you might not want to plant the trees in the first place. Many of the mangoes fall and rot before they are ripe. Others never ripen well, so what's the use? Well, it's like this: some fall and some you will have to throw away, but you plant and take care of the trees. You can eat mangoes today just because it is like this. If you think, Who wants to plant fruit trees when the mangoes just fall off prematurely? you won't be eating any mangoes.

You have to keep coming back to look for the cause of things. But you live in a nice comfortable place, so you won't feel like doing this. You need to live in a place that is not full of conveniences and make real convenience arise. In truth, if you practice correctly, there will always be a way. When people slander you, you have to be able to bear it. If you can't resolve it, you will live with suffering right up till the day you die.

Some people ask me, "Luang Por, if we don't kill any living creatures, how can we survive? If we stop killing mosquitoes, they will bite us."

Hey, how many years have you been killing mosquitoes?

"I've been doing that since I was a child."

Well, are the mosquitoes all gone yet? Even if you spend this whole lifetime sitting here killing mosquitoes, they won't be finished.

If the mosquitoes won't stop, it's better for you to stop trying to kill them. Then there won't be anything. If you want to keep on struggling and competing, you will always be losing. The way of the animal realm is that when they sense a source of food, they go to feed. They don't see things the way people do. So let's elevate our minds above the level of animals. If we want to play with the mosquitoes like this, we are always losing.

I'm just saying these things for you to think about. If you want to kill, go ahead and kill. But you won't make an end of mosquitoes; I guarantee it. If you want to contend with something that can't be finished, when can you reach an end of it? Killing mosquitoes won't make an end of mosquitoes. In a place that has mosquitoes, such as Thailand, I recommend that since they won't cease and desist, we should do so. Then it's finished. Escape in this way.

What will we do if we can't kill mosquitoes? We might think that the Buddha's teaching is too refined, telling us not to kill mosquitoes. What use are mosquitoes? Right. That's our thinking. If we could know the feelings of mosquitoes, they might be saying, "What use are humans?" So what should we do?

I'm just speaking off the top of my head. But we have to think things through, back and forth, and we can come to understand better. What use are mosquitoes? They just come to drink our blood. This is their use. They have to seek their food.

If we build a house for ourselves, really it is not only our house. Lizards come to stay. Mice come to live here. They don't know whose house it is. They only see it as a place of shelter, so they come to live here. Then we get angry: Hey, the mice are biting my pillows and mats! The mice don't know anything about it. They see some usefulness in doing that. They can make a nest, a place for their young. That's just their way. They aren't trying to steal anything from us. If we have wisdom beyond the animal level, we will take care of ourselves and gain some understanding. There will be no problem. Dharma should get to the root of things like this.

Tanha is craving. If we think things through like this, we can quell it. In the books it's called craving. But in my meditation system, I call it "open wide." Open without shutting. This is tanha in meditation practice. It is said, "There is no river equal to craving." Open wide without shutting—there is no end to suffering. Desire is not of the mouth or the stomach. They can be satisfied. If the stomach doesn't have enough, you can eat some rice. That which is tanha is not the stomach or mouth. Craving has no form or self; it is open wide.

I've compared this to a dog. A dog is given some rice and eats it. One bowl, two, three, or even five. Its stomach will be full, but its craving is still there, open wide. Put some more rice in front of it, and it will lie there guarding it. If another dog shows up, it will growl—*grrr*, a chicken comes and *grrr*. It shows that the stomach is not the place of craving, the mouth is not the place of craving. They can be full. But the thinking and feeling that craves is continuously open wide. The Buddha thus said, "There is no river like craving." If it is open like this, it can never be satisfied or filled. If it's closed, when you pour the water, it flows off. If it's open, the water goes in and never fills it, it just keeps on flowing in. It's like this, never satisfied, wanting all manner of things.

Consider a person who is enamored of life and doesn't think about death. When she is seriously ill, she moans and pleads, "Please give me a little more time, if you're going to take me, make it sometime in the future." Then she recovers. She falls ill again and again begs, "May I have a little time? Please don't take me yet." When we're strong and healthy, we don't think about death. We don't feel that we are in danger. Of course we are not beyond danger, because we haven't died. Then when we're sick, "Please, I need a little more time. It's not right to go now." This can happen many times, and still we say, "Please, not just yet!" The truth is, we are afraid. We don't want to die; that's all there is to it. It's a matter of blind craving, people being attached to life. This is an example of desire. If we don't develop wisdom to know this craving, we are always in a state of suffering.

Tanha is called desire. It means not being satisfied, that's a better way to put it. Someone can be free of tanha. He will still have desires, but he can be satisfied. Tanha cannot be satisfied. We carry it along and complain all the way. We complain of the heaviness, but don't want to put down the heavy thing. If we want a lot of things, it gets really heavy. People want a lot, but they don't want it to be heavy. This is not seeking out the facts of the matter. If we understand, there isn't a whole lot to it. It's not a big deal. We can get to the end.

I think Dharma is something difficult. It's troublesome. But if we really contemplate it, it is something that can make an end of our problems. The things the Buddha taught are not impossible to practice. Among all the things the Buddha taught, that which is beyond being practiced by people does not exist. He only taught that which benefits us and benefits others. Things that are of no benefit to us and others he did not teach. Please consider this.

If suffering occurs in your daily life, you should consider why this is happening. It might be that your children don't listen to you. Well, who made these children? If you are suffering because of your children, actually the cause resides with you. You have to think like this, returning to the origin. If you just want to try to fix the situation by forcing them to be a certain way, it will be beyond your means. You won't be able to accomplish it, and you'll end up in tears over your children. In truth, what is the reason? There's a cause. You have to pay attention and see what it is. Things don't just bubble up and appear without cause; but we don't really search it out very seriously.

The Buddha taught us to realize that the world is like this. He could find peace because he knew things according to the truth. What is this about? Let's use an analogy. Have you ever seen monkeys? Are they calm and peaceful? Are there any calm monkeys? That's the way monkeys are, climbing around all the time. Wherever there are monkeys, they act that way. But maybe you get upset when you see them; you feel they should sit still and not be climbing and jumping all over. It might make you so angry you're even ready to kill them. But have you ever seen a tranquil monkey, one that can be still, the way we can train humans to meditate and behave calmly? There's no such thing, apart from a monkey that is dead.

So what should you do? Should you try to force them to be otherwise? You should realize that this is just the way monkeys are. Every monkey in the universe will carry on like this. If you see one and understand it clearly, you know all monkeys. You will let it be what it is because that is the way of monkeys. Whether or not the monkey is calm, your own feeling about it is another matter, and that can be calm. Let monkeys be monkeys without getting emotionally involved. Peace can be born within you because you know the way monkeys are. Knowing the manner of monkeys, you will let go and be at peace, not getting tied up in monkey business. You see them and realize monkeys are like that. You go somewhere else and see monkeys, and you think, Monkeys are like that. There's no ill will on your part, because monkeys are like that. That's all.

But you want monkeys to be calm, and so you reap suffering. That is not how the Buddha wanted you to resolve things. You should resolve them by knowing according to the truth. If you keep looking into it, you will come to realize that it is beyond your ability to alter things, so you have to release them, let go. Wisdom that knows the way phenomena are, knowing they are thus and letting them be thus, brings peace to the mind. There will be no doubt.

The world is the same. The Buddha is said to be the one who knows the world clearly. Just as we know monkeys clearly. The world has to be like that.

Usually people come to recognize this because nature has ripened for them; they have had a lot of experiences. Then they may hear just a little Dharma, and they look back with great regret: "Oh! I've been suffering for so many years, just because I wanted to make things a certain way". And not just many years; it's possible to go on until you die if you keep thinking in the same old way and don't let go. You will never see the place of peace.

You will never see the place where you can let go. Things are a certain way, but you want them to be otherwise and it can't happen. Whatever is the truth of phenomena, that is what you need to see.

———

QUESTIONS AND ANSWERS

STUDENT: Suppose a monkey starts playing with fire. If we just let it be the way it will be, it could burn down our house.

AJAHN CHAH: No, no, it's not like that. That's a different matter. We know monkeys, and we should have greater wisdom than monkeys. Will you let them get hold of fire and burn down your house? When there is a crisis, you will know how to deal with it.

For example, everyone has to die, but still we take care of our lives. But taking care of it the way you doctors do, curing and controlling illness, not to prevent death. There is no such thing. There is no such medicine. If you know this, you care for your patients and treat illness like this.

Maybe a criminal comes to the hospital. He was involved in a robbery and got shot. The hospital has to take care of him. Some will then say that the doctors are supporting a thief, saving him so he can go rob houses. It's not like that. It's the responsibility of the doctors to take care of people. If you take care of them and when they recover they go and commit crimes, that's not your fault. You take care of people according to your function and responsibility as doctors. It's not that you are treating them to continue their careers as criminals. You are only doing your duty to relieve suffering and treat illness and injury.

When people get sick, they rush to find a doctor. Likewise, if a monkey is about to set our house on fire, we will do something to stop it. We have to take care of things and employ caution. But speaking of our house, we don't need a monkey to burn it down; there is already the demon living there. "We don't need to take care of it. Having been born, people must die, so why should we take care of our lives?" There is this question. We should take care of our lives just as doctors treat sick people: to get some temporary relief. Worldly people always complain, saying things like, These doctors are no good. They treated me but I didn't get better; furthermore, you can see that people are always dying. They indulge in this kind of mad talk. Doctors do not treat people to prevent death. They don't have medicine to prevent death. No matter what level of study they go through, they never learn such a thing. That is not the province of doctors. Their responsibility is to alleviate suffering from illness and help people survive one day at a time. That's all. So that's called not letting the monkey burn down your house.

We have to use wisdom to take care of things. When we know what monkeys are all about, if a monkey is bringing fire to the house, will we just sit by and watch? We know the traits of monkeys, and we are able to watch out for them and exert control. Just like with children. We have to know their ways, and we have to take care of them. If we know how children are, we will watch over them carefully. They could burn or cut themselves or fall into ditches—we can't just leave them to themselves. Someone who employs equanimity here is not someone who understands children. Someone like that will let the monkey burn down the house.

You may feel that living at home is troublesome, but when you leave for a while, you start to feel homesick. What should you do? It's strange, isn't it, the way of humans? It's only because when you go somewhere, you don't really reach the place of satisfaction; your thinking doesn't get there. This is what the Buddha called "the cycle." So you come to this monastery for training, to do something worthwhile, but the feeling is still not the same as being at home; no place can be as pleasant and enjoyable as home for you, so you're always thinking of home. It means that the business of good and evil is not yet finished. You are still doing things in a worldly way, so it isn't finished. If it isn't finished, it means you haven't put things down. If you have not put them down, you are still carrying them. Carrying them, you feel the heaviness, and you can see the fault of it.

It comes down to practicing patient endurance. There isn't really anything to it. It is said that patience is the mother of all Dharma. Patience brings good results; but then, when good comes, we are often deluded by it. Strange, isn't it? We should be able to reach a conclusion to all of this. Things are good, but we get deluded, then there is more suffering.

Good and evil, love and hate don't go beyond, but always remain within their limitations. We really ought to think about the Dharma and internalize it to resolve these matters. If we are suffering, we expect another person to cure it for us. But this is not something another person can do. She can explain the path for curing suffering, only that. The matter of really ending suffering is something to be accomplished personally. The Supreme Teacher said, "The Tathagata is only the one who points out the way." He tells you to pick this up from here and put it there, pick this up from there and put it here. He teaches you how to swim. It's not that he swims for you. If you want the Tathagata to swim for you, you are only going to drown.

Last year, some officials came here for a meeting to learn the "right way." Why? Because things were not going well, and they didn't feel good about it. So they came to learn about right understanding. But to get beyond feeling good when things seem right and suffering over things not going well is something not generally understood. The world is like this. Toward the sufferings we create, the heaviness, we need to have some patience and endurance. We know things are heavy, but we have desire, so we pick them up. They will be heavy, so then we really have to endure.

When we were students, we saw adults and thought how happy they must be. We saw them doing all kinds of things, people such as teachers, merchants, employers, or administrators, and we wanted to be like that. So we worked at our studies with the hope of becoming just like them, but now that we are in the same positions, we don't really have such great happiness, do we? The suffering and difficulty are still there. We haven't escaped from that condition of unsatisfactoriness. We haven't escaped now, and we don't really know if we can escape in the future. Things just keep getting heavier as we go along.

This place is called the world. World, or *loko* in Pali, means "darkness." However much the world progresses and develops, darkness develops just that much; the progress of the world is just the progress of darkness. People talk enthusiastically about how the world is progressing, but it is only darkness spreading.

In our monastery, we previously had no electricity. People used to say, "It's really dark here! How comfortable it would be if we had electricity, if we had running water!" But these things don't appear by themselves. They take a considerable investment of money. The ability to get them comes from difficulty. And then when we do have the bright electric lights, it actually enshrouds the mind and darkens it further. Convenience covers the mind in darkness, because it is the nature of people to want everything the easy way. The easier and more convenient things are, the lazier people get.

In the past, when the country was not materially developed, people would build their toilet way out in the forest, and they would have to make some effort to walk out there and use it. Now this can't be done. People won't go out. Wherever they sleep, there must be a toilet right there. I don't know what they want. Does that really bring well-being? The bedroom is here and the bathroom is here, too. People expect this will make for convenience and happiness, but it isn't really so. Being too comfortable just leads to heedlessness. And people want to take it much further than this. But there is never any satisfaction. It's never enough, and then they complain about their suffering.

Speaking of the way we make use of our resources, mostly we feel that we don't have enough money to get by. What should we do to make it enough? It seems to me there is so much money, but it's never enough. That's why I say there are no rich people. At least I've never seen any; I only see people who feel they don't have enough. The Buddha taught about earning and spending money. Earning it is not so hard. The way we use it is what's really important. We should earn our living in a way that is right livelihood. Having earned money, we should make the best use of it, conserving it for meaningful ends. Whatever you may need, don't let it go to excess. The Buddha taught extensively about this, but we don't really pay heed. Whatever we see others getting, we want to match them. However much we earn we are ready to spend.

Suffering—who created it? We don't see. We say it is for this or that reason, but we never point at the source. The root is here, but we are looking all over for it, blaming people and situations, so it doesn't become very clear; we don't really get down to it. We just look at things outside ourselves and are always trying to manipulate externals.

We can look around and see when the house is not clean. We can see when the dishes are dirty. We can clean them up. Then the house is clean, the dishes are clean, but still the mind is not clean. When the house is a mess, we will probably feel uncomfortable and get to sweeping, washing, and so forth. The mind is dark and unpleasant, yet we don't see ourselves. So we go on complaining about our terrible suffering. When you think about it, we are really pretty pitiful.

If we could put effort into cleaning up our minds the way we do sweeping our houses, washing and scrubbing our clothes, and doing the dishes, we would likely be at ease. But when we talk about cleaning like this, people don't know what we're getting at. It's just like someone being indifferent to whether the dishes are clean or dirty. It's an ignorant kind of indifference. We have to go to work and clean, otherwise we never reach the correct point, and the mind remains in this befouled, ignorant condition.

The Buddha spoke of this as the mind not striving to see clearly, but just following its inclinations and tendencies. In our vernacular, we say "following moods." In our families, today we feel love, tomorrow dislike. Today we love our children, but the next day we are exasperated and upset with them. Why is it like this? Why is it not stable? It means that the mind hasn't been trained. Love causes suffering to arise. Aversion causes suffering to arise. Too little and we suffer; too much and we suffer. Where can we stay?

Have you sought your dwelling place yet? Find the right place to stay. How many months and years have passed when you should have been seeking and building the place where you can be at peace, yet you are still in this condition? What is the reason?

A husband and wife live together. There is really no reason they should quarrel. But quarrel they do, even to the point where one of them will get up and leave in the night—though they are likely to come back the next day. It's troublesome, really. I've come to think it's because people don't seek their true dwelling place. We don't clean in the place that really needs it. We scrub and sweep elsewhere. We don't make our minds clean, so there is always confusion. We are always looking outside. The Buddha taught about turning inward: turn inward to look at the mind, to see what is in the mind.

But these days there are only force and hurry. Mangoes are never sweet now. They are forced. Before they're ripe, they are picked and artificially ripened. This is done because people want to get them in a hurry. So when you eat them, you find they are sour. It's trying to match the desires of people, to get things in a hurry. To get something good, something sweet, you have to let it be sour first, according to its own natural way. But we pick them early and then complain that they're sour.

For the most part, things are imitations. We grasp these things that are false and uncertain as real. The Buddha wanted us to see that which is not false but genuine. But these days, understanding is almost completely mistaken. People don't know anything about whether things are real or false, and when it's like this, all kinds of perceptions occur. Things that are false and contrived are taken for real. In this vein, the Buddha taught about turning inward to see. If the mind does not see and realize, there is no path to clarity.

The Buddha said that one who is a teacher, like me, can end up a hungry ghost—a refined sort of hungry ghost. How is this?

There's a story I'd like to tell, a fable that's worth narrating. It's a little long, so try to bear with me.

There was a person who had a very virtuous mind. Whatever was meritorious and skillful, he would strive to do that. Everything he did was refined and somewhat fastidious. Everything had to be neat, everything in its place. When his children, nieces, or nephews came to visit, he would get a little unhappy. The broom that belonged over here would be left over there. The kettle would not be put back where it was supposed to be. If anyone didn't do things his way, he would suffer.

But he was a refined person with a good, orderly mind. One day, he thought about building a pavilion in the forest, a *sala* (hall) where people could take shelter. "Hmm, building a sala here would be a good thing, I would accrue merit. Merchants and travelers could stop and rest here, they would be comfortable and appreciate it greatly." Having thought about this, he went ahead and built it, and people made use of it.

Later, he passed away. After he died, because of his attachment to his virtuous activity, his consciousness returned to reside in that place, the place where he used to live and do his good deeds. He would check out the sala and see whether it was being kept up. When he found parts that were messy, he would be upset, and when he saw that it was neat and clean, he was happy, because his mind was like that—virtuous, neat, and orderly.

Then one day, several hundred merchants came to stay there. After taking dinner, they went to sleep, lying down in long rows.

The owner of the hall was now this refined hungry ghost. He came to check whether they were sleeping in orderly fashion. Patrolling up and down, looking around, he noticed their heads weren't lined up straight. What to do? He thought it over, and then pulled their feet to line up their heads evenly. He kept on pulling and tugging, this row and the next row and the next one, until he had them all adjusted right. But then he looked at their feet; now the feet were out of line. What to do now? So he started pulling the heads up to align the feet.

Once that was finally accomplished, he saw that the heads were out of line again. What's the story here, anyhow? he wondered. He went on like this through the night, bothered the whole time. Finally he gave up, asking himself what the reason was for this. He sat down and thought and saw the light: people are not the same. Their heights differ, so they can't be lined up straight. He then let go of the matter, because he saw that some are short and some are tall; that is just the way it is.

He let go, and he felt better because he saw that people aren't the same. Before, he had expected them all to be the same. When they weren't, he tried to make them the same, but it was impossible, and he suffered for it. Then he stopped and contemplated the matter and saw the truth: "Ah, people are like that. They are not all the same height," and he felt better.

It's similar for us. We have to see the causes of things. We have to see that people are not all the same. This is something worth pondering, because we can't change certain things; it won't do to go cutting off their legs to make them even. Grasping gets us stuck in attachment to how we expect things to be.

We people are like this. We have different work and responsibilities. Some will be fast and efficient, some slow—all sorts of differences. It's easy to become a hungry spirit if you view it wrongly. Me, too. I can become a hungry ghost over this, though I become aware of it quickly: "Hey, you're becoming a hungry ghost, cut it out!"

I have my disciples and I want them to improve, to develop by following our mode of training. Sometimes I suffer over this. When that happens, I remind myself, I've become a hungry ghost again. I teach myself all the time like this.

In this way, we can take birth as hungry ghosts often. We don't give up easily. We have to teach ourselves to become skilled in dealing with things, knowing the causes and results. Then we can let people be as they are, let them do as they do. We let go and can be lighthearted about it. We may want them to be a certain way, but the problem is not because of them, it's because of us. Our own minds are obscured, so we think it is because of this or that person. That's not so. It's because of us. People are not the same, but we expect them to be the same. If we solve the problem of the way we see things, we will be alright.

Someone rides a motorcycle. He loses control and goes down. Then he'll say, "The motorcycle made me fall." Actually, he made the motorcycle fall, because he couldn't drive it well, but he says the motorcycle made him fall.

I'll sum it up. For children and adults, the situation is different. If children do wrong, you can forgive them because they don't really know anything. If adults do wrong, people don't want to forgive because they should know better. The Buddha said that someone who doesn't know right from wrong can be taught to know; someone who knows but doesn't act accordingly is hopeless. The person is called heedless and cannot really be taught.

People end up miserable only because they don't look at themselves. We are always looking at other things and people, looking outside for something that is attractive, trying to make externals pleasing. We never dig internally, never work on ourselves and become bright and clear. The result can only be constant difficulty and confusion. Wherever we look there is darkness. Why? Because the eyes are not good. We complain of the dark; we cannot see light and color, so we say they could not possibly exist. OK, that's true—for the blind. But actually we are upset for nothing. The problem is in the eyes. Nothing is seen clearly, neither light nor color. But if the eyes are good, those things appear, and we will know what they are. We don't really examine this problem. Mostly we look elsewhere, so we don't have happiness. We should learn how to make this life of ours joyous. There really are things that can make that happen.

Monastic Life: Why Do People Ordain?*

DOCTOR V.: I'd like to tell you a story about some relatives of mine. This family had a son whom they recognized as having the potential to be a good student, so they made a lot of sacrifices to

*From a conversation with an air-force doctor in Bangkok.

send him to college. While he was in school, he began to take an interest in learning Dharma and soon found a lot of joy in it.

The parents had great hopes that he would get a good job and become the pillar of the family. Everyone had sacrificed for him to study. But by the time he graduated, he was immersed in Dharma and wanted to ordain. His parents were upset to the point of tears and felt distressed about religion, but in the end they had to agree to let him ordain.

I don't go to monasteries. According to my view, the world has two factions, the laity and the monastics. I have a family to support, and I practice a livelihood. I have my duties to them and to society and the country. When I come here, I get the idea that some people want everyone to ordain. But as a layman, I give benefit to society and people. I support my family and bring them happiness. We can support the sasana (dispensation of the Buddha) in this capacity. But if everyone ordained, the monks and nuns would have to work in the fields and do trading and wouldn't have time to practice and teach.

So when I hear the tale of this young man, who let his parents down so badly, I see it as a sin. A terrible sin. He made bad karma with his parents and so many others. It was a selfish action, following his own desire.

AJAHN CHAH: That's true, Doctor. But I will ask you a question. Which has more value, a kilo of lead or a kilo of gold? Which would you choose if I offered them?

DV: The gold.

AC: Life is like that. When it's so clear-cut, you want the thing with value, the gold. Likewise, this young man made his decision. Why do you choose the gold?

DV: Because it's valuable.

AC: There you are. So don't think like that. I'm not telling you not to think, but investigate to see whether it's correct. And you don't have to worry about everyone ordaining and there being no one left to build the world.

For example, when they need to hire someone to play music, you don't have to be bothered by that. They only hire the ones who can play. They don't hire you and everyone else. Not everyone is going to ordain, and it also won't happen that no one ordains—it just can't happen. Whoever has faith and wisdom will do it. There shouldn't be any sense of oppression.

I used to think like this, too: Killing animals is wrong. How about just eating chilies every day? But who can do that? Who can pound the chilies every day for us to eat? We can't make these sweeping judgments.

The intention in ordaining is not to destroy our parents or our family lineage. We see that our family is still sunk in suffering. But others might see it differently. Like the gold and the lead: one who decides to ordain for life sees the world as lead, just as you chose the gold. We don't want the world, our family, and the rest to be destroyed. But it's difficult to find people who can understand this. There is a palm and back of the hand, but your view is one-sided.

When people ordain with pure intention, they suffer too, because they see things according to Dharma. You can call it bad karma, but then the Buddha really made a lot of bad karma! In the end, the intention is not selfish; it is to be able to teach the family to live in the light.

Right now, in our monastery, there's a monk who studied abroad and then decided to ordain for life. His father was upset at first, but now he comes here and doesn't want the son to leave. At first, we don't see any value to monastic life, but with some wisdom we see that it really has value. Oh, don't worry. There are not so many who want to ordain; there are plenty who want to stay in the world. Don't think the world will empty out.

When someone ordains, he ceases doing evil and works to help people understand and live in happiness and coolness, practice right livelihood and live harmoniously, help each other, live without harming or exploiting. Not everyone will ordain, don't think about it. Not everyone will be alike. The world isn't like that. If it weren't this way, it wouldn't be the world.

DV: OK, I understand. On the subject of making merits, I have this question. Making merits should bring happiness to oneself and others. When I see people do it, they may tell their kids, "Don't eat the most expensive fruit, save it to offer to the monks." Shouldn't it be something that is not a burden to others? This is my objection to the young man who graduated and wanted to ordain: Shouldn't meritorious activity bring happiness and satisfaction to oneself and all others? The way this guy made merit is like me stealing from someone's purse to make an offering, when she needs to take her child to the hospital before he dies.

Monks ordain, they go and teach and spread Buddhism, but these days there are so many ajahns. Others want to make themselves like the Buddha. The Buddha was the one who went first, the one who founded our sasana, for the benefit of the many—others could not see, so he left home to be able to open their eyes. But now there are so many. You and others are teaching the Dharma; it's enough. So it isn't important for this fellow to try to be like you or like the Buddha. If he could wait a few years, it would not upset others. It wouldn't make trouble for them, and he could find happiness for them. My objection is that he did not wait for the appropriate time. He could have waited a few years. He chose the wrong time, so I call it evil.

AC: Who can know the right time?

DV: If he could determine firmly to wait seven years and ordain, fine. Of course, if he waited seven years and became an alcoholic in the meantime, that would be wrong. But apart from something like that, he should wait seven years.

AC: If you say wait, how will you ensure he has the time? You say wait seven years, but will death wait? Is there an agreement you can make with death? Everyone would like to, but who can? So if he sees it like this, he wants to ordain. He doesn't see things the way you do, he realizes the timelessness of the Dharma and the immediacy of the situation, so what can you tell him to do?

DV (faltering): What I think is, he is selfish; he wants the happiness in Dharma for himself. He doesn't think of others.

AC: If it's like that, then think about this. You studied to be a doctor, and that was out of your self-interest, right?

DV: True.

AC: Why? When someone still has self, they will be selfish. The Buddha talked about this. The word *self* is just a concept. We look at others, and we think they have self as we do. But there is just earth, water, fire, and air. The Buddha saw this and taught that there is no real self, no person, being, or individual. So how could there be selfishness? We believe in a self, so we think about selfishness. People who talk about self see the four elements as a person. The Buddha only sees lumps of things momentarily gathered together. But we can't speak about this, people don't understand.

I'll just say a word or two for you to think about: When I say walking forward, backing up, or stopping, you can relate to these words. But if I say none of those, then what is it? One person has reached this point, but others are somewhere else. You hear it, but don't understand at all. There's a problem in understanding, because this is transcendent speech, the words of the awakened ones. When we grow up, we can understand.

The ways of the world and of Dharma don't meet. We have to talk about going forward and such for ordinary people, but that isn't the whole story. We say there is cause and effect for people. True, but it's different for fools and wise people. They get different results. The Buddha said, "I am above cause and effect, beyond birth and death."

Once you were a child. When you saw a balloon, you got excited and wanted to play. But if you see a balloon now, do you want to play?

DV: No.

AC: Why not?

DV: Because it has no purpose.

AC: You grew up, right? When you were a child, you saw a balloon as a very valuable thing. You had so much fun; then it broke and maybe you cried. But now it's different. If someone says, Doctor, do you want to play with balloons? you're not interested.

But still, children will argue with you. They will say, Of course, it's valuable to play with balloons. So who is right? Who will win the argument? The kids are right from their side, the adult is right from his side.

Asking these questions is very good. Let's hear more, and get down to it.

DV: Well, I have another question, about Mrs. B. For ten years or more, she's been running to get sprinkled with holy water. Wherever it's happening, she wants to go. She always invites me, but I refuse. I say, I don't make bad karma, I work hard to help others, and that is one kind of skillful activity that I do with good intention. If there is some mistake or misunderstanding, something inappropriate, I still did not have bad intention to cause harm to anyone, so I believe there is no bad karma. I believe that any religion, whatever it is, teaches people to have lovingkindness, to do good, to help the world and be pure. If we act with selfishness, then we're finished, we give up responsibility for the world.

I believe it depends on our minds whether or not we receive merit. If we act without harmful intent, want to solve problems, are pure enough. . . . We see people ordain according to custom when the time comes for the purpose of being able to get a wife, but their minds may not be pure or pacified. They have anxiety and concerns or some burden from being in robes, so there is really no benefit. If people will ordain and create wholesome karma, it depends on their minds. Like with putting food in the monks' alms bowls, I feel lazy about it. My wife always goes out to do it in the morning, but I don't. I don't like to take off my shoes to offer the food, as is the custom, but in my mind there is no unskillful thought.

Funeral offerings, putting food in alms bowls—people do

these things, but still have greed, anger, and delusion in their minds and still cause suffering for others. Instead of making merit like this, wouldn't it be better to make one's mind peaceful and create happiness for others?

AC: There are two issues here. First, why does your wife like to do those things? Doctor, you have chickens around your house; do you give them shirts and pants or a watch? What do you give them?

DV: Rice grains.

AC: Right. That's useful for chickens. Pants and shirts are for humans, not chickens. Chickens want rice. So you have to know what beings need.
   Second, you talk about being lazy to offer food, but that your mind is good. If people are diligent, will they refuse to go to work or to wash dishes and clean the house? We're talking about a hardworking person, not a lazy person, now.

DV: No need to answer that one.

AC: Right. So we're talking about someone with faith. Your words are reasonable, but they go too far. You should know the middle, otherwise you exceed the cause and get no result. People with faith want to offer food, perform *puja* (chanting), and do other activities. They should do it with wisdom, not foolishness, of course. Anyhow, talking about you as a very hardworking person concerning the things you think are important: If you see the house is a mess, can you just sit there and ignore it? If the dishes are dirty, can you refrain from washing them? If the dog defecates on the floor, will you just leave it there? So people who are practicing Dharma in its various forms are not doing something different. Diligent people see things that need to be done, and they do them. Why do you sweep up the mouse and dog droppings? Because you are an aware and responsible person. So it's not just people living in a different world and doing Buddhist things. Sprinkling the holy water, that's their level; we don't forbid the chickens to eat rice.

Good, very good! An hour is not enough, let's air all those questions.

One Day Passes: A Talk to the
Community of Nuns at Wat Pah Pong

WE WHO HAVE TAKEN ORDINATION should be aware of our responsibilities. What are we supposed to be doing? How should we think and speak? Right now, what are we doing and thinking—is there anger or desire in our minds? Do we have ill will toward anyone? Look in the present. Hurry up and decide about this. As one more day and night pass, will we just sit here and suffer?

The Buddha talked about this. If he were still with us, he would speak in this way. In the texts, he said, "The days and nights are passing relentlessly; how well are we spending our time?" The admonition seems small; it is a brief statement. But he forcefully reiterated that we should know ourselves, each one of us, and having ordained, we should know what our responsibilities are.

We want to give up the afflictions. Do we know the afflictions yet? That which is unwholesome, that which we want to relinquish, do we know what it is yet? Have we given it up, or are we in the process of doing so? Is what we have given up actually done with, merely suppressed, or enduring? What exactly is its status now? Do we yet act like *samanas*, or "renunciants," think and speak like samanas, make use of the requisites for living like samanas? The Buddha asks these questions so we will come to a decision. For what reason? Because the days and nights pass; will we get to work here? We have lust and anger; we must quickly apply meditation practice to eradicate them.

Having ordained as nuns, you have entered a different "gender" from that of laypeople. Will you still think merely in the same way as people who are enjoying sense pleasures? Will that cut it? The time is little; there is not much. There is little time because one day passes by. Things are changing, nothing is stable, nothing remains the same. Will you depend on heedlessness to get you by? Will you live with attachment in your hearts? Will you stir up all sorts of confusion for yourselves? Why won't you let go of these things, craving, anger, and delusion? You have to see the fault of them. Until you see the fault, you can't relinquish. You will still have regrets, regrets over losing the afflictions. People can go on like this, ordained ten years, twenty years, this life, the next life. Just staying like this is easy, if you are not instructed.

Why do we have anger? Because of wrong thinking and wrong understanding. Why do we have delusion? Because we think wrongly. Why do we have desire? Wrong view brings suffering to us, and thus we are not at peace. Peace resides in having right view. If your view is correct, there is only peace. There won't be desire, aversion, or delusion, because you have seen the fault of them and you don't hold on to them anymore. Evil states still arise, but you let them go, give them up, let them pass you by.

Why will you give them up? Because your life is little; your time is little. Why is it little? Because you see that days and nights keep passing. To what end will you create suffering? Why would you grasp things? It would just be a waste of your precious time. Letting go is better. If your thinking is straight like this, you will certainly let go.

Wherever one has right view, that place will be tranquil. Without knowing this, living alone will not bring peace. Living in a group will not bring peace. There will be no peace, because there is wrong view. Within a group, though the members differ from each other, there will be certain common characteristics, such as in the genus of birds. All are birds, though there are different breeds. Some have long beaks, some short; some have great wings, some small. But they are all birds. The genus of monastics is likewise. The characteristics of a bird must be a certain way; the characteristics of a practitioner must be a certain way, which is tranquil.

We are supposed to be practicing to make the mind tranquil. Without wisdom, we won't be able to do this. The dwelling place may be one of plenty, the food abundant, but the mind will not be at peace. All that is wrong within us we have to give up, but we can't because we haven't yet seen the liability clearly.

Having contemplated this, we have to make up our minds to work at it and then get down to making a real effort. These days, you can hear the lay folk say that Wat Pah Pong is a model monastery, a place of exemplary practice. People say the monastics here are of good conduct. We hear about this. Well, are we that good? "The community of nuns are good practitioners, of fine conduct and discipline, worthy of faith and devotion." Are you this good yet, or is the goodness only in their speech? Do we become good merely by their saying so? We all have to examine ourselves and make sure we are thinking and acting properly. If you are praised, you need to consider whether it is accurate. If you are disparaged and criticized as no good, you should also examine to see whether there is truth in this. Rely on yourselves in this way.

If we are not acting well and someone praises our goodness, we should be ready to say they are in error because we are not yet so good. Don't start thinking you are somebody great when you still possess the afflictions, when you still have desires. Instead, you should amplify your practice, paying more attention to the fundamentals and inspecting your actions, words, and thoughts constantly to see where there are deficiencies.

As to what is spoken of as practicing alone, when living with many people, we should be as if living alone. We don't need to be upset or distracted, but should rely on patience instead. If someone speaks in a way that displeases us, we should just know what they are about. Some may not be very skillful; some may not have proper speech or behavior. Be tolerant. When the time is appropriate, we can admonish them. But when it comes to admonishing, we should first be admonishing ourselves. If we admonish others and they don't listen, it leads to anger. If we admonish another person, we should make ourselves right first. Whatever they say about us, whether it is criticism or whatever, we won't mind or doubt, because we know we are doing the right things. Then when the occasion comes to admonish them, we go ahead and do it. If they listen, that is good. If not, that's their affair. One who will instruct others should have this attitude.

And if we are the ones who are admonished—when we hear words such as, "you are wrong, you don't speak well, your actions are bad"—we should be able to listen. Is it true what they say? If it's true, we should accept it. If it isn't true, their thoughts and words are not correct and that is their business. We should let go of it and enter Dharma. We should use such words to enter Dharma, inspecting ourselves to know our minds. We should examine our own minds and know the motivation for our words and deeds and be able to guarantee our speech. If we know that we have good intention, it won't matter what others accuse us of or how they criticize. It is said, "One should admonish oneself by oneself." You shouldn't depend on me to admonish you all the time. That would only make you foolish. Each of you has to control your own minds and do your own practice. My part is to teach you how to do this, how to know whether your actions are correct and whether they are appropriate for a samana.

So they say Wat Pah Pong is a model monastery. And some people say I am an arahant. Isn't that so? But that's just a matter of people's words. Is it really so? The truth of it resides with me. When they say, "There's an arahant! An arahant has appeared!" should I be elated by that? Whether I am or not, that's just others talking. We can't prohibit people from talking, but we have to inspect ourselves, and whatever is really the case only we can know. We don't need to depend on the words of other people. We rouse ourselves like this. They rouse us like this. You should know for yourselves and not just believe the words of others. Please keep this perspective.

Especially for the older people here—sixty or maybe seventy years old—be aware that days and nights keep passing. Today will soon be over; the sun rose in the morning, and now another day is hastening to its end. Have firm determination not to put your mind in turmoil. Don't create distractions and confusion with others. Be one who is easy to speak to, easy to teach, not proud or opinionated. It isn't forbidden to have views—you will always have them—but don't get all bound up by them, firmly attached to your ideas. Release them, let them go. If you don't, they become heavy.

We are taught to relinquish the five aggregates, that they are something heavy. Form, feeling, perception, thought, and consciousness—these are heavy things. If we carry heavy things, they will be heavy for us! Form, feelings, and the rest we see as being self, a person, I and others, and we carry them around. That way they become heavy. The Buddha said, "Please put them down!" Because we hold these bodies as ours; we hold feelings of happiness and suffering, pain and pleasure, as ourselves. Don't do this! It's very heavy! The Buddha wants us to let go of them.

Sanya refers to "perception," recollection of various things. Calling it your self is heavy; let it go. Know it and put it down. *Sankhara* are all conditioned phenomena of body and mind. Don't grasp them—they are heavy. Consciousness, the faculty of knowing, is the same. All five aggregates are heavy if you hold them as self. They are only nature; they are feeling and perception arising, thinking and awareness. No one is their owner. Holding them to be self is the heavy way; put them down. They are merely aggregates. Merely form, feeling, memory. Remember this "merely," and don't grasp so firmly. If you know them like this, liberation appears instantly. Before it was a matter of convention, designation as me and mine. Now there is knowledge that they are merely the aggregates, and liberation is at hand; you go beyond the conventional understanding. Before, you held the five *khandhas* (aggregates), and it was heavy. Now, letting go, there is lightness. When you let go, things are extinguished.

When someone admonishes us, we should accept it gladly and say, "*Sadhu* (How wonderful)." We don't have to hire them to do so; they still admonish us. Even if we are right and they say we are wrong, we should listen gladly. Wisdom can arise. They are giving us something precious.

In Zen, they teach to reduce pride. They don't say that a lot of learning is necessary. When they sit in meditation, someone walks behind them with a stick. If someone is falling asleep, he gets whacked. Then he raises his palms together in thanks: "Thank you, teacher. Thank you for beating me. Thank you for waking me." How about us? Would we be able to offer thanks? Maybe I'll have one of you walk around with a stick and if anyone is sleeping, whack! What do you think? Will you be able to accept it?

Being a teacher or a revered elder is difficult. No one dares to admonish us, because they feel so much awe and deference. You nuns and laypeople get some profit, since I'm always admonishing you and pointing things out. But if I do wrong, it's hard to find anyone who will tell me, because of the traditional fear and respect for the ajahn. So for an elder, practice can become difficult. We may be doing things wrong, but no one will point them out, and we become oblivious to ourselves. There's too much deference.

Here we are all fairly comfortable. So if occasionally we do wrong and someone says something about it, we should feel it is a great thing. Don't try to wiggle away or argue. Look at it and understand what is going on.

We are living in a pretty large group. When you are about to do something, you should recall the head person. Such as here at Wat Pah Pong, the monks and nuns should think about me, since I am the abbot, the one responsible for leading and advising you. If you are about to do something that may not be right and is likely to bring turmoil and distress, think of me first, that I am the one who gives you teachings and good counsel here. Having a place to stay, the monastery and its dwellings, you could say that I was the cause of this because I came here first, and the rest of you were able to follow and live here in comfort. So if you can recollect my virtuous efforts for a tiny moment, that would be good. Then think, Is this right to do? Will it be beneficial?

All of you practicing here should rely on the virtues of the senior people, and then you will have harmony and happiness in your practice. You should think about the head nuns. When you act, recollect me. Do I charge rent for you to stay here? If you go to a hotel, you always have to pay for your room, but there is no such thing in the monastery. It's good for you to consider this.

At night when you are in your *kuti*, or "dwelling," think about it. Am I seeking any gain from you? As a monk, I am indifferent. I received all of you who wanted to stay here. My intentions are good. I have love for you in the way of Dharma, not love in a worldly way, so there needn't be any friction or fear of exploitation. If there is something wrong, you should come forth and speak about it.

Some of you have never asked me anything. Not just among the nuns; I also have never spoken with some of the monks. We have a large group, so this can happen; it can be hard when you are only one of many. So all of you have to depend on yourselves and make your practice strong, taking care of yourselves to your utmost.

We have to realize that the populace will come here and look at the nuns, the monks, and the monastery. They needn't ask you anything. They can just see your kutis and the monastery grounds. The place is neat and clean. Everything is put away where it should be. This is the behavior of samanas, and people will naturally feel faith. We don't have to preach to them. If things are messy, we all lend a hand to straighten it up. When I was younger, I used to walk around the monastery at odd times to take a look at the kutis and the paths in the forest. When I found a kuti and a bathroom that were clean, the paths well swept, I knew this was a person who was a good practitioner; if he had not yet entered into practice, he was certainly going to become good in the near future.

Some make light of this, thinking it's a small thing. It isn't. When I see a dirty bathroom, it shows me that the person is not attentive. It's a sign of extreme coarseness; such a person needn't talk about practicing Dharma at all. I would ask others to find out who it is whose bathroom is such a mess: no water in the barrel, termites all over, spiderwebs hanging, the floor dirty. "It's so-and-so; he says he's too busy practicing meditation to clean the bathroom." What kind of meditation is he doing with a filthy bathroom? So here we all pay attention to our surroundings and help each other to take care of things. This itself is teaching, and it will cause people to have faith and trust.

Do the trees in the forest teach us something? Sometimes we like some of the trees. We may feel they look beautiful and have a nice smell and so forth. The trees are just growing according to their nature, and on our own side, we develop these good feelings about them. It's similar with the situation in the monastery. We don't need to go teaching people, trying to impress something on them. We only need to develop ourselves through our own practice. This will naturally attract them.

I've thought about this for a long time. From my sixth year as a monk, I considered what it entails to establish a monastery, and I came to the conclusion that it is only important to be practicing well. It's not necessary to look to anything else. We don't need to go requesting donations or proclaiming ourselves to the public. If we are really practicing, the requisites of dwelling, food, robes, and medicines will come.

I really feel that if you are practicing well, the gods will know. They will gather around you. At the very least, they will want to offer food. If they don't do this, they suffer headaches, and their heads will split open. They must have this desire to come. Not just here, but even if you are living on a mountain. Wherever you are, this will happen. Though they do not know you and have never seen or heard of you before, they must come because they are attracted by the virtuous quality of your practice.

Thus, practice is the most precious thing for us. If we really practice to the end, there will be no problems or obstacles. If you end up establishing a monastery, you needn't go making requests for anything. People will come to offer what you need. They will come to build the place. We don't have to ask people to lend a hand. They come naturally because we have been creating virtue; it comes flowing in like this. That we are able to live here now is because of our meritorious karma and good practice. If the community is quarreling, if the abbot is a worldly minded person, if there are disputes and contention, what can come of that? They may well come to burn us down.

Understand this. We can stay here now, totally dependent as we are on the support of laypeople, because of our practice. I try to stay to help out. One year, I went away. Everything started running out: no incense, no candles, no kerosene. Just about everything was finished. Nobody was coming to offer anything. Why was that? Because there were few here who were really practicing well. When I returned, you were all glad to see me. "Luang Por's back! Great! Now there will be good meals again." You think that all the good things left when I left. Who is it that takes them away? It's just your own virtue or lack of it that determines this. Make your practice better and this won't happen. You don't need to worry. You only need to create virtue.

Wherever I go, I don't lack for anything. Why? Because of renunciation. If I wanted to, I could fill bags with the offerings, but I prefer to share it all with the monks and nuns at Wat Pah Pong and the branch monasteries. Sometimes people bring medicine that is supposed to be specifically for me. If another monk is sick and needs it, I tell them to give it to him. If he takes the medicine, I feel better. I get well because of the merit involved. I don't need to take the medicine myself.

At one time, Sariputta and Moggallana were residing on a mountain. Sariputta fell ill with severe pains in his stomach. He felt that he might even die. Moggallana asked him, "Have you ever been sick like this before?"

Sariputta answered, "Yes, I have. It's been happening since I was a layperson."

"What medicine did you take for it?"

"Before when this happened, my mother would boil green beans with milk and sugar and some other ingredients. After I ate them, the pains would go away."

There were just the two of them, talking there on the mountain. The deity of that place heard them. Just as evening was coming, he went down to the village to find a lay patron. He grabbed the patron by the neck and dragged his son out, too. He was carrying on and making a great fuss. Why was he giving them such a hard time? "Are you going to prepare some medicine for the Venerable Sariputta? If you don't offer him medicine, he will die. Are you going to let the Venerable Sariputta die?"

The patron understood. He gave his word that he would make the medicine. Then the deity vanished, and the man hurried to find some green beans and spent the night preparing them.

In the morning, Moggallana went for alms. Sariputta could not go because of the pain in his stomach. The patron presented the green beans, along with some other food. "I wish to offer this to the Venerable Sariputta." Then he put it into the alms bowl.

When Moggallana reached the monastery, he took out his own food and offered the bowl with Sariputta's food to him. Sariputta looked in the bowl and saw the green beans, prepared just as he had described the night before. Everything was exactly as he had told Moggallana.

Sariputta was upset. This was not in accord with the rules of a bhikkhu; an inappropriate request had obviously been made. "Venerable Moggallana, please spill this food out on the ground. Food that was requested of a patron without invitation is not appropriate, and I cannot accept it." He was protecting his vows. When he spoke these words, all the deities heard. Moggallana picked up the alms bowl to pour it out, and just as the medicinal food hit the ground, Sariputta's pain and illness disappeared.

This is called the medicine of Dharma. It has power and blessing like this. Sariputta was practicing to this extent. Even when the two monks were alone on a mountaintop the deity heard their conversation. And even when the deity caused the exact food that he needed to be given to him, Sariputta would not eat it because he was afraid of violating his precepts. This was how he guarded his mind

Practice should be like this. Please impress this upon your minds. You will not die! Today, after you finish your meal, you don't need to worry about what you will get tomorrow. It will come. We don't need to store up a lot. If we practice well, the provisions must come. It is said that whoever does not make offerings to those practicing authentically and virtuously will not feel good. They will have headaches. They will want to go to pay their respects and make offerings. Such feelings naturally come about in people because of this power.

4

SEEING
DHARMA

Kondanya Knows

WE ARE PRACTITIONERS OF DHARMA. All dharmas are
nature, existing as it is. Nature is exclusively and completely
Dharma. Those things are not yet clear to us because we haven't
come to know the way to practice, so we need to rely on the instructions and training of a qualified teacher. Nature also teaches
us: things such as trees are born from their causes and grow accordingly. This is nature showing us something, but we are not
yet able to see that the trees are teaching us. All the way from their
birth to growing, blossoming, and giving fruit, we merely see
them as supplying fruit for us to eat. We don't see them as something for us to turn inward and reflect upon. We should know
that Dharma is the tree teaching us, but we don't realize that yet.

When the tree gives fruit, we gather and eat it indifferently
without any real investigation or consideration. The sweet and

sour tastes of fruit are their nature; these characteristics are Dharma, and the fruits are teaching us something, but we don't understand that. When the leaves of the tree wither and die, they fall. We only see it as leaves falling, and we tread on them or sweep them up without any investigation. We don't realize this is Dharma, teaching something for us to hear.

The leaves of the tree fall, then the new buds appear. We see this cycle but don't really think much about it, so we don't learn anything of significance from it. If we were to turn it inward, we would see that our own birth and death are not so very different from that of trees. This body comes into being as a result of various causes and depends on the four elements for its existence. It grows and comes to fruition of different kinds, just like a tree. And the falling leaves and new buds are no different from the lives of people. Take a look at this. We are constantly growing, and conditions are constantly changing. Like the trees; just as trees are, so are we. All humans are born in the beginning, change in the middle—their physical constituents changing into something different from what they were—and pass away in the end. The natural phenomena of trees, vines, and shrubs are continuously and unceasingly in a state of flux, and if we turn this inward, we will understand birth, aging, and death within ourselves, just as we see them externally.

When you understand Dharma from listening to the words of a qualified teacher, it truly pricks your heart: outer and inner are the same. Sankhara (conditioned phenomena), with or without consciousness occupying them, are the same—not different at all. If we understand this, then seeing the way trees are, we will see the nature of our aggregates of body, feelings, perceptions, thoughts, and consciousness. With this kind of understanding we are called people who understand Dharma.

Being people who understand Dharma, we will strive to see Dharma everywhere and in all things, to see the characteristics of our five khandhas—that they are continually in a state of flux, moving, changing, and transforming without any letup. Whether we are standing, sitting, walking, or lying down, we employ mindfulness to guard and watch at all times. Seeing external ob-

Photographer unknown

Ajahn Chah, circa 1982.

jects, it is the same as seeing internal phenomena. Seeing internal phenomena is the same as seeing external phenomena, because they are of the same nature. When it is like this, we are hearing the teaching of the Buddha. With this understanding, it is said

that the Buddha nature, meaning the one who knows, is awakened. There is knowledge of internal and external phenomena
and the ability to explain the facets of Dharma in various ways
according to what we have seen.

We are constantly hearing the teachings of the Buddha
whether we are walking, standing, sitting, or lying down, and
whenever we are seeing forms, hearing sounds, savoring tastes,
and so on. It is exactly as if the Buddha were teaching us, because
the Buddha is just this one who knows dwelling within our
hearts. Knowing and seeing and investigating the Dharma like
this, the Buddha is present. It is not that the Buddha entered final
nirvana long ago and cannot teach us now. The Buddha nature,
which means our own minds when clear knowledge has arisen,
will lead us to investigate and know all dharmas. This knowing
of the Dharma is the Buddha himself. If we establish Buddha in
our hearts, having this awareness and sensitivity, then as we go on
investigating, we will see all things as no different from ourselves.
Living creatures, plants and animals, poor people and those in
difficulty, rich people, dark- or light-skinned people are no different from us, because all of them are of the same characteristics. With this understanding, wherever we stay, we will be
content and at ease. The Buddha will be there, constantly instructing and assisting us.

Without this understanding, we will always have the desire to
hear teachings. We will want to seek out different teachers, one
after the next, and will always be asking when we can get still another teaching, all the while not yet understanding Dharma. The
Buddha said that becoming enlightened to the Dharma is a matter of understanding nature, things as they are. If we don't know
nature, when we meet with situations, we are thrown into turmoil and are always in a state of struggle. We are delighted with
things and get lost, being fooled by them; we are upset by things
and fooled by them. We are deluded in nature, fooled by nature,
and are at the mercy of our moods and emotions. Being deluded
about nature like this means that we do not understand Dharma.
So the Enlightened One explained about what is natural.

This nature is not something mysterious. In nature, things appear, change, and come to an end. It is the same for the material objects created by people. The pots and dishes we use, for example, are also created by causes and conditions, which are the conceptions and intentions of human beings. They are used for a while, they become worn, and finally break and fall apart. That is ordinary for them. Trees, plants, and mountains, as well as animals and humans, are the same: coming into existence; changing and deteriorating; and in the end, breaking up and disappearing.

So when the ascetic Anya Kondanya listened to the words of the Buddha as the first disciple, the realization he had was nothing very complicated. He understood that whatever comes into existence will naturally undergo change and finally cease to be. That is the nature of things. Previously, Kondanya had not realized this. He had not considered this fact and seen it clearly. Or perhaps he had thought about it, but had not contemplated it thoroughly; thus he had not let go. He had still clung to the five aggregates. But when he sat before the Buddha and listened to the teachings for the first time with clear mindfulness, the Buddha nature awakened in him, and he was able to receive authentic transmission of one level of Dharma, which was that all sankhara are uncertain. All things that are born will undergo transformation and finally cease to be; that is what is ordinary and natural for them.

The understanding that arose in Kondanya upon hearing the words of the Buddha was different from anything he had experienced before. He realized the mind as it actually is, so it is said the Buddha arose within him. Then the Lord Buddha proclaimed that Kondanya had attained the eye of wisdom and seen Dharma. What did it mean, that he had seen the Dharma? He had attained knowledge and vision that all things arise in the beginning, change in the middle, and pass away in the end. "All things" means all phenomena of body and mind, and these characteristics apply to all of them without exception.

When this understanding clearly penetrated the heart of Anya Kondanya at the moment when he sat before the Buddha, it became the cause that enabled him to remove all clinging to sankhara from his mind. The view that holds the body to be one's own and to be oneself, and leads one to believe in a self, was clearly seen and uprooted. Once belief in a self was uprooted, the mind of skeptical doubt also came to an end. There was no more bewilderment about phenomena, his knowledge of things having been transformed. As for superstitious attachment to conventions, rites, and rituals, his practice had become correct and straight, so there was no more doubt or hesitation, no more groping or fumbling about cause and effect. If the body were to become sick or experience any other changes, he would not have any hazy notions about it; the ending of doubt had removed attachment and clinging. If there is still attachment, we will still be groping after the meaning of things that happen to the body, and this groping is superstition. But when belief in and attachment to the body as ourselves or our own is removed, there is no longer uncertainty or superstitious notions.

So when the Supreme Teacher expounded Dharma, Anya Kondanya opened the eye of Dharma. He now saw clearly. His view of things was reversed. When this seeing became clear and focused, his clinging was uprooted. When clinging was done away with, the one who knows had truly arisen. Before there had been knowledge, but he had not been able to remove clinging. This meant that he knew the Dharma but did not see Dharma; or we could say that he saw Dharma but had not become one with Dharma, because he did not know the actual condition of things. Thus, the Supreme Teacher proclaimed, "Kondanya knows."

Normally, we are deluded and confused about nature, for example, our bodies. They are composed of earth, water, fire, and air. That is one aspect of nature, material phenomena that can be seen with the eyes. This form of nature is nourished by food, grows and changes, and eventually disappears.

Internally, there is the one who is in charge of the body, the consciousness or faculty of knowing. When this knowing occurs through the eye, it is called the eye consciousness, or the sense of sight. When it occurs through the ear, it is called the sense of hearing. When it occurs through the nose, it is called the sense of smell; and so on for the tongue, body, and mind. There is one knowing, but we call it different things when it occurs through different senses. Six types of consciousness are mentioned in the teachings, but it is only a convention to specify when we are knowing at different points of sense contact, through the eyes, the ears, the nose, the tongue, the body, or the mind. In truth, there are not six. It is one faculty of knowing that is capable of awareness at these six points. And this one mind, this one who knows, has the potential to know things as they really are, which is knowing nature.

Whenever this one who knows is still obscured, its knowing is only the knowing of delusion, knowing in wrong ways, having a wrong understanding of things. It is just the same fundamental awareness, nothing other. Knowing and seeing correctly or knowing and seeing wrongly are functions of this one faculty of awareness. Thus when we talk about wrong view and right view, we are not talking about two separate things, two separate minds or places of origin. When delusion is present, it hides the truth and obscures the mind, and our awareness is mistaken. When our awareness is wrong, our view is wrong. Following that, actions will be wrong, livelihood will be wrong, all will be wrong; and this all begins with wrong understanding.

The factors of the path arise in the same place and follow this same progression. Right view also arises from the one who knows, this faculty of awareness. When it is correct, then the incorrect will vanish. When it is right, that which is wrong will vanish. Thus, when the Buddha was developing the perfections as the bodhisattva, performing great austerities and living on minute amounts of food to the point where his body became severely emaciated, some insight was born within him. He realized that all the buddhas of the past were enlightened through the mind, not through the body. The body by itself doesn't know anything. Feeding it or not feeding it is not the point. Others can even kill this body without harming the mind. So after he had this change of outlook, after he attained enlightenment and began to teach, he pointed out that the enlightenment of all the buddhas was attained through cultivation of mind. When he looked deeply within his own mind, he gave up practicing the extremes of sensual indulgence and self-mortification, and he pointed this out clearly in his first teaching.

His first sermon cut directly through the misconceptions and mistaken practices of ordinary beings. Being immersed in the pursuit of pleasure, comfort, and happiness, in the pride that seeks to elevate and extol oneself, is not the path that one who has gone forth from the world should walk. The state of dissatisfaction and suffering, of negativity, aversion, and anger, is self-mortification. It brings about no benefit at all.

These two paths are not the way a seeker of liberation should walk. They refer to the extremes of elation and depression, indulgence and suppression. The one who walks the path is our own awareness, which should not follow these extreme reactions of mind. The mind should not be left to follow what it supposes to be good or bad because that becomes the cause of joy or sorrow. If it becomes happy over something there is then attachment to what is perceived as good, and that is the extreme of indulgence. If there is something that is perceived as being bad, that is grasped with aversion, invested with negative significance. This is the mind following the two extremes, pleasure on one side, pain on the other, which the Buddha summarized as sensual indulgence and self-mortification.

These two paths are not the way of a samana (a tranquil being). They are the ways of worldly people. All worldly beings are constantly in search of happiness and pleasure. They are habituated to the extreme reactions of attraction and aversion to things and are always being bounced back and forth between the two as they undergo ceaseless change and keep on trading places. This is the way of the world. If there is happiness, there will be suffering. There is suffering, and then there is happiness, and then there is suffering again. These are things that will always be uncertain and unstable. Thus they are the dharma of those who are mired in the world, those who are not at peace. Those who are at peace do not go this way. But they do see and know about these things. They see pleasure and happiness, but not accepting them as real, they don't get attached to or stuck in them. They are aware of whatever aversion there may be to things, but they do not take that as a path either.

These are people who see the path. Those who are tranquil understand the way that is not tranquil while still remaining at peace. The way of seeking happiness with its resultant depression and elation over things is recognized as a mistaken path. The wise also experience such phenomena but do not expect to find any ultimate meaning in them, so they let go of such reactions. The ones who are at peace are unshaken by these things, by happiness and suffering. When there is no more meaning seen in things, one naturally lets go of happiness and suffering, in accord with their nature. When happiness and suffering are known for what they are, they become invalid phenomena. They have no meaning in the mind of the awakened being. There is mere recognition of them, that happiness or suffering are appearing, like hot or cold appearing; it is not that there is no recognition or awareness.

So it is said that the arahant is one far from the mental afflictions. Actually, he or she does not go anywhere far away. She doesn't flee from the afflictions, and the afflictions do not flee from her. It's like a lotus leaf in the water. The lotus leaf exists in the water and lives nourished by the water. The water is in contact with the lotus, but cannot penetrate or submerge it.

The afflictions are the water. The mind of the practitioner is the lotus leaf. They contact each other—the lotus doesn't need to avoid the water—but they remain separate. The mind of the yogin is like this. It does not flee or escape to anywhere. When good comes, it is aware; when bad comes, it is aware. When there is happiness or suffering, like or dislike, the mind is aware; it is aware of everything that occurs. But it merely recognizes these states. They cannot penetrate the mind. This means there is no grasping and no attachment to things.

In Dharma language, it is spoken of as equanimity, keeping the mind balanced and neutral. In ordinary speech, we call it recognition, being informed or notified of what is going on. There is no involvement or taking sides. Just as when we meet someone and he tells us about something, we merely take note of what he has to say. We don't necessarily believe anything, we merely take note.

This kind of attitude must be maintained continuously, because these things exist in this world. The Buddha was enlightened in the world. He taught in the world. He examined the facts of the world; if he had not examined and come to understand the world, when he met with the world, he would not have been able to transcend it. After his enlightenment, the world was still there as before. For example, there was still praise. There was still criticism. There were still material gain, rank, happiness, and suffering. If none of these things existed, there would be no basis for enlightenment, because they are the very opposite of enlightenment. When the Buddha was enlightened, he awakened to the truth of these worldly dharmas that deceive and obscure the minds of human beings. Gain and loss, rank and disrepute, happiness and suffering, praise and blame belong to the world. If the minds of people follow after these things and fall under their sway, that is called worldliness. These eight dharmas destroy the Eightfold Path. Whenever they increase, the path vanishes. When they occupy and fill the heart, there will be no opportunity for walking the path that makes an end of suffering; there is only the world flooding the heart and keeping it in a state of turmoil, anxiety, and distress.

Thus we are taught to develop the path, which is wisdom. The path can be summarized as developing morality to the utmost, developing samadhi to the utmost, and developing wisdom to the utmost. These are the tools and faculties for destroying the fiction that is called the world, the path for destroying the worldliness dwelling in the hearts of deluded beings. Whenever attachment to happiness and suffering, to gain and loss, is present in the mind, the world is there; the mind is the world. A worldly being has been born—born of craving. If craving is extinguished, the world is extinguished, because this blind craving is the source of the world.

The Eightfold Path and the Eight Worldly Dharmas are a pair. These two ways exist in the same place. It's not as if they are in separate realms. The attachment to happiness, status, praise, and gain exists in the mind with the one who knows; but when there is attachment, the one who knows is obscured so its knowledge is mistaken, and it is dwelling in the world; the world comes to be in the mind. The one who knows has not yet awakened the Buddha nature, so it cannot remove itself from worldliness. When we train the body, speech, and mind in morality, meditation, and wisdom, we soon come to see the worldly dharmas buried in the heart. We will see ourselves clinging to them and how that clinging comes about. If we train and make the mind able, we will thus see the world and its origins. The Buddha said, "O Bhikkhus! Look upon this world as an ornamented and bejeweled royal chariot, by which fools are dazzled and entranced, but which is meaningless to the wise." To see the world, we don't have to go traveling all over Thailand and other countries. We need only look at this mind immersed in worldliness. Then sitting under a tree, we can see the world.

When we determine to practice and develop the path, we try to practice samadhi, to focus and pacify the mind. But the mind does not become focused and peaceful so easily. We don't want it to think, but it keeps on thinking. Really, the mind of an ordinary person is like someone sitting on a nest of red ants. Sitting so close to them, they are going to bite. When we who have the worldly dharmas filling our hearts start to practice with our worldly minds, the habits of attraction and aversion, elation and depression, distraction and worry all immediately start to surface. This is quite a natural occurrence for those who have not yet attained the Dharma and whose minds are filled with worldliness. We have not yet seen through these habits and are thus not able to resist their power. So it's just like sitting on an anthill.

We are sitting right on their home, so of course they will come up and bite us. When they are biting, what should we do? We have to find some way to destroy them: put down poison, cover them with earth, or set fire to the nest so they will flee. This is what practice entails, making an effort to combat what torments us. But practitioners don't generally think like this. Whenever they are feeling good about something, they go along with it. If something makes them unhappy, they are affected by that. When they meet with praise and blame and the rest, they react according to habit and pursue them, never quelling them. When that happens, there is the world.

People who study a little bit will look at this and say they just can't do it; it is too hard to let go of these things. That only means they're afraid to exert the effort. When the mental afflictions occur, the Eight Worldly Dharmas suppress and obscure the Eightfold Path. People can't endure things, so they cannot maintain morality, and they can't persevere in meditating to calm the mind. They can't control themselves and endure in order to contemplate the workings of the mind. It's just like the guy sitting on the anthill. He is out of his mind with pain and discomfort from the bites, so there is nothing he is able to focus on or accomplish. Unable to remove the source of his misery, he just remains there, trying to endure somehow.

This is how it is. The worldly dharmas and the Buddha's path of practice are always going to be antagonistic to each other. When ordinary people try to train the mind and make it tranquil, things that have been residing there will come gushing out. If delusion is allowed to remain in control, the mind is in darkness. But when knowledge is born through perseverance, delusion dissipates and the mind is illumined. Knowledge and delusion occur in the same place. When knowledge is born, delusion cannot stay. When worldliness rules and we cannot find the Eightfold Path, we have to make efforts to practice tranquility and insight meditation. It's necessary to keep at it until we can see the attachment, aversion, and confusion that come from contact with the Eight Worldly Dharmas starting to decrease. When they become lighter, we are able to recognize them more clearly and start to remove ourselves from the world, which resides within us as these things and our grasping reactions to them.

One who practices should bear witness as to how much progress is being made on this path. There are only two choices—right view and wrong view—and everything follows from them. The practitioner becomes like two people, meaning the way of the world and the way of Dharma struggle within the mind. The development of the path will gradually and steadily harass and kill off the worldly dharmas, until in the end the wisdom of right view arises and wrong understanding vanishes. The final result is that the path destroys the afflictions.

The two ways continuously contend with each other all throughout our efforts to practice, and this can continue even when we think we are gaining insight through vipassana (special insight) meditation. It can easily turn into *vipassanupakilesa*, the "defilement of insight." What does this mean? When we develop the path, we make efforts to practice virtue and purify the mind. But whatever good results we get, we can become elated over them and attached to them. This elation is just another form of grasping and becomes *vipassanu*, the "wisdom" of the mental afflictions.

Some people will develop a little goodness and then become attached to that goodness. When they attain some sort of purity, they become attached to purity. When they attain knowledge, they become attached to knowledge. This clinging to knowledge and purity is vipassanu infecting the practice. So when practicing vipassana and gaining some insight, beware of vipassanu, because they can be very similar, and you can be misled, unaware of what is taking place. The vital point is that when vipassanu occurs, there will eventually be some suffering as its fruit. If it is truly vipassana, there is no suffering. It is genuinely peaceful, purified of happiness and suffering.

Practice really has to depend on steadfastness and patient endurance. Some people start to practice meditation, and they have ideas and desires as to how they want it to be. They expect the mind to be calm right away. But the old seeds and habits of turmoil are there, so the practitioners will have to experience their ripening. It's important to make efforts where this distress appears. We might feel we would be fine without such disciplines that cause us to feel bothered and oppressed. We could eat and sleep in comfort and at will. We could talk about whatever we like when we have the urge. We could go here and there as we wish, and following our impulses like this would bring well-being.

The teaching of the Buddha talks about resisting, grating

against things. The way of transcendence grates against the worldly; right view grates against wrong view; purity grates against impurity. These things are always going to be incompatible. In the scriptures, there's a fable to illustrate this. Before the Buddha attained enlightenment, when he had accepted and eaten rice porridge from the milkmaid, Sujata, he set the dish on the surface of a southerly flowing river and made the aspiration, "If I am going to become a supremely awakened Buddha, may this dish flow north." The dish flowed to the north.

The dish symbolized his right view, the inherent buddhahood of the mind's basic awareness that does not follow the inclinations of ordinary beings. At that moment, it was able to go against the current of all worldliness in his heart and not be influenced by anything. So now we have his teachings, which go against the flow of our habits. We have impulses of desire and attraction, but he tells us not to crave. We have the impulse to be angry and displeased over things, but he tells us not to be averse. We tend to be deluded about things, and he shows us how to destroy delusion. The teaching is always aimed at uprooting these habits.

The Buddha's mind was going entirely against the currents of the world. The things that are normally said to be attractive and beautiful, he did not see as attractive and beautiful. The world said that the body belongs to oneself, but he did not see it as his own. The things that are said to be meaningful and valuable, he did not see as meaningful and valuable. His view was beyond the way of worldly beings, which merely clings to phenomena. This state of awareness arose in him.

Following that, there is the legend of his receiving eight handfuls of grass from a Brahmin. He made a seat from it and vowed to attain enlightenment there. If the inner meaning of this is explained, the eight handfuls of grass are the Eight Worldly Dharmas. His efforts were to destroy them. This is what a practitioner must do—destroy attachment to gain, status, praise, pleasure, and their opposites.

The grass was offered to him, and he vowed to sit on it and

enter meditative absorption. Sitting on it is a metaphor for suppressing the worldly dharmas. His mind was above them, bent on attaining the transcendental Dharma. The transcendent is that which renders the worldly meaningless, like refuse. To him, gain and the rest were just refuse. He could sit on them, but they did not affect or obstruct him at all.

Sitting in that place many experiences arose in the mind of the Teacher, until he was able to reach enlightenment and conquer Mara, the Evil One. He conquered the world, nothing else. He taught to develop the path, that which can destroy the worldly dharmas, just as the grass was made into his throne of enlightenment.

These days, most of us practitioners have little faith and devotion. We come to practice for a year or two and are full of desire for rapid attainment. We don't think about the Buddha, how he developed the perfections in order to become the Supreme Teacher. After leaving home, he exerted himself to the utmost for six years. Practicing well, really training the mind and developing our qualities, we can gain experience, and then we can appreciate the virtues of the Buddha.

At the very least, we should realize the first level of awakening. It's not just a matter of counting the months and years spent in practice. The mind should attain something. We will have modesty, a sense of shame and fear toward wrong actions. This is extremely important. We who train properly will not dare to do wrong, whether it is in front of others or beyond their sight, in the light or in the dark, because we have approached the Buddha, meaning we have given rise to the one who knows within ourselves. We rely on the Buddha, the Dharma, and the Sangha (the Three Jewels) as our refuge.

If we truly rely on the Buddha for refuge, we must come to see the Buddha. We must see the Dharma and the Sangha. We recite the formula of refuge in the Three Jewels, but still we don't really know the Buddha. Are we close to him? Are we far from him?

What is the Dharma? What is the Sangha? We request their protection as our refuge, but are we close to them yet? Do we know what they are? We request with body and speech, but our minds have not reached there. Once the mind attains and is able, we will know exactly what the qualities of the Three Jewels are. We will know the Buddha has such and such characteristics, the Dharma is thus, and so on. This will be our experience. We will have this refuge because these things have arisen in our minds. Then wherever we may be, the Buddha, the Dharma, and the Sangha are there with us. Thus we will not perform wrong actions.

So the first *ariya* (Noble One), Kondanya, was freed from falling into the lower realms. This was something definite. He could only follow the straight path, and there would be no eighth rebirth, because the path had been shown and he had attained certainty. Sooner or later, he was bound to reach the end of the path. There was no way he could ever return to performing wrong actions by way of body or speech. He had gone beyond the sort of turmoil that is actually hell itself. So it is said that the ariya is freed from the lower realms. Even if he or she is mistaken about something, it is nothing strong enough to throw him or her into a lower rebirth. The mind cannot go that way anymore; it cannot return to its old ways. This is called the ariyan birth, and it can happen in this life.

These are things that can only be known by the individual through direct experience. We all talk about Dharma and are supposedly practicing Dharma, but we don't really know what Dharma is. Understanding Dharma, seeing Dharma, practicing Dharma—what is it all about? This is really a problem for us. It is nature, the ordinary that is already present, things existing as they are. Why are we now under the sway of happiness and suffering, gladness and dejection? Because we don't know Dharma, we do not see Dharma.

The Buddha intended for us to be free of attachment to the five aggregates, to lay them down and give up involvement with them. We cannot give them up, however, because we don't really know them for what they are. We believe happiness to be our-

selves; we see ourselves as happy. We believe suffering to be ourselves and see ourselves as unhappy. We can't pull the mind out
of this view, which means we are not seeing nature. There isn't
any self involved, but we are always thinking in terms of self.
Thus it seems that happiness happens to us, suffering happens to
us, elation happens to us, depression happens to us. The chain of
self is constructed, and with this solid feeling that there is a self,
everything seems to be happening to us.

So the Buddha said to destroy this conception, this block
called self. When the concept of self is destroyed and finished,
we are free of the belief that there is a self in the body, and then
the condition of selflessness is naturally revealed. Believing that
there is me and mine and living with selfishness, everything is
understood as being a self or belonging to a self or somehow relating to a self. When the phenomena of nature are seen thus,
there is no real understanding. If nature appears to be good, we
laugh and rejoice over it; if phenomena appear to be bad, we cry
and lament. Thinking of natural phenomena as constituting
ourselves or something we own, we create a great burden of suffering to carry. If we realized the truth of things, we would not
have all the drama of excitement, elation, grief, and tears. It is
said, "Pacification is true happiness," and this comes when attachment is rooted out through seeing reality.

Reality exists in the phenomena of nature, in their appearing,
changing, and disappearing. That is their truth. It is people who
are not true. We become excited by things, but phenomena are
not excited in themselves. We become attached to things, wanting them to be a certain way, taking them to be ours. We react
with extreme emotions depending on whether they seem to
turn out in the right way or the wrong way, meaning whether
they turn out according to our desires.

Thus, Anya Kondanya saw the nature of all things. His view
was transformed in the moment when he first heard the teaching of the Buddha. He saw clearly and truly. From that moment
on, whatever he encountered, he just saw arising and passing
away. Pleasant and unpleasant phenomena still kept appearing to

his mind, but he merely recognized their appearance. There was no way he could again fall into the states of extreme suffering that are called the lower realms. His mind firmly established in awareness, he could no longer react to things with gladness or dejection. So it is said that Kondanya received the eye of Dharma that sees according to reality; wisdom knowing the truth of all existence was born in him. This is one who knows and sees Dharma. When one knows one renounces and lets go of things, lays down the burden. We try to bear giving things up, employing forced endurance and renunciation, but we don't see Dharma through this. When one really attains and sees, there is nothing to be endured or given up. When one sees Dharma, there is only Dharma, and in Dharma there is no enduring or re-nouncing. But when we don't yet know and realize Dharma, when it is not our being, we have to apply the conventions of Dharma, exerting ourselves in various practices. We have to apply effort because of the tendency to laziness. We employ endurance and forbearance because of a lack of determination and an inability to bear things and restrain ourselves. But if one has practiced well and is habituated to it, no kind of forced effort is needed.

Fumbling and Groping

ONE WHO HAS PASSED BEYOND doubt no longer needs to grope. If doubt hasn't been removed, you sit and try to develop samadhi, reciting verses to invite the deities and invoke their help. It's just superstitious attachment to rites and rituals. This is talking on a subtle level.

The stream enterer has no doubts. There are still things he has not realized, but he has no doubts. He has removed the first three fetters—belief in a self, doubt, and superstition. The mental afflictions of the stream enterer are of one type, those of the once-returner (at the next level) another. These afflictions become more refined and subtle. What is heavy for a child and what is heavy for an adult are different. Through the stages to attaining the full awakening of the arahant level, it is all different. The afflictions may have the same name, but the weight is different. However, they will all eventually be finished and gone.

Even though there still is something remaining, it doesn't matter; there will be no ill effects. The groping mind that doubts and wonders, Is this right? Is that wrong? is done with. When one realizes the truth of cause and effect, there is no more doubt as to what is right and wrong. If people at this level act correctly and someone else calls them wrong, they will not be moved by that; but they also won't argue with anyone over it. An argument between someone with doubt and someone with no doubt will probably not get very far.

Belief in the body as being or belonging to oneself, doubt, and superstition are all simply groping. For example, when we sit in samadhi for a long time, do long periods of walking meditation, confess our transgressions of the precepts, and thus feel that we have purified our minds, this is all blind belief in rites and rituals. It is just groping.

It's like if you walk along in this cramped little hall, and you keep bumping into the corner of a bench—then there is groping. If you were just sitting there and didn't go and bump into something, there wouldn't be this reaction. For this groping to occur, there has to be something to set it off. Others don't walk into the bench, so their legs won't hurt and they won't have this reaction. I'm trying to illustrate it as simply as possible.

Why is there groping? There is doubt, so there is this discomfort in the mind. Did I do this? Did I do that? It depends on intention as the cause. A mosquito bites you and you brush it away, then you notice, Oh! My hand is full of blood. The mosquito is dead! You don't need to start groping at this point: Did I create some bad karma here? Did I have intention to kill it? Even if there was no intention, I am supposed to be mindful. You can get really worked up over it, groping around. If you just see that the mosquito died and you are aware that it was an unintended happening on your part, you let it go. You can return to your dwelling later and not be chewing it over. Tomorrow, you won't be bothered by second-guessing. You get straight about your intentions in this way and conquer the anxiety. Then when you sit down to meditate, you needn't return to this memory and worry over it. It's like not walking into the bench. If you walked into it, you would have to put some balm on your leg. There is something here, some pain, so there is this reaction. The mind is apprehensive and unsettled over something, so there will be this groping.

There is the view that the body is ours. The Buddha says it isn't ours, and we come to yield on this point. We recognize that this is true and don't need to grope anymore. The next fetter is doubt. Previously unsure about all phenomena, we are no longer in doubt now that we have relinquished the belief in a self. Then there is attachment to rites and rituals, blind belief in the efficacy of conventional modes of behavior. The three are connected, one leading to the other, three types of mental affliction. From seeing the nature of the body and letting go, doubt disappears. And when there is no doubt, there is no more groping. This applies to all the aggregates—body, feeling, perceptions, conceptualization, and consciousness.

Let's speak about it in terms of the Eightfold Path. It begins with right view. If your view is right, then thinking will be right, and all the other factors will be right. But it will be right to a limit, depending on the individual. There is the right view of stream entry, the right view of a once-returner, and the right view of the nonreturner. None of these have yet reached the supreme right view of the arahant. On each level of the path, there is a corresponding level of right: right view and the rest. But there is no doubt from the beginning of entering the stream; there is right view for each level. That of the stream enterer is limited, unlike that of an arahant, but such a person still will not have any wrong understanding. When there is right view, wrong view cannot also be present. When there is no wrong at all within a person's being, that is the arahant level. When there is still some wrong within the person, she is at stream entry or some other lesser level. She cannot yet go where the arahant can go, but she has reached a certain level of right. When right comes to fulfillment, she will be an arahant. Saying,

"I have reached the limit of my strength, I have lifted as much as I can," has a different meaning when it is spoken by a child and by an adult. They are the same words, but the meaning is different.

Getting to the end, doubt is finished. Mind and body are relinquished. Everything is exhausted and finished with. You don't desire the body, don't desire the things of mind. Their power over you is finished, and nothing remains. Why would there be anything left? If there is, let the dogs and cats have it.

We have to hear the teachings and then let go, cast the concepts aside and really practice. The knowledge that will dry up doubt comes from doing, from effort in practice. It doesn't happen from asking questions of someone else. But it's hard to maintain enthusiasm for exerting ourselves in practice. We want to get attainment quickly, but we tend to be lazy. The Buddha said, "Doubts will be exhausted in the mind of the Brahmin because of unflagging practice. . . ." It won't come from anywhere else. So he urged us to apply ourselves with consistent effort.

Whatever arises, pick it up, examine it, and see it clearly. If you can't yet see it for what it is, put it aside for the time being. Today you meet it through this explanation, but only on the level of knowledge. What you don't yet understand, you have to put it aside and practice. Too hot, too cold, neither is right. Not fast or slow, that's not it. You can't find where it is. This is something that only you can know; when you try to explain it to someone else, it doesn't work. Another cannot truly believe simply by hearing. It is something to be contemplated with constant, even mindfulness.

If you practice unceasingly, there will come a moment when you know this clearly. But you have to give up desire for it to happen. If you don't give up this desire, you won't come to know. Right now, all you know is desire. When you let go, that's it. Instantly things are different, and you can practice with the attitude that if you attain some realization, that is fine, and if you don't, never mind. That way you have ease and comfort in your practice; it lies in this direction, not in the direction of wishing and struggling.

You may own a diamond, for example. It falls into the water, and you get very upset. You keep on searching in the water, trying to find it, not caring how hungry or tired you get. Finally, you may think it over and decide, Never mind if I get it back, that's OK. If it's lost, that's OK, too. Then you can return home without the burden of worry.

The crucial moment is when you let go and give up your obsession with it. If you keep on thinking, Oh, what a terrible loss! Where can I find it? This is really bad! Why did this have to happen? you are only increasing your suffering. If you can accept whatever happens, whether you get the diamond back or not, you will feel better. There will be some calmness then. You don't need to waste too much energy on it.

Take care of yourself, pay attention to the things you have, and keep developing and increasing mindfulness. If you develop it first and foremost above other things, you won't be mistaken and your formal meditation practice will certainly not suffer. You probably have doubts about what you're supposed to do in your practice—this is it, right here. But you really have to keep at it to make mindfulness complete, increasing it gradually until you can be aware fully and clearly of everything that happens. When your mindfulness becomes really clear and bright, knowledge will be born. Then you are aware of whatever occurs.

This knowledge that comes from having firm, clear mindfulness will be the cause for wisdom as you come to know and see things as they really are. Without mindfulness, this won't happen. So make your mindfulness as great as you are able. It is the extraordinary treasure that can support your knowledge and awareness and enable you to enter a state of peace. It is the Buddha himself. It will help support and admonish you. You can call it being near to God or Buddha because when you have mindfulness you will be awake. You will know and see, and you will have restraint and caution.

When the more subtle afflictions are still in the heart, lying hidden from your sight, it is because mindfulness is not complete. You do not see them, so they are able to hide from you. Whenever mindfulness is there in sufficient force to clarify things, it makes the mind bright, it makes your wisdom clear. It's like putting water in a bowl. You can look into the bowl and see your face in it when the water is still and clean, just as with mindfulness you can see yourself. And not just yourself—your awareness will extend to many things. Even if a tiny insect falls into the water, you see it. If the water is stirred up or unclean, you can't see much at all. You won't be able to see your reflection clearly. If the water is still and clean, you can see the ceiling. If there is a lizard on the ceiling, you will see it reflected in the still water. Having mindfulness is similar to that. There will be restraint and caution because of the knowledge and sensitivity that has been born of mindfulness.

This mindfulness we have been discussing and practicing can be called recollection. There could be some confusion over the terminology here. When mindfulness arises and knows something, it becomes perception or memory, and this is impermanent, something that can deteriorate. For example, I may want to call the monk named Jagaro, but I say, "Pamutto." I know what I want to do, but when it comes to speaking, I say something else. And I am aware of this happening. That's the impermanence of perception. This change and instability occur as time passes, we get older, and the brain weakens. It's only the natural decay and worsening of the elements, according to the principle that perception is impermanent. We can see this happening clearly, but it happens by itself. We see it is like that, and we accept it. The Buddha taught that memory is impermanent, as are the other aggregates of body and mind. So we don't hold tightly to all these things as being self or other.

If there's nothing happening, you don't need to investigate anything. Just remain in an ordinary state. For example, when you are sweeping your dwelling, if no one calls to you, of course you don't need to look. If someone calls, "Hello there!" then you look, and you are aware of what is happening and what business the person may have with you. After that, you just keep on sweeping. If something is there, we investigate. If not, there's nothing to investigate. We are just mindfully aware of our own abiding. There is careful attentiveness; we are not simply letting ourselves go. Whatever may occur, we will know. It isn't dwelling in unawareness. But we don't have to go thinking and seeking, trying to find something or to figure anything out. When there is contact through the senses, we have the inner awareness to watch it.

When mindfulness is in charge and protects us in this way, there is tranquility in the mind, which will lead to wisdom because of seeing all these things. Please look into this.

When it's time to sweep up leaves, then sweep. Maintain your awareness as you sweep and contemplate whatever occurs. Don't merely sweep with a blank, indifferent mind. If you keep your mindfulness up, the mind can enter a concentrated state. You will think, Well, sweeping the grounds is good, after all. We keep the monastery clean, and we practice meditation to sweep the afflictions out of the mind. Your mind will converse with itself like this, and wisdom will keep on growing.

When the mind is in a settled and awake state resulting from proper meditation, it's like a freshly swept path: as soon as a few leaves fall, you will notice them. They will be easy to see on the ground. But if the mind is not guarded or controlled, it is like a forest floor covered with leaves: if a few more leaves fall, they are lost among those already on the ground.

Wisdom grows as we see the nature of phenomena. We see there is no way to solve, undo, or adjust things. We accept the transitory nature of existence, accept things as they are, and the result is peace. Suffering is quelled because of this surrender and acceptance. When we surrender, clinging attachment is uprooted, and we see there is really nothing there; there is nothing left. We have perceptions of self and others, beings, people, and so forth, but in fact these are only conventions, appearances. In ultimate transcendent reality, there is nothing. The body we perceive is only a coming together of the elements. Men and women are like that. Asians and Westerners are like that. Everyone is actually like that. All are the same, and seeing this leads to a state of ease.

For example, we are taught to meditate on the food we eat. Looking at it and contemplating properly, we can see there is nothing really special, not a whole lot there. There is the food, and there is us, the two parts that are just the elements, and then they get put together. That's it. You won't get too worked up over your food now. But if you cannot see it like this, if you cannot accept that this is all there is to food, you will suffer. The person who accepts that the food and the one who eats it are the same mere combinations of elements will have lightness, but for the person who cannot accept, there is heaviness.

In your practice, you should aim at this kind of understanding. Seeing things in this way can alleviate and reduce your experience of suffering. Before you can end suffering, you have to reduce it first, little by little. All of you who have undergone the training should be able to verify this. I've observed some of you changing over the years, and you can compare what it was like for you before and now. Look at the condition of your mind. There are big differences now. Why is it like that? The things you grasped at so much have been losing their power over you.

But still desire wants instant realization and accomplishment. It's pretty ordinary that everyone wants to be liberated right away, but it can't happen. I remember how one monk used to read stories of people who attained the arahant stage merely through hearing a little teaching or meditating briefly; then he would start to wonder, What's the matter with me? Am I practicing in the wrong way? This would make him confused and upset, so he would shoulder his bowl and mosquito net umbrella and go into a forest. His practice didn't work any better there, so off he would go to another forest. But he wasn't able to pacify his mind in that forest, so he went to yet another forest, and still it wasn't peaceful. It wasn't peaceful in the mountains, either. Wherever he went, there wasn't any peace for him, and there didn't seem to be a way to find peace, so his mind never got out of this turmoil. It was because he was thinking that peace is in the living environment. Yes, it does have a part in it, but the larger part lies with right view. That is where peace will really be found.

If there is wrong view, the mind is always at work, scheming how to find peace. "Oh yeah, I've heard that mountain is a really peaceful place, that's where I will make an end of the afflictions."

It has a part in it, as I've said, but it is a condition for only a little bit of tranquility. So you keep on going when the mind is unsettled. Someone tells you, "You really ought to go to such and such mountain." You will believe this and go there. When it doesn't work out, you will try other places, always finding disappointment. On and on you go. "You should visit this ajahn, you should study with that ajahn." It keeps you on the move, until you have gone through all the mountains and all the teachers. Finally, you might decide there is no such thing as enlightenment and quit. But really, where is tranquility to be found? It is in right view. Dwelling in right view, you will be at peace no matter where you are.

When people stay in quietude, it may be uncertain whether they have finished the afflictions or if something remains. There might actually be a lot left, but they are completely unaware of it and feel fine, enjoying their calm state. They are comfortable only because they are accustomed to the place. If they go somewhere else, they don't feel right and have to go looking for the so-called right place again.

Actually, when good people try to practice, it will make them mad. All kinds of suffering and turmoil flare up. I went through this. Mind filled with pride, wandering all over, always wanting things to be other than they were. Everything was always too big or too small, too long or too short. Nothing was ever right; there was no moderation, no middle ground. It was outside the natural balance of Dharma, always in a condition of struggle. You have to practice to stop the insanity in order to feel better.

5

BEING
DHARMA

Beyond Cause and Effect

ONCE IN THE PAST, I was living with a small group of monks.
We stayed in the forest, where we had a small sala (meditation
hall) and altar without much light. One monk was reading a
book there, and when his candle burned down he left the book
and went away. Another monk came along and stepped on the
book in the dark. He picked it up and thought, Hmm, that monk
doesn't have much mindfulness. Why didn't he know to put the
book away?

He found the first monk and asked him, "Why didn't you put
the book away? I came and stepped on it." The first monk
replied, "You didn't have self-control. You weren't careful, so you
stepped on the Dharma book."

And the other responded, "Why didn't you take care of the
book and put it away?"

They went back and forth, one blaming the other for not taking care of the book properly, the other blaming him for not being careful and stepping on the book. It's like this if you are only looking for logical answers. There will be no end.

In the matter of real Dharma, you have to discard cause and effect. Dharma is higher than this. The Dharma the Buddha was enlightened to can quell the mental afflictions and remove suffering. It is above cause and beyond effect. There is no suffering and no happiness. The Dharma the Buddha taught can pacify our lives, purge causes and results. If you just rely on the logic of cause and effect, there will be endless dispute, like the two monks arguing over stepping on the book. They could go on forever, logically discussing their reasons. There is no peace this way.

We who study should learn about cause and effect: happiness comes from such and such causes, suffering comes from such and such causes. We come to know that there is always cause and result in actions. But the Dharma realized by the Buddha is pacification, that which is above cause and result, beyond happiness and suffering, beyond birth and death. But now you have even more doubts when you hear about this. This is something really important. This is the Dharma that brings peace.

Our desire, our wish to know things quickly, is not Dharma. It is only our desire. If we act according to desire, there is never any end. You know the story of Ananda, the Buddha's attendant. His faith was as strong as anyone's. There was to be the *Sanghayana* (Sangha Council) after the passing of the Buddha, and only arahants would be allowed to attend. Ananda was determined to attain the stage of arahant and began strenuous practice so he could join them. But his mind would not do what he wanted it to. He was in this coarse state, and over and over again he was only meeting with frustration. "Tomorrow is the Sanghayana. All my Dharma friends, the arahants, will be attending, but I am still an ordinary person. What should I do?"

He decided to meditate from dusk to daybreak. He went at it, but he was only getting fatigued. Coming to the end of his tether, he decided to take a brief rest. At dawn, he set down a pillow and made ready to rest.

Stupa containing Ajahn Chah's relics,
Wat Pah Pong, Thailand.

Having made the determination to rest, his mind had already started letting go, putting down his business. Then, lying down, even before his head hit the pillow, his mind let go completely and he saw the Dharma; he was enlightened to the arahant stage.

Seeking to let go, we can never do it. We could try for years and it wouldn't happen. But in that moment, when Ananda had decided to stop, to take a rest and put down his burden of wanting attainment, just resting with mindfulness established, the mind let go and he was able to see and awaken. He didn't have to do anything special. Before, he wanted something to happen, and it didn't work. There was no occasion to take a rest, no occasion to awaken to the Dharma.

Understand that becoming enlightened to the Dharma is a matter of letting go, letting go with wisdom, with knowing. It doesn't come about through wanting and struggling, but from letting go in full mindfulness. When there is this taking a rest, nothing is bothering the mind. There is no desire to disturb it. Then instantly the mind can awaken, as in Ananda's case. Ananda was practically unaware of himself. He knew only that he wasn't getting what he wanted; desire for enlightenment was thwarting all his efforts. So he decided to take a break.

Enlightenment is not something easy to talk about and make people understand. It's difficult to practice if people have the wrong idea. For example, the Buddha said this place is not a place for people to dwell. There are the floor and the roof. If there is no roof and no floor, then there is nothing, right? There's nothing to talk about. The space in between is not the place where people can live—there is no becoming there. Becoming is the upper story or the lower story. If people are going to live somewhere, they must live upstairs or downstairs. "No becoming?" People aren't interested.

People are not interested in letting go. With letting go, is there anything being born? When you go upstairs, that is becoming. You may feel it's nice up there in the high place; coming down is not so pleasing to you. You feel it's nice, but it is the root of suffering. You don't want to put down this pleasure and pain and experience normalcy because you prefer the place where there is becoming. The place without becoming is not of interest to you. Even just to try to conceive of it is hard.

What the Buddha was referring to when he spoke of the place without becoming and birth was just the state of nonattachment. Attachment is the cause for suffering to arise. We can't let go of this grasping attachment, and still we want peace. But it is not peaceful. We live with becoming. No becoming is something we can't conceive of. That is the habit of people, the mental affliction of humans.

Nirvana is said by the Buddha to be beyond becoming and birth. People don't understand this. They only understand matters of becoming and birth. If there is no becoming, there is no place to live. If there is no place to live, what will I do? How will I exist? Ordinary people think it's better to stay here. They want to be born again, but they don't want to die. Is there such a thing? If you want something that cannot be, you will have a big problem. People think like this because they don't understand dukkha (unsatisfactoriness of life). "I want to be born, but I don't want death." It boils down to no more than this.

The Buddha said that death comes from birth; if you do not want to die, don't be born. People think, Well, I don't want to die. I want to be born again; but I don't want to die. You might conclude they are stubborn. Speaking with people who are under the sway of desire and attachment is difficult. Getting to the point of letting go will really be hard.

Defilement and craving are like that. The Buddha taught about the state where things don't really exist. If there's no place to set a pillar, how can we talk about building something? That is like no becoming and birth, no place to be born. But when we talk about this, people cannot listen and understand. When talking about self, it is emphatically pointed out that there is no such thing. Self is simply a convention. On the absolute level, the level of liberation, it does not exist. There is just elemental nature arising only for the reason that causes and conditions are manifesting. We suppose that this is a self arising, and we grasp at it. When there is this supposition, we grasp at me, then there is mine arising together with it. But we don't even know how this is taking place. So people say things like, "I want to be born, but I don't want to die."

Speaking of entering the stream to nirvana, if there is genuine knowing within you, there is no one desiring anything. And further, nirvana is not a matter of wanting. It isn't something you can desire. This characteristic is not easy to understand.

This Dharma isn't something you can explain or give to people. Our parents might want to give it to us, but even they don't know what it is, and they have no means to do this. This is something to be known within yourself. You can tell others about it, but there is this problem: will they really know what you are talking about? If they don't have the realization in their own minds, they won't get it. Thus, the Buddha said, "The Tathagata merely points the way." Just as I am doing these days—I am one who explains, not the one who does it for you. Having been told, you need to practice and realize. Then the marvelous will arise and be known in your mind. There's a story in the scriptures of people asking the Buddha about nirvana. When he refused to elaborate on it, they began to say it was because he didn't know. How could the Buddha not know? The point is that such a thing is to be realized by each individual.

When I speak like this, if you just hear it and believe me, that is not so good. It's not yet genuine. Those who believe others are said by the Buddha to be foolish. He said to listen to things and then contemplate to experience the truth of them. You should be able to listen without merely denying. Receive the words, not merely believing but investigating their meaning. It isn't a matter of believing or not believing. Put those aside for the time being and contemplate to the best of your ability.

There are the two extremes. We lean toward either side, but we don't like to stay in the middle. The middle is the lonely way. When there is attraction, we go that way. When there is aversion, we go that way. Putting them down is lonely. We refuse to go there. The Buddha taught that neither extreme is the way of one who is tranquil. We need to be free of pleasure and pain, for neither is the way of peace. Once free of these things, we can be peaceful. Thinking, I am so happy, is not it. That is just happiness for suffering in the future. These are things we have to be wary of. Walking the path, we see the two extremes and keep going. We keep to the middle without desiring them, because we want peace, not pleasure or pain. This is the correct path.

The practice of Dharma is leading to the point of letting go. But we must have knowledge of things according to the truth in order to let go. When real knowledge arises, there will be endurance in the practice of Dharma. There will be enthusiastic, consistent effort. This is called practicing.

Once you have gotten to the end, you don't need to use the Dharma. Like a saw that you sharpen to cut wood. Once the wood is cut, you put down the saw. You don't need to use it then. The saw is the Dharma. Dharma is the tool to help you attain path and fruition. Once we have accomplished this we put it down; once the job is done, why would you keep holding the saw?

The wood is the wood. The saw is the saw. This is about stopping, having reached the essential point, the end of all the taints of craving and ignorance. The wood is cut. You don't have to cut any more; you can put the saw down. One who will practice must rely on the Dharma. That's someone who is not yet finished. But if the job is done, you don't have to do any more. You can naturally let go at that point. With no more attachment and giving meaning to things, there is no need for any more doing. It is the state of peace.

When we hear about it, we are full of doubts. What can it be? It seems so far away, but it's actually very close. It is something you can discover in your own mind. Things arise, and you come to realize they are not certain. "This is not real. That is not real." Where is the real? Right there! Trying to surmise—this is like this, that is like that—is not right. Let go of things, put down the judging and guessing. We go back and forth, passing it by again and again, and we are always in a state of suffering.

End your doubts here. End your doubts and stop. Make an end of it right here.

Nibbana Paccayo Hotu

THE PROFOUND TEACHING OF BUDDHISM is that morality is necessary. Morality resides with the intentions of people. If you have the conscious determination to refrain from harmful activities and wrongdoing by way of body and speech, morality is coming about within you. You should know this within yourself. It's fine to take vows with another person, and you can also recollect the precepts by yourself. If you don't know what they are, you can request them from someone. It's nothing very complicated or distant. So really, whenever you wish to receive morality and Dharma, you have them right at that moment. It is just like the air that surrounds you everywhere. Whenever you breathe, you take it in. All manner of good and evil are like that. If you wish to do good, you can do it anywhere at any time. You can do it alone or with others. Evil is the same. You can do it with a large or small group, in a hidden or open place.

When there is morality, you should pursue Dharma. Morality means the precepts as to what is proscribed and what is permissible. Dharma refers to nature and to humans knowing about nature, how things exist according to nature.

The Buddha taught Dharma for us to know nature, to let go of it and let it exist according to its conditions. This is talking about the material world. As to the mind, it can't be left to follow its own conditions. It has to be trained. We can say that mind is the teacher of body and speech, so it needs to be well trained. Letting it go according to its natural urges just makes us animals. It has to be instructed and trained. It should come to know nature, but should not be left merely to follow nature.

Born into this world, all of us naturally have the afflictions of desire, anger, and delusion. Desire makes us crave various things and causes the mind to be in a state of imbalance and turmoil. It won't do to let the mind go after these impulses of craving. That can only lead to torment and distress. It's better to train in Dharma, in truth.

When aversion occurs in us, we want to express anger toward people, and it may get to the point of physically attacking or even killing someone. But we don't just let the impulse go according to its nature. We know the nature of what is occurring. We see it for what it is and teach the mind about it. This is studying Dharma.

Delusion is the same. When it happens, we are confused about things. If we merely leave it as it is, we remain in ignorance. So the Buddha told us to learn about nature, to train the mind, to know exactly what nature is.

People are born with physical form and mind. In the beginning these things are born, in the middle they change, and in the end they are extinguished. This is their nature. We can't do much to alter these facts. We train our minds as we can, and when the time comes, we have to let go of it all. It is not within the power of humans to change this or get beyond it. The Dharma the Buddha taught is something to be applied while we are here, for making actions, words, and thoughts correct and wholesome. He was teaching the minds of people so they would not be deluded in regard to nature, to conventional reality and supposition. The Teacher instructed us to see the world. His Dharma was a teaching that is above and beyond the world. We were born into this world; he taught us to transcend the world, not be prisoners to worldly ways and habits.

It's like a diamond that falls into a muddy pit. No matter how much dirt and filth cover the diamond, they do not destroy the radiance, the hues, and the worth of it. Even though the mud is stuck to it, the diamond does not lose anything, but is just as it originally was. There are two separate things.

The Dharma the Teacher expounded was for going beyond suffering. What is this going beyond suffering all about? What should we do to escape from suffering? It's necessary for us to do some study; we need to study the thinking and feeling in our hearts. Just that. It is something we are presently unable to change. We can be free of all suffering and unsatisfactoriness in life by changing this one point, our habitual world view, our way of thinking and feeling. If we transform our sense of things, we transcend the old confused perceptions and understanding.

The authentic Dharma of the Buddha is not something pointing far away. It teaches self. It teaches about the concept of self, and that things are not really self. All the teachings the Buddha gave were pointing out that "this is not a self, this does not belong to a self, there is no such thing as ourselves or others." When we contact this, we can't really read it, we don't translate the Dharma correctly. We still think, This is me. This is mine. We attach to things and invest them with meaning. When we do this, we can't disentangle from them; the involvement deepens and the mess gets worse and worse. If we know that there is no self, that body and mind are really not self, as the Buddha taught, when we keep on investigating, we will eventually come to realize the actual condition of selflessness. We will genuinely see that there is no self or other. Pleasure is merely pleasure. Feeling is merely feeling. Memory is merely memory. Thinking is merely thinking. They are all things that are merely themselves. Good is merely good, bad is merely bad. There is no real happiness or real suffering. There are merely existing conditions: merely happy, merely suffering, merely hot, merely cold, merely a being or a person. We should keep looking to see that things are only so much. Only earth, only water, only fire, only air. We should keep on reading these things and investigating this point. Eventually, our perception will change. The tight conviction that there is self and things belonging to self will gradually come undone. When this sense of things is removed, the opposite perception will keep increasing steadily.

When the realization of selflessness comes to full measure, we will be able to relate to the things of this world, to our most cherished possessions and involvements, to friends and relations, wealth, accomplishments and status, just as we do to our clothes. When clothes are new, we wear them; they get dirty and we wash them; after some time, they are worn out and we discard them. There is nothing out of the ordinary there; we are constantly getting rid of the old things and starting to use new garments.

We will have the exact same feeling about our existence in this world. We will not cry or moan over things. We won't be tormented or burdened by them. They will remain the same as they were before, but our feeling toward and understanding of them will be changed. Our knowledge will be exalted and we will see truth. We will have attained supreme vision and authentic knowledge of the Dharma. The Buddha taught the Dharma that we ought to know and to see, and this Dharma is right here within us, within this body and mind. We have it already; we should come to know and see it.

Whatever we gained by our birth into this human realm, we are going to lose. We have seen people born and seen them die. We see this happening, but don't really see clearly. When there is a birth, we rejoice over it; when someone dies, we cry for them. It goes on in this way, and there is no end to our foolishness. Seeing birth, we are foolhardy; seeing death, we are foolhardy. There is only this unending foolishness.

Let's take a look at all this. These things are natural occurrences. They are the Dharma you should know and see. Make up your minds about this, and exert restraint and self-control now while you are amid the things of this life. You shouldn't have fears of death, rather you should fear the lower realms, be afraid of falling into hell because of doing wrong while you still have life. Some people are alive but don't know themselves at all. They think, What's the big deal about what I do now? I can't know what's going to happen when I die. They don't think about the new seeds they are creating for the future. They only see the old fruit. They fixate on present experience, not realizing that if there is fruit, it must have come from a seed, and that within the fruit they have now are the seeds of future fruit. These seeds are just waiting to be planted. Actions born of ignorance continue the chain in this way, but when they are eating the fruit, they don't think about all the implications.

Whatever we are experiencing as part of our lives now, one day we will be parted from it. So don't just pass the time. Practice spiritual cultivation. Take this parting, this separation and loss, as your object of contemplation right now, until you are clever and skilled in it, until you can see that it is ordinary and natural. When there is anxiety and regret over it, recognize the limits of this anxiety and regret, knowing what they are according to the truth. If you can consider things in this way, wisdom will arise.

Whenever there is happiness or suffering, wisdom can arise at that moment. If we know happiness and suffering for what they really are, we know the Dharma. If we know the Dharma, we know the world clearly; if we know the world clearly, we know the Dharma. But for most of us, if something is displeasing, we don't really want to know about it. We get caught up in the aversion to it. If we dislike someone, we don't want to look at his face or get anywhere near him; just to see his house or even his dog can make us angry! This is the mark of a foolish, unskillful person; this is not the way of a wise person. If we like someone, then of course we want to be close to him. We make every effort to be with him, taking delight in his company. This is foolishness also. They are actually the same, like the palm and back of the hand. When we turn the hand up and see the palm, the back of the hand is hidden from sight. When we turn it over, the palm is not seen. Pleasure hides pain, and pain hides pleasure from our sight. Wrong covers up right, right covers wrong. Just looking at one side, our knowledge is not complete.

Let's do things completely while we still have life. Keep on looking, separating truth from falsehood, noting how things really are, getting to the end of it, and reaching peace. Eventually we will be able to cut through and let go completely.

We have not yet left this world, so we should be careful. We should contemplate a lot, make copious charitable offerings, recite the scriptures a lot, cultivate a lot—cultivate reflection on impermanence, on unsatisfactoriness, and on selflessness. Even if the mind does not want to listen, we should keep on breaking things down like this and come to know in the present. This can most definitely be done. We can realize knowledge that transcends the world. Even while we are living in this world, our view can be above the world. To put the Buddha's teaching in a nutshell, the point is to transform our view. It is possible to change it; it only requires looking at things and then it happens. We don't need to look up at the sky or down at the earth. The Dharma we need to see and to know is right here within us, every moment of every day.

This is what the Buddha taught about. He did not teach about gods and demons and *nagas* (water deities), protective deities, jealous demigods, nature spirits, and the like. He taught the things we should know and see, truths we certainly should be able to realize. The truth can be seen in the hair, nails, skin, and teeth. Previously they flourished; now they are diminished. The hair thins and becomes gray. Will you say it is something you can't see? Really, we don't want to see, because we feel this shouldn't be happening. But the Buddha called these "divine messengers," or *devadhuta* (literally, the excellent bearers of news). Here they are, telling you, "Your hair has turned gray now. Your eyesight has become weak. Your back is bent. . . ." They are the excellent teachers of impermanence, showing you the transitory nature of life and leading you to dispassion. You certainly should be able to see with a little investigation.

If we really take an interest in all of this and contemplate seriously, we can gain genuine knowledge. If this were something that could not be done, the Buddha wouldn't have bothered to talk about it. Normally we speak in terms of self—talking about me and mine, you and yours—but it is possible for the mind to remain uninterrupted in the realization of selflessness. How many tens and hundreds of thousands of the Buddha's followers have come to realization over the centuries? If we are really keen on looking at things, we can come to know. The Dharma is like that.

So the Buddha said you should take the Dharma as your foundation, your basis. Living and practicing in the world, will you take yourself, your ideas, desires, and opinions as a basis? Taking yourself as the standard, you become self-absorbed. Taking someone else as your standard, you are merely infatuated with that person. Being enthralled with yourself or with another is not the way of Dharma. Dharma doesn't incline to any individual or follow personalities. It follows the truth. It does not simply accord with the likes and dislikes of people; such habitual reactions have nothing to do with the truth.

If we really consider all of this and investigate thoroughly, we will enter the correct path. Why is it that we have suffering? Because of lack of knowledge, not knowing where things begin and end, not understanding the causes; this is ignorance. When there is this ignorance, various desires arise and, driven by them, we create the causes of suffering. Then the result must be suffering. When we gather firewood and put a match to it, then expect not to have any heat, what are our chances? We are creating a fire, aren't we? This is origination itself.

If you understand these things, morality will be born within you. Dharma will be born. So prepare yourselves well. The Buddha advised us to prepare ourselves. You needn't have too many concerns or anxieties. Just look within. Look at the place without desires, the place without danger. The Buddha taught: "*Nibbana paccayo hotu* (Let it be a cause for nirvana)." Being a cause for the realization of nirvana means looking at the place where things are empty, where things are done with, where they reach their end and are exhausted. Look at the place where there are no more causes, where there is no more self or other, me or mine. This looking becomes a cause or condition, a condition for attaining nirvana. Then practicing generosity becomes a cause for realizing nirvana. Practicing morality becomes a cause for realizing nirvana. Listening to the teachings becomes a cause for realizing nirvana. Thus we can dedicate all our Dharma activities to become causes for nirvana. But if we are not looking toward nirvana, if instead we are looking at self and other and grasping without end, this does not become a cause for nirvana.

When we deal with others and they talk about self, about me and mine, about what is ours, we immediately agree with this viewpoint. We immediately think, Yeah, that's right! But it's not right. Even if the mind is saying, Right, right! we have to exert control over it. It's like a child who is afraid of ghosts. Maybe the parents are afraid, too. But it won't do for the parents to talk about it; if they do, the child will feel she has no protection or security. "No, of course Daddy is not afraid. Don't worry, Mommy is here. There are no ghosts. There's nothing to worry about." Well, the father might really be afraid. But if he starts talking about it, they will all get so worked up about ghosts they'll jump up and run out of the house—father, mother, and child—and end up homeless!

This isn't being clever. You have to look at things clearly and learn how to deal with them. Even when you feel that deluded appearances are real, you have to tell yourself they are not. Go against it. Teach yourself inwardly. When the mind is experiencing the world in terms of self, saying, It's true, you have to be able to tell it, "It's not true." You should be floating on the water, not submerged by the floodwaters of worldly habit. The water is flooding our hearts; if we run after things, do we ever look at what is going on? Will there be anyone watching the house?

Nibbana paccayo hotu—one need not aim at anything or wish for anything at all. Just aim for nirvana. All manner of positive results, merit and virtue in the worldly way, will naturally come as well. Don't end up like someone with a stick and a basket struggling to get mangoes off a tree: if the stick isn't the right length, the mangoes remain out of reach, or they will be knocked haphazardly to the ground where they get bruised and end up rotting. Making merits and skillful karma, hoping it will cause you to attain some better state, you don't need to be wishing for a lot of things; just aim directly for nirvana. Wanting virtue, wanting tranquility, wanting all sorts of results, you just end up in the same old place. It's not necessary to desire these things—you should only wish for the place of cessation.

Throughout all our becoming and birth we are so terribly anxious about so many matters. When there is separation, when there is death, we cry and lament. I can only think how utterly foolish this is. What are we crying about? Where do we think people are going, anyhow? If they are still bound up in becoming and birth, they are not really going away. When children grow up and move to the big city, they still think of their parents. They won't be missing others' parents. When they return, they will go to their parents' home, not someone else's. And when they go away again, they will still think about their home here in Ubon. Will they be homesick for some other place? What do you think?

So when the breath ends and we die, no matter through how many lifetimes, if the causes for becoming and birth still exist, the consciousness is likely to try and take birth in a place it is familiar with. I think we are overly fearful about all of this. So please don't go crying about it too much. Think about this. It is said, "Karma drives beings into their various births." They don't go very far. They cycle back and forth through the round of births, just changing appearance, appearing with a different face next time, but we don't recognize this. We're just coming and going, going and returning in the round of samsara, really just remaining where we are. Like a mango that is shaken off the tree and falls to the ground with a thud: it is not going anywhere. So the Buddha said, "Nibbana paccayo hotu." Let your only aim be nirvana. Strive hard to accomplish this; don't end up like the mango falling to the ground, going nowhere.

If you can transform your sense of things like this, you will know great peace. Please make this effort to change, and come to see and know. These are things you should see and know. If you do see and know, then what else do you need to do? Morality will come to be. Dharma will come to be.

When you transform your view, you will realize it's like watching leaves fall from the trees. When they get old and dry, they fall. When the spring comes, they begin to appear again. Would anyone cry when leaves fall or laugh when they grow? If you did, you would be insane, wouldn't you? If you can see things in this way, you will be OK. You will know it is just the natural order of things. It doesn't matter how many births you undergo, it will always be like this. When you study Dharma, gaining clear knowledge and undergoing a change of worldview in this way, you will realize peace and be free of bewilderment about the phenomena of this life.

Listening to the Dharma should resolve your doubts. It should clarify your view of things and alter your way of living. When doubts are resolved, suffering can end. You stop creating desires and mental afflictions. Then, whatever you experience, if something is displeasing to you, you won't suffer over it because you understand its changeable nature. If something is pleasing to you, you won't get carried away and become intoxicated by it because you know the appropriate way to let go of things. You maintain a balanced perspective because you understand impermanence and know how to resolve things according to Dharma. You know that good and bad conditions are always changing. Knowing internal phenomena, you understand external phenomena. Not attached to the external, you are not attached to the internal. Observing within yourself or outside yourself, it is all completely the same.

When we know the truth of things and don't get caught up in happiness and suffering over them, we don't need to apply forbearance because Dharma is already present; our experience is Dharma. Whatever occurs is Dharma, and the one who is aware of it knows according to truth. There has been a process of learning Dharma and seeing Dharma, and now things are appearing as

Dharma. When experience is Dharma, we can stop. There is peace. There is no need to apply any Dharma, because everything is Dharma. External and internal phenomena are Dharma. The one who is aware is Dharma. Conditions are Dharma. This knowledge is Dharma. There is oneness, liberation. This nature is not born. This nature does not age or decay. This nature does not die. This nature is not happy or sorrowful. It is not big or small, high or low, black or white, light or heavy. There is nothing to compare it to, no way to illustrate it. No conventions of speech can approach it. So it is said that nirvana has no form, no color or caste. All these are matters of convention, the relative reality of appearance. Beyond all these things, there is no convention that can apply to it or touch it. So when the Buddha talked about the plane of transcendence, he said, "The wise will realize it individually for themselves." It cannot be proclaimed or shown to others; there is only the giving of skillful means. Those who attain it will make an end of things. To use the ordinary conventions of speech and concepts will not suffice; all convention ends here.

In this way, we can dwell in a natural state, which is peace and tranquility. If we are criticized, we remain undisturbed. If we are praised, we are undisturbed. We let things be; we are not influenced by others. This is freedom. Knowing the two extremes for what they are and not stopping at either side, we can experience well-being. This is genuine happiness and peace, transcending all things of the world. We transcend all good and evil and are above cause and effect, beyond birth and death. Born into this world, we can transcend the world—this is the aim of the Buddha's teaching. He did not aim for people to suffer. He desired people to attain peace, to know the truth of things and realize wisdom. This is Dharma. There is no need to be in confusion or have doubts about it. Wherever we are, the same laws apply.

So while we are still living, we should train the mind to be even in regard to things. We should be able to share wealth and possessions. When the time comes, we should give a portion to those in need, just as if we were giving things to our own children. Sharing things like this, we will feel happy. If we can give away our wealth, then whenever our breath may stop, there will be no attachment or anxiety because everything is finished with. The Buddha said to "die before you die," to be finished with things before they are finished. Then you can be at ease. Let things break before they are broken, let them end before they are ended. This is the Buddha's intention in teaching the Dharma. Even if you listen to teachings for a hundred or a thousand eons, if you do not understand these points, you won't be able to undo your suffering and you will not find peace. You will not see the Dharma. But understanding these things according to the Buddha's intention and being able to resolve things is called seeing the Dharma. This view can make an end of suffering. It can relieve all heat and distress. Whoever strives sincerely and is diligent in practice, who can endure, who trains and develops to the full measure—such people will attain peace and cessation. Wherever they stay, they will have no suffering. Whether they are young or old, they will be free of suffering. Whatever their situation, whatever work they have to perform, they will have no suffering, because their minds have reached the place where suffering is exhausted, where there is peace.

The Buddha thus said to change your perceptions, and there will be the Dharma. When the mind is in harmony with Dharma, Dharma enters the heart. The mind and the Dharma become indistinguishable. This is something to be realized by those who practice, the changing of one's view and experience of things. The entire Dharma is something to be realized individually. It cannot be given by anyone; that is an impossibility. If you hold it to be difficult, it will be difficult. If you take it to be easy, it is easy. Whoever contemplates it and sees the one point does not have to know a lot of things. Seeing the one point, seeing birth and death, the arising and passing away of phenomena according to nature, you will know all things. This is a matter of the truth.

This is the way of the Buddha. The Buddha gave his teachings out of the wish to benefit all beings. He wished for us to go beyond suffering and to attain peace. It's not that we have to die first in order to transcend suffering. We shouldn't think that we will attain this after death. We can go beyond suffering here and now, in the present. We transcend within our perception of things, in this very life, through the view that arises in our minds. Then sitting, we are happy; lying down, we are happy; wherever we are, we have happiness. We become without fault, experiencing no ill results, living in a state of freedom. The mind is clear, bright, and tranquil, like the sun or the full moon emerging from behind the clouds. There is no more darkness or defilement. That is when we have reached the supreme happiness of the Buddha's way. Please investigate this for yourselves. All of you, please contemplate this to gain understanding and ability. If you have suffering, practice to alleviate your suffering. If it is great, make it little; if it is little, make an end of it. Everyone has to do this for themselves. May you prosper and develop.

6

TEACHING
DHARMA

IT'S ALL UPAYA (skillful means). It is as if we're advertising medicine to sell; we have to talk about its effectiveness. "Whoever suffers from headaches, whoever has indigestion. . . ." Then whether or not people will buy is up to them. But we do have to go to the villages and say something, otherwise they won't know about it. It is just skillful means to get people to take a look.

Dharma has no body or substance, but we have to find some way to get people to come to it and understand. We make analogies and comparisons to say that it is like this and like that; it is totally a matter of upaya. The real Dharma cannot be shown or seen like this. Think about it. No one can really give Dharma to another. We can only give upaya to help people understand, speaking in ways they can relate to. So where is the Dharma? You'd better investigate this anew.

The Buddha didn't praise those who merely believe others. He praised those who come to know for themselves. This latter kind of knowledge is clear, and when you know in this way,

problems and questions come to an end. If you only know because of what someone told you, the questions remain.

For example, when you were coming here, you had to ask
someone the way to Ban Gaw village and Wat Pah Pong, what the
monastery is like, and so forth. But just hearing their answers is
not knowing clearly. You know, but not for real. You could spend
your whole life thinking about it without knowing until you actually get here. If someone else asks you about Wat Pah Pong,
what can you say? Nothing is really clear yet, because you have
only heard what others had to say. Your knowledge does not
reach the actuality; it hasn't arrived. So there are still questions.

When you do arrive, and see for yourself, there is nothing
more to be puzzled about. You can say what Ban Gaw is like,
what Wat Pah Pong is like, what the ajahn is like. The questions
have come to an end because you see for yourself.

So the Buddha taught us to meditate and realize for ourselves.
Just believing others' words he called foolishness. We may believe
the words of others, but we have to investigate and come to believe a second time through really seeing the truth of those
words.

Like some people, I've often thought about how people like
to make merit through offerings these days. It's a popular practice, and people feel good about it. And it is good, true enough.
But think about giving up evil. Actually, giving up evil is a big-
ger thing than the meritorious activity of giving. A thief is unable to stop doing bad deeds; but he might offer food to monks
or do some other charitable acts. He might steal from one person and then distribute some of his gains to others and feel good
about it. But to get him to give up stealing is not so easy. Making merit and doing evil are of different weight in this way. Anyone can give things, isn't that so? In our culture, it's a deeply
ingrained tradition. But giving up evil—well, think about it. A
thief won't do that unless he undergoes a genuine transformation. You can consider the matter from this little example.

Practicing and living the Dharma are like that. Listening is not
so difficult; doing is difficult. We need to see and realize through
practice, not only through hearing. We have to hear and gain un-

Portrait of Ajahn Chah by Gerry Rollason, late 1970s.
From Forest Sangha Newsletter, *Commemorative Issue, April 1993.*

derstanding from hearing, but then we have to take it inside to
see more clearly, to see a second and a third time. There will be
no problems then. We are likely to continuously have doubts and
problems precisely because of reading texts. "This teacher says
this, that one says that, the disciples of the Buddha said this. . . ."
But what about our own minds? We don't yet know. Yes,
Sariputta was good, Moggallana was good. But are we as good as
they? Have we gotten down to practicing as they did yet? "No,

but let me read this first." We might well die first, just reading texts and listening to teachings.

Can you really experience the truth of Dharma from reading a text? Learning about anger from a text isn't the same as knowing anger. One who really sees anger will give it up, but just knowing the word is not real knowing. You can hear the teaching and think, yes, it's probably true, but when you meet situations and have sense-contact, you lose control. At that level, you still can't let go. "I know, but I can't give it up. When the time comes to practice, I will let go, but now I can't."

The way I see it these days, it's better to go back and make yourself normal. Whoever has faith will come and do it. We don't need to talk about it a lot. We need to practice a lot. If there is a wound, you'd better clean it deep down, all the way, not just on the surface, or you'll end up amputating.

It's not that we can just talk about Dharma and people will see instantly. It isn't like that. Such as with talking about nirvana. It only brings confusion. People even criticize the Buddha. He knew it perfectly, so why did he speak about it indirectly? Why didn't he show it directly for us to see? There's a problem here. This is not something you can explain for others to know clearly, so he had to speak as he did. Otherwise, we would have to accuse him of being ignorant or unskilled. If it were the case that knowing for oneself would enable one to make everyone else understand, why would the Buddha leave us in confusion?

It's the same as trying to show colors to someone who is totally blind. What will you tell him about red or yellow or green? "Green is like this." Is that sufficient for a blind person? "Red is such and such." Will the blind person understand? Yes, you can talk and explain in the greatest detail, but what will he understand from that? What is the reason he is unable to understand? It's only because of his blindness. You can't really be faulted for not explaining it.

There's no way to give this to someone else. The Buddha elucidated for people to be able to come to realization by themselves. But people fault the Buddha, saying he was ignorant or unskillful. "OK, if you know it, then explain it to me clearly." It's like the blind person who keeps on asking about colors and keeps grumbling that you aren't doing a good job of explaining. You say, "Hey, this is yellow. This thing is really a perfect yellow." What's the use? The more you talk, the more confused he is about it. So what's to be done? It would be better to come back to the salient point and ask, "What's wrong with your eyes? Let's find a way to restore your sight." Then you won't need to try and explain about red and green and yellow. Otherwise, just trying to point things out with words is a futile exercise and nothing meaningful will result. The darkness of ignorance is much more terrible than being blind.

So in the end, it's a matter of practicing. You must do it yourselves; the Dharma is really only upaya. If you have never been inside the hall here, but I have seen the Buddha statue and other things and feel that you should see them too, I should find a way to get you to come here rather than just telling you about it. I can describe the splendid statue to you, but you may not believe me. So I have to find a way to get you inside, and once you have seen, you will believe.

It can be difficult to convince people of anything real if they are self-absorbed and firmly trust their own views. They may say there is no sense or logic to the Dharma when we try to explain it to them. Having no sense in themselves, they ascribe that to others. So how can we tell them about Dharma? We can only teach those who will give it a try. Those who will not do anything, who won't practice to find out for themselves, cannot be taught; they are what is called *padaparama*, or "idiots."

What kind of person is a padaparama individual? Does it mean someone without schooling? A person can have a doctorate and clearly belong in this category, or it can be someone who has stayed in the woods all her life. Yet the illiterate forest-dweller can also have the capacity to understand Dharma; she can be of the type who sees easily. It's not always necessary to have a lot of study. People can be highly learned in a number of disciplines and still be hopeless, refusing to trust anyone's words; for all their knowledge, these people can be the hardest type of padaparama.

People can be difficult, really. Everyone wants to know easily.

University students often come here. They ask, "Luang Por, what should we do to gain realization quickly? What's the very fastest way?" Well, if you're interested in fastest, you don't need to bother at all. Just forget about it. What do you think you will get with this attitude?

Some practitioners like to dispute over meditation methods, over precepts, over what tranquility is and what insight is. Don't go arguing with them. I don't argue with people. I do my practice according to what I understand, and what others believe is up to them. Don't make a big deal out of it. I practice the way I do. If you are interested, you may try it. I can't make a law about it. If you are curious to know whether there's something to it, you have to find out for yourself. Otherwise there's no end to it: samatha and vipassana, meditating on the rising and falling of the abdomen, Buddho, Dhammo. . . . Everyone will go mad, discussing and arguing as to what is the right way to practice, what is the best way. It's excessive, really. But this is what some people like. When it comes to practice, they like to ask questions. They have endless questions over the smallest thing. They like to try every meditation method they hear of. It's like there's a fire underneath them, a fire they lit themselves.

We tell them, "Sit in meditation and you can calm the mind"; practicing samadhi makes the mind peaceful. It sounds good, so they try it. They get the idea that as soon as they sit down, they will become tranquil. They sit and try to fix the mind, but it starts running all over, so they say it's a lie, it doesn't work. "Yeah, I've tried that, sitting to practice samadhi, but my mind wouldn't stay still. It got really agitated, even worse than if I didn't try to meditate. These meditation people are putting across a lot of deception." Have you heard this? What would you say to them?

That kind of thing is simply due to the desires and ignorance of people. It doesn't happen the way they'd like it to. Look at the accounts of the way people practiced, the way they lived, in the Buddha's time. It isn't like that now. These days people just look at books. They memorize things and then start teaching. I don't know where they get their ideas. They go ahead and teach all kinds of mistaken things without knowing what they're doing, not knowing what is correct or what is incorrect. It's because they haven't gained knowledge from within their own minds.

When the members of Parliament are up for reelection, they all say,"I am a good person! I work hard to help all of you!" Well, how many years has the populace been voting for these folks? What has come of it? Maybe we've seen a tiny bit of improvement because of them. And the only reason they do anything at all for us is so we'll vote for them. They have the desire to be MPs. If they didn't have the desire, they wouldn't run. They have to have desire as a motivation to do anything; that's how things normally work. "Oh, I'm the very best there is . . . trust me!" Who is the best one, really? Everyone will say they are. But if we examine them thoroughly, will they really be so good?

I'm not speaking ill of anyone, but this is the way people are. If it were arahants in that situation, you wouldn't hear them talking like that, stirring up confusion and turmoil. We don't get arahants in Parliament. Only worldly people want to be MPs, where they can play their worldly games. How good can you expect them to be? Just as good as they are, with their worldly motivation, good within the limits of worldliness. Or should we try to find some arahants to run for Parliament?

It's the same with medicines. No matter what the medicine, how good can it be? Good within the limits of medicine itself. There are no medicines to stop death. They can alleviate the suffering of illness a little and help us feel better for a while. That's all. Eventually the Lord of Death is going to take the doctors, too. It's like this, so don't make your thinking complicated and expect too much.

We seek tranquility, but we have to think correctly. It's mostly a matter of relying on endurance and patience. If we can't bear the difficulties, it all falls apart. We can't take the confinement in the forest, so we want to give up and escape, get out and start talking with people and doing all our old activities again.

Those who call themselves Buddhists today, what are they

like? I've taken a good look. It doesn't really seem to touch people's hearts. Those we can point to and say their minds are one with the Buddha's way are indeed very few. Some Westerners ask me, "Luang Por, you've done your study and practice and attained knowledge, so why do you still live in the forest? There are few people here." I think they're trying to take me to the slaughterhouse. "If you go to the big city, there are many people you can help. You can't accomplish much benefit in the forest." Setting a trap, waiting to kill me.

If you go to the cities, the places of "progress," to speak about Dharma, the people there will think you are mad. "The crazy monk has come. The mad monk is here!" If you try to talk about anything other than self, other than me and mine, they will say you're crazy. Anyone who talks about things not being self or belonging to a self they will call insane. So I think those Westerners are trying to trick me, sending me to the slaughter. Most people aren't going to listen.

People ask if I teach the foreigners about nirvana, or what I tell them. I'm only trying to get them to become a little more comfortable with themselves. There's no point in talking about selflessness right off the bat. I just instruct them as to what to do. It's like I tell them, "You have to put this glass here. Leave it here for two minutes, and don't pick it up. After two minutes, pick it up and put it over there. Do this."

"But why should I do it?"

"Don't talk about it! Just do it! That's good enough! Why do you need to ask? Knowledge will come to you through doing this."

"What will happen from doing it, then?"

"Don't ask! You came to study with me, and now your responsibility is only to lift up the glass and put it down."

Wisdom will come about from this. Practicing for months and years, some reaction and change will take place in the mind. There will be some feeling, some awareness. Then wisdom will appear. The person doesn't need to ask me questions, only do the practice. What's the point of asking about a lot of things? I just teach you to do this, and your job is to do it. "Pick it up and put

it here for two minutes. Then pick it up and put it over there."
By keeping at it, some knowledge will come. Through the arising of awareness, the person will come to know something. But
it's necessary to endure. A person who endures must come to realization. When she does, then never mind what kind of teachings we give her.

So in my meditation these days, whatever comes about, I just
say, "This is not certain." That's enough. Good experience—this
is not certain. Bad experience—this is not certain. That person
is nice, I like him—not certain. That person is really repulsive—
this is also not certain. It all comes down to this. These things
that are uncertain will not become otherwise. If you take something to be exceedingly good, some problems will come about
for you. If you see something as extremely bad, will that help
you? If you follow these two ways, you are experiencing the two
extremes the Buddha warned about. You have indulgence and
self-torment within you. But if you put them both down, good
and evil, where will you dwell? When you are not following the
ways of good or bad, what is there? It's nothing that can be fixated on and objectively known. If you practice in this way, the
realizations will come about.

Please think about this. When you see that all things are truly
uncertain, what will you try to cling to? You will let go, leaving
things to follow their own conditions. If you need to solve problems, you will act to an appropriate degree, not react with elation
or depression over them. When you see them all as uncertain,
they lose their value. Isn't that so? Uncertain things won't entice
you; they will just be like refuse or leftovers. "This is trash, that is
trash. Who would want them? This is not certain, that is not certain." Why would you grasp things that aren't certain? What
would you want with things that have no value? So the fact of
uncertain can forcefully bring you to enter into something that
is certain. This is what you need to do. If you do this, I will say
without hesitation that you will be able to practice meditation
with success.

We don't need to study a lot. Living in an ordinary way, we
don't need to control the mind too much. When we see that

everything is uncertain, we don't accept things through attraction or aversion. We let go. Why would we get involved with uncertain things? We lose the path only by thinking that things are certain.

If we don't practice this and instead go asking questions, seeking knowledge from different people, what will we get? Who can speak the words that will cause knowledge to be born within us if we are not practicing correctly?

The Buddha was not so ambitious. He just taught a few people at a time. At first, it was the group of five ascetics. He didn't teach them a lot. They learned from practice. When a person practices, he has experience, and this experience creates enthusiasm. There will be a happiness for which he is willing to dedicate his life and make great sacrifice. Others cannot understand why he feels like that. They don't have any idea what the person experiences. If he tries to tell them about it, they may get some superficial knowledge from the words, but they can't really relate to the experience. The practitioner alone realizes the fruit; others cannot see it.

If you try to get it only through others' words, you are likely to become discouraged and give up. I feel it is really necessary to work in practice. You don't need to do a lot of complicated thinking about it. Follow the trainings of sila, samadhi, and wisdom. Whatever various teachers may say, don't get confused. They have to teach in different ways, employing skillful means to get people to understand the path, to practice, to feel satisfaction in practicing. Then disciples will gain realization for themselves through enthusiastic practice.

Perhaps you have not come to realization yet and this troubles you. You are being bound by tanha (craving). You wish to progress in a hurry. Don't worry, it will progress by itself. If you plant a tree today, do you expect it to be fully grown tomorrow? Could that happen? Your work is to water and fertilize it; whether it grows fast or slow is not your business. That's the tree's affair, not yours. You can stand there and complain until you die that it's taking too long to grow. You'll start thinking that the soil is no good, so you uproot it and plant it somewhere else.

But you will again think it's not growing fast enough. Must be the soil again; you pull it up and try to plant it elsewhere. Keep doing this and the sapling will die.

What's your hurry? Wanting something to happen in a hurry is tanha. If you want things to go slowly, that is also tanha. Will you practice according to tanha or according to the Buddha? It's your choice. Troubles come only from straying like this. You need to employ patience and consistency in the practice of Dharma. When you arrive, there won't be any Dharma. You won't need to practice anything, and you won't need to endure or use patience. But now you are trying to practice Dharma. You haven't yet reached it; you just use Dharma as a tool. When you let go, there's no more need for patience or endurance or any other efforts. All of that is finished. You *are* Dharma. Now you want to be something, and everything is too fast or too slow. Where are you going in such a great hurry? You need to stop.

Don't speak with tanha. Don't act with tanha. Don't think with tanha. Don't eat with tanha. But everything we do is with tanha, so when can we expect to meet the truth and attain realization? When will tanha come to an end? We keep on rearing it, feeding it every day, somehow thinking it will die in this way. It only keeps on growing. Think about the things you do. Why do you do anything? It is exclusively because of tanha.

Think deeply about this. If you let go and stop the stream of craving, your actions become steady. Whether you are feeling diligent or lazy, you will still do your practice. Whatever your mood, you just keep working. You don't follow your feelings. But if you only practice when you're in the mood, taking it easy when you feel lazy, this is just following tanha. When will you follow the Buddha instead? If you are feeling lazy, never mind that, just do your practice. If you're feeling diligent, practice. You don't need to depend on these feelings. Following moods, practicing according to your whims, you are not bowing to the Buddha. If you are bowing to the Buddha, laziness will not stop you from practicing. How long do laziness or diligence last in the mind? Take a look at their characteristics, their way of appearing. They keep changing, and you keep on going back and forth between them. Following changing impulses, you are constantly bowing to tanha.

The great disciples of Ajahn Mun, as well as the Buddha and his followers, practiced with determination. In the Buddha's life story we see how, after long years of austerity, he sat beneath the Bodhi Tree and made the vow, "Let flesh and blood dry up, I will not rise from this place until supreme enlightenment is attained. . . ."

These were the words of the Buddha. We read the story in a book and think, Oh, he really went for it. I should do that, too. We may have been meditating only a year or so, but we feel inspired and decide to get right down to business. So we light a stick of incense and think, Until this incense has burned down, I will not get up, even at pain of death. We use the words of the Buddha. We're really going to do it. But it doesn't turn out to be so easy. We start to feel that three hours must have passed, so we open our eyes to look, but the stick is still quite long. We're sweating and in pain. Oh! But I said I would die rather than stop. So we close our eyes again, go through the misery another two or three times. But the incense is still burning. Discouraged, we start feeling we don't have sufficient good karma behind us. Our thinking runs like this. We have this big idea to be like the Buddha. But how long and hard did the Buddha work to cultivate the perfections?

After the Buddha was enlightened, he wanted to vanish, didn't he? He didn't want to teach people. Contemplating the way things were, he saw that the afflictions of beings are very dense. There is so much darkness, the condition of things even goes beyond darkness. Whatever one tries to say is not likely to be understood. Then he considered the four kinds of lotus; he saw that there were beings ready to be awakened, like the lotus about to bloom, and was moved to teach.

But we are not at that level. Just think about the five precepts. Merely teaching this much, people will say they can't do it because they live in the world. The important point is to refrain from certain actions. But people have no restraint. Those who are in positions of authority and responsibility, with power over others, are usually the worst. There is no sila, no Dharma, in the hearts of people, even though they may know all the words and can practice the forms of various Dharma activities. There are those who have studied in great depth and can teach on any subject, but their minds are not where their words are.

So what should we do? The Buddha said that we should wish for things that are appropriate. If people don't believe us yet, don't go thinking they are stupid or worthless, as some teachers do. Actually we are stupid, because we don't have the skill to teach them. You have to cultivate the practice yourself, improve yourself, and make yourself really know and believe first. Through practice, you can develop the wisdom and skillful means to instruct others according to their needs. You can't just go trying to rearrange the world, forcing people to be as you would like them to be. Don't make a big issue out of nothing. All people in the world have a reason for being as they are. Many Buddhas have trained themselves here, putting down this burden. They didn't go carrying the world with them. So don't worry too much about this. Do what you can. Help yourself and help others to the best of your ability. Give up what you should give up and do what you should do. Don't worry about teaching the whole world to follow Dharma.

There's one monk who is a good example of this. You might have seen him here in the past—he used to come listen to me teach when he was a layperson. He wanted everyone to be well behaved and was always pointing out how he felt everyone should or shouldn't act. I just let him be. Then he decided to ordain. He would give Dharma talks, and he hoped to inspire people to believe in the teachings. It did not go well for him.

I told him, "Two oxen are pulling one cart. If the two work together, the cart is lighter for them. Think about this. If one ox is faster than the other, it ends up pulling the cart as well as the other ox. How far can it get? If you were the lead ox, you would be better off slowing down to let the other one keep up with you. Pulling so hard all by yourself only increases the load for you. Wouldn't it be easier to let up a little so you're pulling with the other ox?"

He came back sometime later, and this little talk had gotten to him, because this was what he'd been trying to do. He wanted to train the laypeople. On the lunar observance days, he would try to get them to sit up and meditate all night. "Hey, Sir! Hey, Miss! Don't sleep tonight, we are all sitting up." But they would be falling asleep in their seats or going to lie down. No one seemed to want to practice hard. They didn't have the correct determination. No matter how hard he tried to pull, he couldn't get them to move along at the proper pace, and this started to make him tired. When he was sufficiently worn out, I think he remembered my words. "Hmm. It seems I'm pulling a cart and I'm pulling an ox; maybe I should slow down and let the other ox pull with me." So he came back and wanted to hear some Dharma from me. I told him that I don't have Dharma, only upaya, some words to speak.

I said, "When the time has not yet arrived, what can you do? If a child is born today and you want her to be grown up by tomorrow so she can help you with your work, she isn't likely to satisfy your expectations. So what can you do? Obviously you should care for the child and raise it patiently. Otherwise, you are headed for madness. You can't have it right away." This is just tanha, wanting, pushing, ignoring cause and effect, and struggling meaninglessly.

In regard to livelihood, people these days want to do a little and get a lot, or better yet do nothing at all. The whole world will raise their hands for this. The Buddha said, however, that it is necessary to be diligent in whatever we do. We should be aware of income and expenses. There needs to be some training, and there needs to be moderation in the way we spend and consume. But when we are playing with tanha, there will be no moderation. Our income is never enough; it's as if we are giving money to a mad person. He could consume everyone's salary and not be satisfied, just like we were throwing the money in the ocean.

So who can be satisfied with what they have? The mad person will just go and request more from whomever he can. One's thinking has to go a little deeper. I've considered this; for people who don't understand, it is really a profound matter. They get what they deserve. The meditation masters talk bluntly, expressing it like this: "Serves you right!" Haven't you heard? People complain that we only want to talk about Dharma when they are in such dire straits. . . . What will you say to these mad ones? It's hard to make them see, as I've said, like telling a blind person about colors. We mention white, and they want to know, "What is the color white like?"

"It's like gypsum."

"And what is gypsum like?"

"Oh, it's the same color as the clouds in the sky."

"And what are the clouds like?"

"Well, they're white in color."

Foolish ones just continue on like this until they get frustrated. It would be better to find out about the person's blindness, when it began, what may have caused it, and so on, and try to find a cure. We won't have to explain about all the colors in the world. When one day they open their eyes and see the world, they will know for themselves. There will be no more questions. This way is probably better.

What will you employ to solve the problems and answer people's questions and get to the end of things? Especially with those who have a lot of education, there's nothing you can tell them. Sometimes we poor meditators will be driven to desperation when the university students come and ask questions. They want a quick solution to everything. You tell them to practice something, and they say they just can't manage it. Well, they have to go back to the beginning and endure until they can manage to do it.

Believe me, over the years, I've been seeking all kinds of means to instruct people. Now, I just try to do what I am able to. Things that are beyond me, I will put aside for the time being. And there are some things I simply have to let go of. Some people are easy to teach, some are difficult. And there are some who don't need to be taught; they can realize the truth by themselves, without much prodding from others.

You can see what I do these days with the monks who come here. I'm not teaching a lot now. People who have the capacity to see don't need a lot of teaching. You can leave them in the forest. They will look at the trees and think, Ahh, trees are like people: the leaves and branches of a tree eventually dry out, and such is also the case for humans. This is called the *ugghatitanyu* (intuitive) type of person. Just staying in the forest, they can come to knowledge by themselves. They can see the nature of human life. They have this kind of mind and don't need to be taught very much.

Other people must come to sit here and listen. The *vipacitanyu* (intellectual) people need to hear analogies and comparisons to ignite their understanding. They can't be left alone. With some teaching, they can see. With the right instruction, they will come to have a change of viewpoint and realize what they did not see before.

Then there's the *neyya* (trainable) person. For this type, you really have to instruct and train at great lengths, but it can be done. It's like in a group of one hundred students, perhaps eighty will be able to pass, and this is the eightieth. He can still pass and move along with the rest of the group and eventually make use of the knowledge he has gained.

But beyond this, there are people who are going to remain on the outside.

"Today, you must not do such and such."

"Yes, sir."

But in a couple of days, they are back to doing those things again.

"Don't do that anymore."

"Yes, sir."

And before long they're doing it again, so again you say, "You must not do that."

"Yes, sir."

It's, "Yes, sir" all the way along. Eventually, you have to let go and release them to their previous owner. Who is that? It's karma.

Sometimes there's nothing you can do, and you really have to give up and leave people to deal with the karma they've made for themselves. You have to stop trying to change them and leave them alone. The old karma is too powerful. You can't fight with the old owner.

Don't forget this in your dealings with people. Sometimes people seem to develop little by little, only to fall back. When the truck gets to the end of the road, you can't try to force it to carry the load any further. If you are still not satisfied and want it to keep going, it will only end up stuck or overturned. You have to know your own abilities and strengths and be satisfied with what you can do. Otherwise, you end up as a hungry ghost.

The world goes the way it will. We do what we can to solve problems. Still, the nature of things is that they appear in the beginning, change in the middle, and vanish in the end. Just do what you can, what is appropriate to the situation and your ability. Trying to do more than this is only creating a lot of grief for yourself. Think about this. It's not being selfish. Some people will say, "This guy is so selfish, he doesn't want to help." You have to look at yourself to know whether it's true or not. Don't simply react to what someone else says, but look to see what is going on with you. If it's true that you are being selfish, you can accept the criticism as valid. Depend on yourself in this way; what's the use of relying on someone else's words? If someone says your virtuous activities are no good, how will you react to that? It's not a matter of arguing or getting angry over what someone says about you, rather you have to be aware of what is really the case with yourself and measure the words appropriately.

But these days, it's a little difficult, especially for those in positions of responsibility. Perhaps the police arrest two people in a case of theft. One of them actually did it; the other is innocent. But when they are interrogated, they will both profess their innocence.

"Did you steal it?"

"Oh, no."

"And what about you? Did you steal it?"

"Oh, no."

It's the same answer from both people, but only one is telling the truth. It might not be easy for the detectives to determine the facts of the case. One person is innocent and says, "No, I didn't do it." The other person actually committed the theft, and he also says, "No, of course I didn't do it." So what can the cops do? They have to make their own investigation without merely relying on the suspects' words. The minds of people tend to be crooked and tricky like this, so it's better to know yourself and be able to believe in yourself. Don't be too ambitious; know what is appropriate and what you can do.

These days, I am not so keen on trying to interest others in my words. There doesn't seem to be much benefit in trying to convince people. I am here in the monastery, where this way of life has been established; if someone wants to come and look into these things, they are welcome.

If there's a fire spreading in a neighborhood and some houses are burning to the ground, the firefighters will first try to protect the houses that have not yet caught fire. They can't do much about the buildings that are almost gone. Many are still standing, so there's more value in saving those. That's how firefighters work.

If we try to solve everyone's problems, no matter how intractable, we are likely to end up running out of time. The first thing we need to do is make a good example of ourselves. Instead of doing things in a worldly or selfish way, if we do things according to Dharma, someone who has the right karmic conditions may take notice and have some interest in listening to our words. They will attract that type of person.

Whenever Dharma arises in someone's heart, it will benefit the world. Good people will appreciate that, but evil people won't. Some things you might not like, but worldly people will call them Dharma. You don't see it like that, so you won't have faith in their way and they won't believe in your way. They will take delight in doing the worldly things you see no value in. In all ages, it has been like this. We need something to measure by; if everyone is good, there are no bad people. If there are no bad people, there won't be any problems, and without problems to resolve, it might be difficult to develop wisdom.

Since I came to Wat Pah Pong, I've been thinking about this. With a monastic community living in the forest, it has become a place where people are forbidden to seek animals for food. I thought it would be good to have a protected spot like this, where animals can live free of fear and the forest can remain intact. I thought it was a good thing; but still I met with criticism. "What are you living here for? Did you just come here to protect trees? Is that all a monk does? You are supposed to be renouncing all things of this world, so why are you so concerned about trees and animals?"

I listened to their words, but I felt some compassion for the squirrels and other small animals and didn't want them being shot by hunters. "Are you raising animals? Aren't they wild animals? This isn't the business of monks."

I thought it over—suppose we build a wall around the monastery? So we did, but people got upset with me. My intentions were good, really. Then there were the village dogs. They came here and chased the squirrels. They hurt and killed a lot of them. This was very painful to see. What could we do about it? We needed to find a way to keep dogs out of our monastery. Finally, after many months, I realized my thinking was wrong.

This is just the nature of these animals. If we could drive the dogs away, the squirrels would become stupid. When there is some danger for them, they become more clever and careful. They get their own kind of wisdom from the dogs being around.

In this way, wrong is good, because it is paired with right and leads us to what is right and good. We examine our actions and consider whether they are right or wrong. When a carpenter is cutting wood, he has to measure his lengths. Short will instruct long, and long will instruct short. The world is like this, all things existing along with their opposites. I came to realize that I had to let go, leave the dogs and the squirrels to sort things out according to their natural existence. And yet now the squirrel population is thriving. They have become more resourceful and clever.

So the problem was mine. I wanted to prevent the dogs from biting the squirrels. I wanted to prevent people from criticizing. But it's natural for people to have criticism according to their point of view. I decided I had to solve the problem right where it was. I learned to stop struggling with things.

Living in the forest at Wat Pah Pong, there were difficult situations. Things troubled me here, so I had to learn to settle them here. Malarial fever was pretty serious, bringing me close to death for several years. But I was content to be here. Staying and seeing it through, you learn something. When your strength of mind increases, difficult situations and problems become less powerful. Why does their strength decrease? Simply because yours has grown, so theirs is less by comparison, even if it's the same as before.

This is all quite ordinary. You don't need to think about it too much. Instead, you should just do what you can do. You don't need to do things that bring you suffering. If you are creating suffering in your heart, there must be something wrong with the teachings! The point of Dharma practice is to make an end of suffering, so why are you increasing your suffering? We need to see where we are wrong. If someone doesn't want to listen to our words and we get upset over that, we are in the wrong. We're supposed to be practicing to be free of suffering, so why are we creating suffering? We are very mistaken indeed. Look at this point. You don't need to have lofty thoughts of nirvana. Just look within. Where else should you be looking to conquer? Please consider this.

GLOSSARY

AFFLICTIONS (P. *kilesa*)   The mental defilements of desire, aversion, and delusion.

AJAHN (P. *acarya*)   Teacher.

AJAHN MUN (1870–1950)   The most renowned meditation master of the twentieth century in Thailand, and the teacher of most of the great masters in the Northeast of Ajahn Chah's generation.

ANANDA   The Buddha's attendant and close disciple.

ARAHANT   The final level of enlightenment in Theravada Buddhism. Literally, "the one far from the afflictions" or "one who has destroyed the enemy."

ARIYA   The Noble Ones, those who have attained the levels of enlightenment and thus are no longer ordinary beings.

BHIKKHU   A fully ordained monk. Literally, "one who sees danger in the round of samsara."

P = Pali; Th = Thai.

BUDDHO   The name of the Buddha, commonly used as a meditation object in Thailand, meaning "the one who knows."

DEITIES   (P. *devata*) Worldly gods subject to birth and death;
the highest of the six realms of samsara.

DHAMMO   A meditation object, similar to Buddho.

DHARMA   The teaching of the Buddha; ultimate truth. Literally, "that which exists." (With uppercase *D*.)

DHARMA   Phenomena. (With lowercase *d*.)

DUKKHA   Unsatisfactoriness, the suffering nature of existence;
the first of the Four Noble Truths taught by the Buddha.

EIGHTFOLD PATH   The fourth of the truths taught by the
Buddha; the way leading out of unsatisfactory experience,
consisting of right understanding, right intention, right
speech, right action, right livelihood, right effort, right
mindfulness, and right meditation.

EIGHTH REBIRTH   One who enters the stream to nirvana will
be reborn no more than seven times before attaining final
enlightenment.

EIGHT WORLDLY DHARMAS   Gain and loss, praise and
blame, fame and disrepute, happiness and suffering.

FIVE AGGREGATES   Bodily form, feelings, perception/mem-
ory, mental formations, and consciousness.

FOUR FOUNDATIONS OF MINDFULNESS   The basic meditation system in Theravada Buddhism, which includes mindfulness of the body, feelings, mind, and dharmas.

FOUR NOBLE TRUTHS   The first teaching of the Buddha: the
truths of suffering, its origin, its cessation, and the path
leading out of suffering.

HUNGRY GHOSTS   Unfortunate beings who cannot find food
or drink, usually depicted as having huge bellies, tiny
mouths, and limbs like sticks. The cause of such birth is said
to be greed and miserliness.

KHANDHA   Aggregate: the classification of psychophysical
components mistakenly thought to constitute a person or
self. Literally, "heap."

KUTI   A monastic dwelling, usually a small cabin raised on
pillars.

LOWER REALMS   States of extreme suffering.

LUANG POR (TH.)   Title of respect and affection for an older monk. Literally, "Revered Father."

MAGHA PUJA   Major Buddhist holiday commemorating the formation of the Sangha.

MERIT (P. *punya*)   Positive qualities of mind and the activities that accumulate them.

MOGGALLANA   One of the Buddha's two foremost disciples, known for his magical powers.

NAGAS   Serpentlike water deities in Buddhist mythology.

NEYYA   A person who is trainable.

NIRVANA   The enlightened state, the unconditioned; the extinction of greed, hatred, and delusion.

NONRETURNER (P. *anagami*)   The third level of enlightenment, before arahant; a being who is not reborn into the world, but completes the path in an immaterial realm.

ONCE-RETURNER (P. *sakadagami*)   The second level of enlightenment after stream entry; a person who will have only one more rebirth in the world.

PACCEKA BUDDHA   One who attains enlightenment without a teacher and does not have the ability to teach others; usually depicted as living in solitude.

PADAPARAMA   A person who understands, at most, the words of the text; an idiot.

PALI   The dialect of Sanskrit in which the Buddha taught.

PERFECTIONS (P. *parami*)   Spiritual qualities that are cultivated as a support for realizing enlightenment. In Theravada Buddhism, there are ten: generosity, morality, renunciation, wisdom, effort, forbearance, truthfulness, resolution, lovingkindness, and equanimity.

RAINS RETREAT (Th. *Pansa*; P. *vassa*)   A three-month period (mid-July through mid-October) corresponding to the Asian monsoon season, during which the monastic communities reside in one place without traveling; traditionally a time of intensive practice.

REQUISITES   The material supports for monastic life: robes, alms food, a dwelling place, and medicines.

SAMADHI Concentration meditation; meditative stability.

SAMANA An ordained person, a renunciant. Literally, a "tranquil one."

SAMATHA Tranquility meditation.

SAMSARA The round of birth and death, the cycle of unsatisfactory conditioned existence.

SANKHARA All conditioned phenomena, that is, anything that has a beginning and an end, birth and death. As the fourth of the aggregates, it refers to thought or mental formations. In the Thai vernacular, it can refer to the body.

SARIPUTTA The other of the Buddha's foremost disciples, known for his wisdom.

SASANA (Sometimes Buddhasasana.) Buddhism, traditionally translated as "the dispensation of the Buddha" but commonly known as "the Buddha's way."

SILA Virtue or morality, and the code of conduct and precepts that is in accord with and leads to virtue.

SKILLFULNESS (P. *kusala*) Intelligence that discerns what is wholesome and skillful; positive actions that are accompanied by understanding.

SONGKRAN (Th.) Traditional Asian New Year on April 13. Coming at the end of the dry season, it involves water ceremonies.

SOTAPANNA One who attains the first level of enlightenment. Having entered the stream to full enlightenment, this person will be reborn seven times at most. Literally, "stream enterer."

TATHAGATA An epithet for the Buddha. Literally, "the One Thus Gone."

THREE JEWELS The Buddha, the awakened one; the Dharma, his teachings; and the Sangha, the community of practitioners who have realized the truth of the teachings.

TUDONG (Th.) (P. *dhutanga*) Ascetic observances permitted for Theravadin monks.

UBON UBONRACHATANI the province in Northeast Thailand where Ajahn Chah lived and where Ajahn Mun was born.

UGGHATITANYU   A person of quick understanding or intuition; a genius.

UPAYA   Skillful means, helpful ways of teaching and training others.

VIPACITANYU   A person who understands a concept after a detailed explanation; an intellectual.

VIPASSANA   Insight meditation. Literally, "special seeing."

VISAKHA PUJA   Holiday commemorating the Buddha's birth, enlightenment, and death (parinirvana).

WAT (Th.)   Monastery.

ABOUT THE TRANSLATOR

Born in Brooklyn in 1948, Paul Breiter traveled to Thailand in 1970 where he took ordination as a monk. Shortly thereafter, he met Ajahn Chah and became his student. Breiter learned Thai and the local Lao dialect (Isan) and served as Ajahn Chah's translator for the many Western students who came to study with him. He kept a journal of his translations of Ajahn Chah's Dharma teachings, some of which he published with Jack Kornfield as *A Still Forest Pool* (Quest Books, 1985). He also translated a volume of a text on monastic discipline, known as *Vinayamukha* (Entrance to the Vinaya; Mahamakuta Royal Academy, 1983). Breiter traveled with and translated for Ajahn Chah when he visited the United States in 1979. He later published an account of his time studying with Ajahn Chah called *Venerable Father: A Life with Ajahn Chah* (self-published, 1993; Buddhadhamma Foundation, Bangkok, 1994).

After disrobing in 1977, Breiter returned to the United States and continued his Buddhist studies with Roshi Kobun Chino Otogawa of the Soto Zen school, and then with Lama Gonpo Tsedan of the Nyingmapa lineage of Tibetan Buddhism. He currently works for the U.S. Postal Service.

CREDITS

———

THANKS TO THE FRIENDS who provided pictures of Ajahn Chah from their personal collections. Thanks particularly to the monks of Bung Wai International Forest Monastery, Ubon, Thailand; and to the monks of Abhayagiri Monastery, Redwood Valley, California, who generously provided their only prints of precious historical photographs.